Southern Literary Studies
Louis D. Rubin, Jr., Editor

Kate Chopin Reconsidered

Kate Chopin Reconsidered

Beyond the Bayou

EDITED BY
Lynda S. Boren and Sara deSaussure Davis

Louisiana State University Press
Baton Rouge and London

Copyright © 1992 by Louisiana State University Press
All rights reserved
Manufactured in the United States of America
First printing
01 00 99 98 97 96 95 94 93 92   5 4 3 2 1

Designer: Amanda McDonald Key
Typeface: Times Roman
Typesetter: G & S Typesetters, Inc.
Printer and binder: Thomson-Shore, Inc.

Library of Congress Cataloging-in-Publication Data

Kate Chopin reconsidered: beyond the Bayou / edited by Lynda S. Boren
    and Sara deSaussure Davis.
        p.   cm.—(Southern literary studies)
    Includes bibliographical references and index.
    ISBN 0-8071-1721-8
    1. Chopin, Kate, 1851–1904—Criticism and interpretation.
    2. Feminism and literature—United States—History—19th century.
    I. Boren, Lynda S. (Lynda Sue), 1941–   . II. Davis, Sara
    deSaussure, 1943.   III. Series.
    PS1294.C63K385   1992
    813'.4—dc20   91–29368
                                                        CIP

The essays in this book by Jean Bardot, John Carlos Rowe, and Doris Davis originally appeared in
somewhat different form in *Perspectives on Kate Chopin: Proceedings from the Kate Chopin International Conference* (Natchitoches, La.: Northwestern State University Press, 1990).

Grateful acknowledgment is made to the editors and publishers who granted permission to reprint
certain passages contained herein:
Excerpt from *Approaches to Teaching Chopin's "The Awakening,"* by Elizabeth Fox-Genovese, reprinted by permission of the Modern Language Association of America. Copyright © 1988 by the
Modern Language Association of America. Excerpt from "The Open Cage: Freedom, Marriage and
the Heroine in Early Twentieth-Century American Women's Novels," by Shirley Foster, in *Women's
Writings: A Challenge to Theory,* ed. Moira Monteith, reprinted by permission of St. Martin's Press.
© Moira Monteith, 1986. Excerpts from *The Quintessence of Ibsenism,* by George Bernard Shaw,
reprinted by permission of The Society of Authors on behalf of the Bernard Shaw Estate. Excerpts
from *Kate Chopin: A Critical Biography,* by Per Seyersted, reprinted by permission of Louisiana
State University Press. Copyright © 1969 by Louisiana State University Press. Excerpts from *The
Complete Works of Kate Chopin,* edited by Per Seyersted, reprinted by permission of Louisiana State
University Press. Copyright © 1969 by Louisiana State University Press. Excerpts from "'Development of the Literary West': An Undiscovered Kate Chopin Essay," by Heather Kirk Thomas, re-
printed by permission of McFarland & Company, Inc., Publishers, Jefferson, North Carolina. Vol-
ume 22:2 of *American Literary Realism.* © 1990 McFarland & Company, Inc. Excerpt from *All the
King's Men,* copyright 1946 and renewed 1974 by Robert Penn Warren, reprinted by permission of
Harcourt Brace Jovanovich, Inc.

The paper in this book meets the guidelines for permanence and durability of the Committee on
Production Guidelines for Book Longevity of the Council on Library Resources. ∞

Contents

Foreword

Kate Chopin did not exist when I was in graduate school, at least not in any institutional sense. Her name never appeared on syllabi or examination reading lists. In the huge "bullpen" where graduate students had desks, we often debated literature and critical theory, but *The Awakening* we discussed in whispers in the women's room. In my first teaching position in 1974, as one of the only women faculty members at a formerly all-male liberal arts college, teaching Kate Chopin raised eyebrows. I had proposed a women-and-literature course, the first "women's studies" course in the university's history. Included in the nineteenth-century portion of the course were Jane Austen, the Brontës, George Eliot, Emily Dickinson, Edith Wharton, and Kate Chopin. One colleague scoffed that he had never even heard of Chopin and borrowed my copy of *The Awakening*. "She's good," he said, returning the book the next morning, "but I'm not sure I want my wife to read this." He was joking, of course, but nonetheless declined to keep *The Awakening* a few days longer in case his wife might want to read it too.

There is a point to this anecdotal recitation of a personal literary history. Now, in editing a journal of American literary studies, I see almost as many submissions on Kate Chopin as on any other author. I have not done a quantitative analysis, but it certainly seems that we receive essays on Chopin with nearly the same frequency as those on Melville, James, and Faulkner. It is a rare month that goes by without a submission on Chopin and an unusual issue that does not contain an article, note, book review, or allusion to Chopin's work. In less than a generation, she has gone from obscurity to canonization. And this collection continues that process of ensuring that her work will continue to be read and evaluated in the next generation.

Kate Chopin Reconsidered: Beyond the Bayou provides a range of fascinating engagements with Kate Chopin's work—biographical, New Historicist, materialist, poststructuralist, certainly feminist. And it shows that

Kate Chopin's work continues to be intellectually, emotionally, and critically compelling. Will this volume render her, once and for all, a respectable writer? I hope not. As these essays suggest, Kate Chopin now fills a crucial chapter in American literary history not only because of her life and work but also because of the story of how her work was lost and found. Allegorized, hers is a story of the high cost of literary feistiness *and* a story that feistiness can pay off in the long run.

Especially in our own historical moment when cultural conservatives mount their charge against a newly gendered and multicultural canon, a collection such as this reminds us (just in case we've forgotten) that *politically correct* and *excellent* are not mutually contradictory terms. Along with nineteenth-century writers such as Harriet Wilson, Harriet Jacobs, Elizabeth Stoddard, and Frederick Douglass, Kate Chopin enlarges and enriches that ever-fluctuating entity known as "American literary history." Her rediscovery serves as a compelling reminder that at its best, the work of the literary critic is significant, visionary, and like Kate Chopin, always a little feisty.

Cathy N. Davidson
Duke University

Acknowledgments

We wish to acknowledge the encouragement and assistance of friends and colleagues as we worked to bring this project to completion. Much gratitude to Leonard and Doris Schoenberger for giving over the sanctuary of their home in Louisiana to the incessant whir and clack of computer and printer, and to Veronica Makowsky of Louisiana State University and her husband, Jeffrey Gross, for moral support and gourmet meals along the way. To Ada Jarred and Carol Wells of Northwestern State University's Watson Memorial Library for their interest and participation in the early stages of this effort, and to Emily Toth of LSU and Cathy N. Davidson of Duke University for serving as preliminary readers and advisers.

To Sheri Washington, program assistant in the Arts and Sciences dean's office at the University of Alabama, who took on not only word processing but organizing and worrying, we owe special thanks for her good nature and her good work. Thanks also to Karyn Bullard, Sheri's successor, who ably took over in the second round of manuscript preparation, and to David Klemmack, who readily interrupted his own work to provide essential computer advice. The Alabama Arts and Sciences dean's office also generously allowed many assaults on its copying and printing capacities. We are also grateful to two friends and colleagues who provided library help: Nancy C. Michael at the University of Wisconsin and Guy Hubbs with the University of Alabama Special Collections.

Abbreviations

ATA	*Approaches to Teaching Chopin's "The Awakening,"* ed. Bernard Koloski
KCA	Kate Chopin, *"The Awakening": An Authoritative Text, Contexts, Criticism,* ed. Margaret Culley
CW	*The Complete Works of Kate Chopin,* ed. Per Seyersted
CB	Per Seyersted, *Kate Chopin: A Critical Biography*
CS	Daniel Rankin, *Kate Chopin and Her Creole Stories*
KCM	*A Kate Chopin Miscellany,* ed. Per Seyersted and Emily Toth
NEA	*New Essays on "The Awakening,"* ed. Wendy Martin

Kate Chopin Reconsidered

Introduction

LYNDA S. BOREN

Until fairly recently, scholars have shied away from a preoccupation with the motives and strategies that inform Kate Chopin's art; her day-to-day struggles and obsessions seemed peripheral, somehow nonrelevant. The same curiosity, however, that impels scholars to want to know and yet never to despise the "true" living Shakespeare spurs us to a greater involvement in Chopin studies. As is usually the case with rediscovered writers previously dubbed "marginal" by the establishment, it was largely by word of mouth and through the increasing popularity of courses in southern and regional literature, American studies, and feminist studies that Kate Chopin achieved her present eminence. Along with that process of canonization and progress to status, however, was the struggle for "ownership" of the writer's psyche. Lurking questions about the validity of biographical interpretations of her fiction surfaced during the past two decades, inciting debates and exchanges that have served only to stimulate further speculation and a wide diversity of approaches to reading and teaching Chopin.

With the proliferation of women's studies, feminist critics with new perspectives on Chopin's life and art have opened the doors to many "rooms" of complexity and interpretation previously marked *do not enter.* From such critics, whose introduction to Chopin was no doubt simultaneous with their awakenings to a host of other American women writers, for which Charlotte Perkins Gilman's "The Yellow Wallpaper" became the symbolic epitome, comes the inspiration to pursue to the furthest limits the siren call of Chopin's mystery.

Equally fascinating with recent feminist and theoretical explorations is the multifaceted nature of Chopin's art: its lucid reflection of Louisiana life, language, and spirit; provocative subtexts and structural brilliance; obvious incursion into the themes and techniques of naturalism, realism, and modernism. The chimerical properties or strategies of Chopin's art can indeed breed frustration, an unsatisfied desire to penetrate the obviously polished, meticulously crafted surface in search of a profounder message or an encoded text of Chopin's sufferings. Chopin has remained maddeningly inscrutable, as if to demonstrate sardonically the consequences of Mark Twain's tongue-in-cheek injunction in his preface to Huck's adventures: Anyone finding a plot would be shot; a moral, banished. Frustration is an honest response, however, perhaps more honest than the impassioned rhetoric that colors some readings of the novel, ultimately more liberating than the smugness that claims to have the final say in Chopin criticism.

Frustration often grows out of a lack of confidence in dealing with Chopin. Most readers find her clever and insightful, but also detached from polemics. For this reason, Chopin's art demands a better understanding of the forces that motivated it. Delighting in Chopin's lyricism, her obvious affinity with Whitman and Emerson, some readers sense that her insights into a particular type of feminine response to life were almost exaggeratedly intense. It is easy to sympathize with the discomfiting knowledge that there is much left to be uncovered about Chopin. Opinions about where she belongs in the canon are nebulous. Clearly she belongs to that tradition of women writers, including Emily Dickinson, who transcended through their wit and irony any inducement to propagandize: Jane Austen, Mary Wilkins Freeman, Constance Fenimore Woolson, Ellen Glasgow, Edith Wharton, Elinor Wylie, Virginia Woolf. Neither was she a slavish idolator of region or local color, even though she absorbed and transformed it so uncannily in her depiction of Louisiana's Cajun-Creole milieu. In the final assessment of where to put Chopin, it is startling to discover that one has been forced back into one's personal history, into participation with Chopin's most intimate creative moments.

Chopin's creative moments were inspired by the place in which she lived and worked. A journey to this region opens yet another door to the artist's psyche. Starting from the Cane River town of Natchitoches, not far from the old Chopin plantation in Cloutierville (reputed to have been the notorious McAlpin plantation of *Uncle Tom's Cabin*), one heads southwest toward the hills of Louisiana's pine country and even farther south to the bayous that helped to inspire Chopin's local color (*CB,* 36). Coming into Natchitoches up a narrow highway spawned from the vestiges of the old El Camino Real, one encounters a sleepy, seemingly deserted little village the fame of which appears to rest on the town's privileged status as the oldest settlement in the Louisiana Territory. Once a year its riverfront banks twinkle with Christmas lights. Fireworks explode as contented revelers munch on highly seasoned meat pies.

To encounter Natchitoches for the first time is to step back, however ephemerally, into the past. Graceful willows hang serenely over placid water rippled here and there by leaping fish and surfacing turtles. White herons spread their slow-motion wings in liquid flight, and time seems suspended in a shimmering dazzle of green and gold and blue.

> The bayou curved like a crescent round the point of land on which La Folle's cabin stood. Between the stream and the hut lay a big abandoned field, where cattle were pastured when the bayou supplied them with water enough. Through the woods that spread back into unknown regions the woman had drawn an imaginary line, and past this circle she never stepped. This was the form of her only mania.

Chopin's opening words from "Beyond the Bayou" insinuate themselves, like a palimpsest, onto the peaceful scene, dark lines drawn in heavy charcoal over one's naive impressionistic vision.[1]

Chopin takes away as much as she gives. She imbues the landscape with shadows, circumscribing its apparent endlessness with mental circles, transforming it with the darker tapestries of conflict and self-denial. This ominous sensation—of darkness and confinement—clashes paradoxically with Chopin's experience and helps to shape one's eventual perspective on her intentional pathos.

One is as dazzled by the beauty and serenity of the region as Chopin had obviously been. The banks of the Cane River lake offer changing panoramas of color and motion—pinks, golds, silvers, brilliant greens, billowy white clouds, migrating fowl—a testament to Chopin's powers of depiction. Her lyricism was mimetic, not bathetic as some might have supposed. The region has its own esoteric language. When night falls, it falls like a curtain of velvet. A chorus of singing creatures vibrates intensely, rising and dying with compelling, almost supernatural crescendos of intensity. On the river's shores, lawns slope down to quaint piers with

---

1. *"The Awakening" and Selected Stories* (New York, 1981), hereinafter cited parenthetically in the text as *SS*.

graceful canopied boats. Even the profound stillness has a sensuous palpability.

> She stopped to find whence came those perfumes that were assailing her senses with memories from a time far gone. There they were, stealing up to her from the thousand blue violets that peeped out from green, luxuriant beds. There they were, showering down from the big waxen bells of the magnolias far above her head, and from the jessamine clumps around her. There were roses, too, without number. To right and left palms spread in broad and graceful curves. It all looked like enchantment beneath the sparkling sheen of dew.[2]

These Edenic reveries from Chopin's brief sketch in "Beyond the Bayou" of La Folle—the "large, gaunt black woman, past thirty-five," who "in childhood . . . had been frightened literally 'out of her senses' "— contrast sharply with the bleaker violence of her character's psychological torment. La Folle, or Jacqueline, suffering from agoraphobia, had chosen to dwell alone "in her solitary cabin" when "the rest of the quarters had long since been removed beyond her sight and knowledge" (*SS*, 19). Jacqueline's childhood trauma was induced by the sight of P'tit Maitre, owner of Bellisime plantation, "black with powder and crimson with blood," as he staggered into her mother's cabin.

Refusing to travel beyond the bayou, Jacqueline subjects herself to a geographical prison, a regional boundary that while offering sanctuary to her wounded soul, confines her to unspeakable loneliness. Jacqueline's exile is finally broken when she overcomes her paralyzing fear to save the life of Cheri, P'tit Maitre's only son and the love of Jacqueline's life. When Cheri is wounded with his own rifle while hunting squirrel, Jacqueline, overcoming her terror, carries him in her arms to the great house of those unknown regions that had haunted her since childhood. "At the foot of the stairway, which she could not have mounted, she laid the boy in his father's arms. Then the world that had looked red to La Folle suddenly turned black—like that day she had seen powder and blood" (*SS*, 24). Chopin's yoking of trauma and rebirth to the regional landscape of Jacqueline's life is decidedly Faulknerian. Region becomes an extension of man's nightmares and his dreams; it liberates and terrifies.

2. Kate Chopin, "Beyond the Bayou," *ibid.*, 26.

In this tiny slice of one woman's life, Chopin demonstrates her talent for universalizing an ostensibly "local color" tale. Although La Folle's struggles with a paralyzing fear and her subsequent overcoming of that fear parrot conventional themes of heroic quest literature, the poignancy of her dilemma is revealed in the effects of that "morbid and insane dread she had been under since childhood" (*SS*, 22).

La Folle's final plunge into the unknown is strikingly similar to Edna Pontellier's courageous conquest of the Gulf: "La Folle gave a last despairing look around her. Extreme terror was upon her. She clasped the child close against her breast, where he could feel her heart beat like a muffled hammer. Then shutting her eyes, she ran suddenly down the shallow bank of the bayou, and never stopped till she had climbed the opposite shore" (*SS*, 23). The sympathetic rendering of such a struggle and the resultant dignified portrait of Jacqueline are quintessential Chopin. This rendering is what gives Chopin's art its life and ensures its canonization. The flora and fauna are there, of course, with an animus of their own, but they are also brilliant psychological accoutrements to the pathos of Chopin's characters. Without the human struggle, the encroaching violence and ever-present anticipation of death, Chopin's bayou folk would be little more than curiosities, relinquishing their individuality to the overwhelming presence of drooping live oaks and honeysuckle.

No doubt Chopin, no native to the region, understood intuitively the fact that lush description and the accurate recording of dialect and manners needed a touch of irony for the sake of realism. Not that Louisiana's rich mixture of races and customs was likely to vanish. The history of this region of Louisiana where Chopin lived with her husband after leaving New Orleans has been preserved by those scholars and writers who felt compelled to share with the outside world their knowledge of its unique character. In at least one particular aspect, as Gary B. Mills's history *The Forgotten People: Cane River's Creoles of Color* illustrates, the society that Chopin encountered was unknown to the rest of North America.[3] Louisiana, particularly the Cane River region, had been conquered and colonized by peoples whose values and fierce pride contributed to the closed

3. Gary B. Mills, *The Forgotten People: Cane River's Creoles of Color* (Baton Rouge, 1977).

nature of its social structures. Without an understanding of the complex caste system that dominated, and to some extent still dominates, both the Cane River region and Louisiana as a whole, a newcomer often feels that he has ventured into an unknown continent.

As so many of Chopin's stories show us, the strata of hierarchies were multilayered and multicolored. Glimpses into the problems and resentments nurtured by this stratification can be seen in characters like *The Awakening*'s Mariequita, whose rustic, dark-eyed beauty is an implied threat to the avowed superiority of the white aristocratic women of Grand Isle and in Neg Creole, the little black outcast who nourishes in isolation the pride of his noble lineage. In writing of the Cane River's Creoles of color, Mills reveals much about the workings of such a society. In a caste system that labeled its members according to the percentage of Negro blood that flowed through their veins—using such legal designations as *Negro, sacatra, griffe, mulatto, quadroon, and octoroon*—the Cane River's freemen of color constituted a third racial caste "seldom recognized outside Louisiana."

> Under the title of *gens de couleur libre,* free part-white Creoles were accorded special privileges, opportunities, and citizenship not granted to part-Negroes in other states.
> Preservation of this third racial class in Louisiana society was contingent upon strict adherence to the caste system by its members. Just as the whites entertained feelings of superiority to Negroes, so did Louisiana's *gens de couleur libre*. Often possessing more white blood than black, and quite often on good terms with and publicly recognized by their white relatives, most members of this third caste in Louisiana were reared to believe that they were a race apart from the blacks, who occupied the lowest stratum of society. Countless testimonials reveal their inherent pride in their French or Spanish heritage and their identification with the white rather than the black race.[4]

This was the milieu into which Chopin ventured as a young bride. Through stories told by her great-grandmother Mme. Charleville, she had already formed a semifictional, highly romantic version of life in Louisiana; and at the age of eighteen she spent three weeks in New Orleans,

4. *Ibid.,* xiv.

which she "liked immensely." It was "so clean—so white and green," and it was there she learned to smoke and became infatuated with the famous German singer Mrs. Bader (*CB*, 30). When she married Oscar Chopin and moved with him to New Orleans, then, Kate was able to navigate safely—with her fluent French and gracious manner—through the discriminating society of the Creoles. As an outsider, she had an added advantage. She maintained her independence and refused to take seriously many of the duties and restrictions of the Creole wife. For this reason, she was also afforded an aesthetic distance that enabled her to summon up, with cool irony, the detached perspective of art.

It is tempting to imagine what Chopin's secret thoughts must have been upon entering a society so rigidly defined and so little given to the candor of her father's Irish heritage. In spite of Chopin's gay, witty manner, which feminist critics are coming more and more to comprehend as a form of defensive armor, her daughter's observation forces us to acknowledge the "other" Chopin, perhaps that romantic side that yearned for a solace that only nature could give.

> When I speak of my mother's keen sense of humor and of her habit of looking on the amusing side of everything, I don't want to give the impression of her being joyous, for she was on the contrary rather a sad nature. She was undemonstrative both in grief and happiness, but her feelings were very deep as is usual with such natures. I think the tragic death of her father early in her life, of her much loved brothers, the loss of her young husband and her mother, left a stamp of sadness on her which was never lost. (*CB*, 48)

Seyersted hints at the artist's "difficulty." She "had a strong will of her own," he tells us, and she was subject to moodiness. "These negative moods made Kate Chopin an enigma to those around her," and "one of the few things to cloud her gay insouciance was the duty of a weekly reception day. She seems at times to have resented this obligation, and her husband could not have stopped her had she, like Edna, decided to escape from it" (*CB*, 39). Without her music, her sense of humor, and her vivid imagination, it is doubtful that Kate Chopin could have endured the prejudiced, incestuous atmosphere of Louisiana's Creole elite.

The darker tapestry keeps emerging in the search for Chopin. She was surely forced to modify her youthful claim that her chief desire in life was to be "really just a girl completely happy with her home, her husband, and in the eager expectation of . . . her first child" (*CB,* 39). The question lingers: How sucessfully could Chopin have endured life in Louisiana, particularly after her departure from New Orleans, had she not taken the romantic's characteristic pleasure in those darker moments of interior sadness, the projection of her own fears and longings onto the characters and the landscapes of her fantasies? Even in Seyersted's depiction of Chopin's New Orleans life, Kate emerges less a contented, settled wife than a restless, alien observer. There appears to have been little motivation behind Kate's long rambling walks, particularly in the evenings, other than a frustrated desire for excitement and escape.

> Like Whitman, she loved to ride on streetcars and observe people, and she seems to have covered the routes of all the carlines at her disposal. In the little notebook she kept in New Orleans, which is now lost, she occasionally jotted down brief remarks on things seen and done during her outings, but she added no personal opinions or reflections. Nowhere did these unpretentious notes suggest any literary intentions. (*CB,* 41)

A woman satisfied with hearth and home as the all-encompassing realm of her existence would not have been driven, as was Chopin, to roam the streets and devour the sights as though for her very life.

In her diary for 1894, after the return to St. Louis, Chopin reveals her essential romanticism and desire for solitude.

> I am losing my interest in human beings; in the significance of their lives and actions. . . . I want neither books nor men. They make me suffer. Is there one of them can talk to me like the night—the summer night? . . . The night came slowly as I lay out there under the maple tree. . . . My whole being was abandoned to the soothing and penetrating charm of the Night. —The katydids began their slumber song. . . . How wise they are. They do not chatter like people. They only tell me: "sleep, sleep, sleep." . . . It was a man's voice that broke the necromancer's spell. A man came to day with his "bible class." He is detestable with his red cheeks and bold eyes & coarse manner of speech. I hate people who teach lies. Can he tell . . . me things of Christ? I would rather ask the stars: they have seen him. (*CB,* 67–68)

It is "a man's voice" that disrupts Chopin's mood, so strongly bound to a wish for death. If she is awakened into life again only by the vulgarity of a paternalistic Bible-thumping proselytizer, what choice does she have, as this episode demonstrates, other than a desire for escape and a greater harmony with the "voices" of nature?

If a woman lives long enough in Natchitoches, she will find occasion to visit the home of the local seamstress, who turns out costumes and billowy gowns at amazing speed. Customers are led back to her tiny sewing room strewn with patterns and half-finished dresses. Standing as still as possible, arms lifted in an attitude of crucifixion, as measurements are taken, one notices a plaque that hangs directly above the sewing machine.

> To succeed in life a woman must
> Look like an angel,
> Act like a saint
> And work like the devil.

For the seamstress encaged in her makeshift sewing room, survival means *pleasing* her clients. The Natchitoches seamstress is socially bound to that image handed down to her from the women she serves. A fleeting vision of Chopin's "mother-women" distracts. "They were women who idolized their children, worshipped their husbands, and esteemed it a holy privilege to efface themselves as individuals and grow wings as ministering angels" (*KCA,* 10). Natchitoches and Cloutierville abound with women who work ceaselessly during the Cane River region's many tours and festivals, rushing here and there in their long skirts, serving food, answering questions, and welcoming tourists. They are gracious and untiring throughout, even with soaring temperatures and drenching humidity.

At Bayou Folk, which has been preserved as a historical museum, the principal guide answers a multitude of questions about Chopin, leading her guests through each room, telling stories about the region, and explaining the history of the furniture and memorabilia contained in the museum. She talks endlessly about the attractiveness and independent spirit of Kate, how she scandalized her neighbors by riding through the streets of Cloutierville, the plume of her hat fluttering in the breeze.

One's respect for Chopin grows with the knowledge of what she must have endured as a wife and mother in the Cane River region. In Cloutierville, according to her daughter, she had been known as the "Lady Bountiful of the neighborhood, dispensing advice and counsel, medicines, and, when necessary, food to the simple people around her" (*CB,* 45). After her husband's death from swamp fever in 1883, in the words of William Schuyler, Kate "had to carry on correspondence with the cotton factors in New Orleans, make written contracts, necessitating many personal interviews with the poorer Creoles, the Acadians, and the 'free mulattoes,' who raised the crop 'on shares,' see that the plantation store was well stocked, and sometimes even, in emergencies, keep shop herself" (*CB,* 46). Apparently, it was not the hard work and responsibility that depressed Chopin but the restrictions that were often placed on her as a woman. To "work like the devil" was *self*-satisfying; angels satisfied *others*. She particularly enjoyed the role of businesswoman and abandoned her home in Cloutierville only at the prompting of her mother in St. Louis.

Living in the Cane River region is different from visiting it as a tourist. Cloutierville and Natchitoches are literally and symbolically close to Huey Long's old stumping grounds. Willie Starkism has left its mark on everything, replacing the aristocratic domination of wealthy Creoles with a new order. Robert Penn Warren captured both the image and the words in his satirical portrait of Louisiana's most celebrated populist:

> "No, I'm not here to ask you for anything. A vote or anything else. I reckon I'll be back later for that. If I keep on relishing that peach ice cream for breakfast in the big house. But I don't expect all of you to vote for me. My God, if all of you went and voted for Willie, what the hell would you find to argue about? There wouldn't be anything but the weather, and you can't vote on that." [5]

The geography of power has changed since Chopin's day.

The justification for offering this collection of essays on Chopin rests on the assumption that region is both psychological and political. The Cane River region of Chopin's fiction is only now becoming accessible in scholarly terms, more understandable, at least from Chopin's perspective as a writer, particularly with the publication of Emily Toth's definitive biography. [6] However, much remains to be rethought and recreated in Chopin studies. The international conference at Northwestern State University in

5. Robert Penn Warren, *All the King's Men* (1946; rpr. New York, 1974), 11.
6. Emily Toth, *Kate Chopin: The Life of the Author of "The Awakening"* (New York, 1990).

April of 1989 was merely a beginning to what promises to be a resurgence in Chopin scholarship. Crossing all disciplines and engaging multiple perspectives, the conference in Natchitoches combined Louisiana culture and cuisine with history and critical thinking. The "Ladies in Calico" once again donned their antebellum gowns to host jazz brunches and elegant dinners under the live oaks.

Advances in Chopin studies could not have occurred, nor the conference at Northwestern funded, without the foundations laid by earlier scholars, particularly Chopin's biographers. Introductions by Barbara Solomon, Sandra Gilbert, Lewis Leary, and Nina Baym have been supplemented by Barbara Ewell's study of Chopin, Bernard Koloski's edition of *Approaches to Teaching Chopin's "The Awakening,"* and Wendy Martin's recent edition of essays for Cambridge University Press.[7] Although Martin's edition examines *The Awakening* within the context of Chopin's search for autonomy, it also reinforces one's original perception of Chopin's darkness, the "other" Chopin of moods, sadness, and night. "In many respects," Martin writes, *The Awakening* is about death, not life" (17). And the summation to Andrew Delbanco's "The Half-Life of Edna Pontellier" in the same volume acknowledges this darker strain that in itself constitutes a modern, enlightened sophistication about the plight of women in the American South. According to Delbanco, we must "acknowledge majesty in Edna's recognition that her 'awakening' is becoming a new form of degradation. . . . Most important, we may feel how insufficient is her death as an expression of a human being's need to find some third way between the alternatives of submission and emulation when faced by those who regard power as the ground of all human relations" (106).

The essays in this volume were derived from an array of events and individuals. Some of the essays were presented at the New Orleans MLA; others were discussed at the Northwestern conference. All seek to move beyond reductive applications of theory, offering provocative insights into Chopin's unique talent. We have gone beyond *The Awakening* to a consideration of Chopin's lesser-known but equally important fiction and "beyond the bayou" in our search for that complex region that transcends, as it defines, the interior landscape of a woman artist's search for fulfillment.

7. Barbara C. Ewell, *Kate Chopin* (New York, 1986); *ATA; NEA.*

I Biographical Approaches

Kate Chopin Thinks Back Through Her Mothers: Three Stories by Kate Chopin

EMILY TOTH

Especially by the first critics who rediscovered her, Kate Chopin has been lauded as a detached, "objective" writer, definitely not autobiographical. She had no causes, no opinions, we are told. She was a serious-minded child raised among pious Catholic widows. She became a serene St. Louis widow who just imagined rebellious women. And among Kate Chopin scholars there have always been gender gaps. Chopin's male critics of the early 1970s in particular were prone to claim that Chopin's works are "universal" rather than feminist, about the human condition rather than women.[1]

Virtually all of these claims are wrong.

Chopin's first biographer, Daniel Rankin, failed to notice and even denied that much of her fiction echoes events and people in her life, although he did sometimes confuse Kate Chopin with her characters (CS, 81, 83). He claimed, for instance, that Edna's moods in The Awakening were directly transcribed from Kate Chopin's feelings. He alleged that the Ratignolles' marriage in The Awakening, a satirical portrait of bovine contentment, was an exact replica of the Chopins' perfect union. Rankin often missed ironic and critical statements about marriage and woman's lot in Chopin's works. He also created a sunny narrative of Chopin's life that belied and denied her tensions and passionate struggles.[2]

Per Seyersted, Chopin's second biographer, continued the view that Kate Chopin did not draw much on real life. Trained in New Criticism,

---

1. Priscilla Allen, "Old Critics and New: The Treatment of Chopin's The Awakening," in The Authority of Experience: Essays in Feminist Criticism, ed. Arlyn Diamond and Lee R. Edwards (Amherst, 1977), 224–38; Emily Toth, "Comment on Barbara Bellow Watson's 'On Power and the Literary Text,' " Signs, I (1976), 1005.

2. Emily Toth, "The Shadow of the First Biographer: The Case of Kate Chopin," Southern Review, XXVI (April, 1990), 285–92.

reluctant to make biographical leaps, Seyersted reported (in a footnote) that only four Chopin stories were "taken more or less directly from life" (*CB*, 217–4).

Yet certain parallels between Kate Chopin's life and works are readily apparent. The image of Kate Chopin as the serene widow of St. Louis, faithful to her husband's memory, is a myth. In Chopin's writings, characters' names are frequently the same as or very similar to those of real-life people. The Cane River country storekeeper Chartrand gets his name from the real-life Charles Bertrand. The boatman, Coton Mais, bears the same name as an Isle Brevelle family. The playful "Chouchoute" has the nickname of a Chopin relative. Chartrand appears in *At Fault* and "Love on the Bon-Dieu"; Coton Mais is in "Desiree's Baby"; Chouchoute is in "For Marse Chouchoute." Chopin also drew on a man she knew intimately for the character of a planter in several Louisiana stories.[3] An examination of the 1880 U.S. Census and documented research by diligent Chopin scholars provide extremely useful resources for finding Chopin place-names, characters, and the like.[4]

Similarly, most of Chopin's characters live, as she did, in St. Louis or Louisiana, either in New Orleans or in Natchitoches ("Nak-i-tush") Parish, the Cane River country in northwest Louisiana. During her New Orleans years (1870 to 1879), Kate Chopin was, like her character Edna at Grand Isle, an outsider among the city's Creoles and dominated by motherhood. When the Chopins moved to the tiny village of Cloutierville ("Cloochyville," 1879 to 1884), Chopin, like her character Melicent in *At Fault,* brought big-city fashions and ways to unappreciative locals. Only later did she realize how peculiar she had seemed.

Kate Chopin was suddenly widowed, as is the case with half a dozen of her characters, and for the most part she wrote about widowhood as a rather cheerful state. Of Chopin's widowhood stories only "Madame Martel's Christmas Eve" presents a widow who wallows in her grief. Other Chopin widows, such as the title figure in "A Lady of Bayou St. John,"

3. Emily Toth, *Kate Chopin* (New York, 1990).
4. Thomas Bonner, Jr., *The Kate Chopin Companion, with Chopin's Translations from French Fiction* (New York, 1988); Elizabeth Shown Mills, *Chauvin dit Charleville* (Oxford, Miss., 1976); Gary B. Mills, *The Forgotten People: Cane River's Creoles of Color* (Baton Rouge, 1977).

Therese in *At Fault,* and Louise in "The Story of an Hour," find their situation a challenge and an opportunity. Kate Chopin wrote in her diary that the deaths of her husband and her mother had freed her for her "real growth" (*KCM,* 92).[5] She was liberated to become an author, to draw on her past life for inspiration, and to meditate freely about what might have been.

She also looked into her family's past. "For we think back through our mothers if we are women," Virginia Woolf has written, and some of Chopin's stories are clearly motivated by a desire to reconstruct her female past. Born in St. Louis in 1850, Kate O'Flaherty was raised by her widowed mother, maternal grandmother, and maternal great-grandmother. The great-grandmother, Victoria Verdon Charleville, was her first teacher.[6] Mme. Charleville entertained young Kate with stories from early St. Louis history, including the era of her own mother's life, and Chopin's sole historical story, "The Maid of Saint Phillippe" (written 1891, published 1892), takes place during that tumultuous time, the 1760s.

Chopin's "Maid" is an intrepid young woman who wears boyish buckskin clothing, carries a gun, and hunts in the woods. She is a motherless child whose father has never stopped grieving for his dead wife: "the better part of himself went with her," a friend says (*CW,* I, 119). At home, the maid wears her dead mother's skirt, bodice, and cap. When her father dies, the maid realizes that she has "no will to obey in the world but her own," so "her heart was as strong as oak and her nerves were like iron" (*CW,* 120). Like countless later Chopin heroines, the maid is strongest when she is alone, and when a handsome devoted captain begs to take her back to France and bedeck her in jewels and silks, she refuses. She has breathed free air and "was not born to be the mother of slaves" (*CW,* 122). In the end, she strides toward the rising sun, alone.

Mme. Charleville's mother, a contemporary of the maid's, was a woman of courage and daring who also had good reason to reject marriage

5. See also, Per Seyersted and Emily Toth, eds. *Kate Chopin's Private Papers* (Bloomington, Ind., forthcoming).

6. Virginia Woolf, *A Room of One's Own* (New York, 1929), 79; See Emily Toth, "A New Biographical Approach," in *ATA,* for a discussion of erroneous 1851 birthdate for Kate Chopin. See also Maryhelen Wilson, "Kate Chopin's Family: Fallacies and Facts Including Kate's True Birthdate," *Kate Chopin Newsletter,* II (1976–77), 25–31.

and prefer solitude. A widow, Victoria Verdon had taken an ill-tempered carpenter as her second husband, and their fierce quarrels were so notorious that the two obtained the first legal separation ever granted in St. Louis. After their separation agreement, which she had signed with an *X*, the newly independent Mme. Verdon learned to write, gave birth to a child out of wedlock, and operated a highly profitable keelboat line out of St. Louis. Although she was known as Victoire, or "La Verdon," the imperious name she used for signatures, her first name was Marianne, the same name that her great-great-granddaughter Kate Chopin gave to her independent heroine in "The Maid of St. Phillippe." [7]

However, historical fiction was not Kate Chopin's forte. She abandoned it, never looked back, and sometimes made fun of her own efforts. But she remained fascinated by the lives and the choices of her female ancestors, and she continued to write their histories through her own imaginings.

Four years after "Maid," Chopin wrote an evident meditation on the life of her maternal grandmother Mary Athenaise Charleville Faris. According to Chopin's notebook, "Athenaise" took longer to write than any other short story. She spent eighteen days on it (April 10 to 28, 1895). [8] Chopin did spend several years writing and rewriting the story "Euphrasie," eventually published as "A No-Account Creole," but that was at the very start of her publishing career. Chopin may have had trepidations, for her grandmother was still alive. Mrs. Faris, who had been a widow for half a century, died in January, 1897, at the age of eighty-eight, four months after the story was published in two installments in the *Atlantic Monthly*.

We cannot know whether the very elderly Mary Athenaise Charleville Faris, living in the household of Chopin's aunt Josephine, was able to read "Athenaise." Nor can we know how she would have reacted to the story, but her early life suggests that like the fictional Athenaise, she had gone into marriage naïvely and been wounded by it.

In Kate Chopin's story the title character is a young, high-spirited Louisiana bride, the second wife of a much older husband. He is the generation

7. Mills, *Chauvin dit Charleville;* Maryhelen Wilson, "Women's Lib in Old St. Louis: La Verdon," *St. Louis Genealogical Society,* XIV (n.d.), 139–40.

8. See Chopin's manuscript account notebook in Seyersted and Toth, eds., *Chopin's Private Papers,* courtesy of the Missouri Historical Society, St. Louis.

of Chopin's mother or grandmother, for he grew up with slaves. His young wife has come to "detes' and despise" being married (*CW*, 431). Athenaise is disgusted with having a man's clothes and presence about her, and seeing his dirty bare feet. She has a "constitutional disinclination for marriage" (*CW*, 431). Chopin's readers in the mid-1890s would understand that she has a particular loathing for sex, for she tries to find out, through hints to her friends, whether "marriage were as distasteful to other women as to herself" (*CW*, 436). Her husband, apparently understanding, chooses not to "compel her cold and unwilling submission to his love and passionate transports" (*CW*, 438), but he cannot make her love him.

So Athenaise, who lives in the Cane River country, absconds to New Orleans with her brother's help. In a boardinghouse she is befriended by the journalist Gouvernail, whose neatness and soft white hands she notices. Although he has advanced ideas—"A man or woman lost nothing of his respect by being married" (*CW*, 444)—Gouvernail does not go beyond the bounds of friendship with Athenaise. When she discovers she is pregnant, Athenaise's whole being is "transfigured" with "wonder and rapture" (*CW*, 451). She returns, ecstatic, to her husband, who feels her "lips for the first time respond to the passion of his own" (*CW*, 454).

To my knowledge, no critics have said that Athenaise's pregnancy cements her oppression in a difficult marriage. She is still young and unformed, with a severe and silent husband. Moreover, Chopin's story contains many ironically couched comments on marriage in general. The narrator calls it "a social and sacred institution" (*CW*, 432). Athenaise's parents consider it "a wonderful and powerful agent in the development and formation of a woman's character" (*CW*, 434). But Athenaise calls it "a trap set for the feet of unwary and unsuspecting girls" and blames her mother (*CW* 434).

Still, Chopin's ironies were often missed by her readers. The editors of the *Atlantic*, where the story was published in 1896, no doubt found the ending in keeping with the genteel tradition as enunciated by William Dean Howells. The smiling, happy aspects of life were preferred, and adulteries and unhappy marriages were to be shunned. Athenaise's awakening to passion at the end was presumably acceptable because it was triggered by approaching motherhood.

"Athenaise," as Chopin's manuscript notebook shows, was one of only three Chopin stories accepted by the *Atlantic,* although she submitted more than a dozen. The other two, "Tante Cat'rinette" (1894) and "Neg Creol" (1896, 1897), also use conventional themes. Both are about former slaves who are devoted to their former owners' families. The thought that slaves would be loyal to their masters was pleasing to American editors in the 1890s, and so, evidently, was Athenaise's final submission to a woman's traditional role.

But "Athenaise" can also be read as the story of a woman's enslavement by her own body, her submission to motherhood, and there it seems to have direct application to Kate Chopin's grandmother. In her youth, Mary Athenaise Charleville, perhaps as impractical as her fictional namesake, had also made an unfortunate marriage, nearly seventy years before Kate Chopin wrote her story. In the mid-1820s, the Catholic Mary Athenaise Charleville (whose name is sometimes given as Marie Anne Athanaise in legal documents) had married a Protestant, Wilson Faris, the well-educated son of a Virginia state representative. Although Athenaise Charleville and Wilson Faris were married in the Catholic Church, her French-speaking father never forgave her for marrying an "American."[9]

Faris was also an incompetent businessman whose chronic failures enraged his father-in-law, who aided his other daughters' husbands but did nothing to help Athenaise and Wilson Faris. At one point, the hapless young Faris even signed over all his worldly goods to his father-in-law, including his furniture and his horse, to repay "rent of a house and boarding."

In "Athenaise" Kate Chopin gave her heroine the chance to escape, but in life it was the husband who deserted the marriage. Like her fictional counterpart, the real-life Athenaise had found that biology was destiny and motherhood inevitable. When Wilson Faris departed, some six years before his granddaughter Kate was born, he left his wife with little money and seven children. Eliza, the eldest, was barely in her teens. Eliza was not greatly educated, but she was pretty, charming, gentle, and soft-voiced, and spoke English with a French lilt. Although her mother had been married at eighteen, and her sisters much later, Eliza Faris became a bride a little after her sixteenth birthday. On their wedding day in 1844,

9. Mills, *Chauvin dit Charleville,* 51–53; Wilson, "Chopin's Family," 25–31.

Thomas O'Flaherty was thirty-nine, four years older than his mother-in-law, Athenaise Faris.

In the eyes of the old French of St. Louis, including his own grand-mother-in-law Mme. Charleville, who spoke only French and never could pronounce "O'Flaherty," Thomas was an upstart at a time when Irishmen were widely assumed to be drunkards and rowdies. But Thomas O'Flaherty was a self-made man, a Galway immigrant who had become a successful merchant and civic leader. He had married a young woman from a prominent "French" family, but she died young. Six months later, he married Eliza Faris. (Their daughter Kate, born in 1850, was evidently named for his first wife, Catherine).

Whether Eliza Faris resisted marrying a man just a year younger than her father and a bare half year after the man's first wife died, is not recorded. But her reason for marrying is obvious: As the eldest child, she was providing for her family. A year after the wedding, her impecunious father died, but Eliza's marriage had solved the Farises' desperate financial need.

If Eliza ever regretted her marriage, she left no record, but her daughter Kate Chopin included more than a few hints. Chopin's fictional wives are often discontented and attracted to other men. Some yearn for the freedom of their single days, like the heroine in "Athenaise." Some, like the "Maid of Saint Phillippe," refuse to give up that freedom. Chopin may also have been thinking of her mother's marriage when she wrote *The Awakening,* for Edna, after several youthful infatuations, marries an older man who is safe, secure, and rich, thereby "closing the portals forever behind her upon the realm of romance and dreams" (*KCA,* 19). But it was in "The Story of an Hour" that Chopin wrote her mother's story, in the most radical revision of her female past.

By the fall of 1855, five-year-old Kate O'Flaherty had begun boarding school at the Sacred Heart Academy. Besides her half brother George, she had an older brother, Tom, and a younger sister, Jane. Eliza O'Flaherty was noted for her charm and lavish hospitality, and Thomas O'Flaherty's net financial worth qualified him as one of the "solid men of St. Louis."

Captain O'Flaherty, as he had come to be called, was on the inaugural train on November 1, 1855, for the ceremonial opening of railroad connections to Jefferson City over the new Gasconade Bridge. Among the other

celebrated passengers were the ministers Artemus Bullard and John Teasdale and the banker Louis A. Benoist, the wealthiest man in St. Louis and
owner of a great country estate, Oakland Plantation. (At Oakland, over a
decade later, Kate O'Flaherty would meet a charming Benoist grand-
nephew from Louisiana named Oscar Chopin.)

But as the ceremonial train chugged onto the Gasconade Bridge, the
bridge's floor timbers suddenly gave way, and ten of the cars plunged into
the river. Thirty men died, including the ministers Artemus Bullard and
John Teasdale (whose granddaughter Sara would be the greatest St. Louis
poet of the generation after Kate Chopin). The telegraph first brought the
news to St. Louis, and then the newspapers. The Missouri *Republican* later
retracted the reports of two deaths. A Mr. Moore from Cape Girardeau was
injured, not killed, and a Mr. Bryan, a St. Louis lumber merchant, had not
been on the train at all.

But Thomas O'Flaherty had indeed been on the train, and he was dead.
Later, Eliza O'Flaherty seemed to be a pious widow, devoted to her husband's memory. Kitty Garesche, Kate's friend, recalled that Mrs. O'Flaherty was "sad and beautiful. . . . This I explain to myself by knowing that
her soul must have been shrouded in grief at her dear husband's untimely
death" (*CS*, 35). But Eliza, only twenty-seven when her husband died,
now controlled a large estate. She had four children and had already buried
at least one infant. She had not married for romantic reasons, and a widow
mourning the loss of her husband was always respected in society (as in
Chopin's story "A Lady of Bayou St. John"). There were many reasons
for a widow to remain single, and Eliza never remarried.

Meanwhile, her daughter evidently brooded over her father's death and
her mother's life, for thirty-nine years after the Gasconade in "The Story
of an Hour" Chopin used a husband's reported death in a train accident as
a catalyst for a wife's "monstrous joy" (*CW*, 353). The newly widowed
Louise Mallard revels in being "free! Body and soul free!" (*CW*, 354).
She had loved her husband, she tells herself, but that hardly counted "in
the fact of this possession of self-assertion which she suddenly recognized
as the strongest impulse of her being!" (*CW*, 353). But then her husband
walks in, having been nowhere near the crash. The wife's weak heart fails,
the doctors come, and they conclude that she died of "heart disease—of
joy that kills" (*CW*, 354).

Chopin called the piece "The Dream of an Hour," and it was published under that title in the December 6, 1894, issue of *Vogue*. The title was evidently changed by Per Seyersted for the *Complete Works*. The story has also been filmed twice, both versions much longer than the story: Marita Simpson and Martha Wheelock's *The Story of an Hour* (Ishtar Films) and Tina Rathbourne's *The Joy That Kills* (Cypress Films). Both versions create plots that are not in Chopin's story. Simpson and Wheelock add water imagery from *The Awakening;* Rathbourne shows the stultifying relationship between the Mallards, not unlike the marriages in Charlotte Perkins Gilman's "The Yellow Wallpaper" or Henrik Ibsen's *A Doll's House*.

Kate Chopin never wrote about her father in her surviving diaries and letters. She would scarcely have remembered him. In fact, she wrote very little about fathers, although she did write about mothers who refuse to sacrifice themselves for others, most notably in "A Pair of Silk Stockings" (1896, 1897) and *The Awakening* (1899). But in "The Story of an Hour" Chopin used a woman's solitude, as she had in "The Maid of Saint Phillippe" and "Athenaise," as a sign of the character's awakening to her own choices and her place in the universe. The maid chooses solitude, and Athenaise chooses to run away, but Mrs. Mallard is denied the new identity she has chosen.

In life, Thomas O'Flaherty did not return from the railroad crash, yet "The Story of an Hour" is more than a series of hints about what the newly widowed Eliza O'Flaherty might have thought. "Story" also contains details clearly drawn from Kate O'Flaherty's childhood memories.

As noted earlier, Chopin frequently relied on mnemonic devices and name similarities. In "The Story of an Hour," the protagonist's name is Louise, and Eliza O'Flaherty's French-speaking relatives called her "Eleeza," a name that would sound very much like Louise to a frightened eavesdropping child. Likewise, Chopin called the protagonist's sister Josephine, the name of Eliza O'Flaherty's youngest sister. For the husband's name, Brently Mallard, Chopin used a name resembling that of one of the real-life victims, Artemus Bullard, but she gave her character the same initials as Bryan and Moore, the two men falsely reported dead at the Gasconade Bridge. Through "The Story of an Hour," Chopin was openly and subtly remembering.

Like many writers, Chopin used her stories to ask and resolve questions—in her case, about marriage, motherhood, independence, passion, life, and death. Where she seems to make choices, she favors *solitude,* a word that appears some fourteen times in *The Awakening,* nearly always in positive contexts. As she came of age, Kate O'Flaherty lived in a household where her mother, grandmother, and great-grandmother were the central figures (the only males were her brother, half-brother, an uncle the age of her brothers, and servants). There were no adult males and no married couples in the household until she was fifteen when her aunt Zuma and Zuma's husband, John, joined the ménage, and by then, Kate was immersed in school activities at the all-girls Sacred Heart Academy.

Until her marriage, then, Kate O'Flaherty grew up in a world of women. When she became a widow, she had numerous admirers but made the same choice her mother, grandmother, and great-grandmother had made: She would not marry again. Although she never had a room of her own until the last years of her life, Chopin always valued the nourishing solitude of her own mind. She peopled her imagination with the women before her. She looked at what they had chosen, and out of her meditations she created extraordinary stories of women in crisis and in fulfillment.

But she also grew pessimistic as her career progressed. The unmarried Marianne in "The Maid of Saint Phillippe" shoulders her gun at the end and goes off happily, alone, to join the Cherokees. There are few people in the story, and few family members to influence the bold Marianne. Such is not the case with Louise in "The Story of an Hour," which Chopin wrote three years later. Although Louise's death is an occasion for deep irony directed at patriarchal blindness about women's thoughts, Louise dies in the world of her family where she has always sacrificed for others.

The claims of family and community are even more unavoidable for the very young wife in "Athenaise," written a year later, in what is chronologically the last of Chopin's reconstructions from her family. Athenaise's world is full of people—parents, brother, friends, relatives, boardinghouse keeper, fellow boarder, servants—and all are watching her and gossiping about her. Her story appears to have a happy ending, but unlike Marianne or Louise, Athenaise has sacrificed her independence, has given her self to the expectations of others.

Although she had commercial ambitions and was pleased to publish "Athenaise" in the prestigious *Atlantic,* Chopin was looking for other kinds of truths beyond the traditional claims on a woman's time and faculties. The women of her family had through widowhood evaded in some ways the claims of family, community, and husbands. All were independent and unusual women, survivors who escaped patriarchal imperatives. Certainly it is no accident that all three of Kate Chopin's ancestor stories present rejections of traditional marriage.

Kate Chopin also kept pushing at the boundaries surrounding freedom of expression. "Athenaise," the last of her ancestor stories, was published in August and September of 1896. In January, 1897, the real-life Athenaise died. Chopin's mother had by then been dead for twelve years, her great-grandmother for thirty-four. By early 1897, Chopin's children were grown. The youngest, her only daughter, Lelia, was seventeen and was famous for her dashing manner and unconventional ways.

That June, Kate Chopin began writing *The Awakening*.

French Creole Portraits:
The Chopin Family from Natchitoches Parish

JEAN BARDOT

I have established a new connection between the Louisiana and French branches of the Chopin family. Newly located sources of biographical information concerning the Chopin family of Natchitoches Parish offer a better understanding of this microcosm of Creole society and its influence on Kate Chopin's literary world. These sources, which include genealogical trees, photographs, and letters in the possession of Julie Chopin Cusachs of Baton Rouge and her cousin Renee Antonia Chopin of Nangis, France, enable us to see a more accurate and complete picture of the Chopin family with whom Kate Chopin maintained close ties throughout her life.[1]

Among the rare family photographs from Julie Cusachs, two are of particular interest for us. The first represents Oscar at the age of nineteen at Derry plantation, and the second is a picture taken by Kate Chopin in the spring of 1904 during her last visit to Louisiana. It shows the Derry plantation home, her brother-in-law Lamy Chopin's residence, which she used as the setting of her first novel, *At Fault*. This document is all the more precious as the house was destroyed by fire in the early 1940s. Lamy and Frances Chopin are standing on the gallery, and their children are below. The little girl in the foreground next to the rosebush is their daughter Julie.

The letters written by Dr. Chopin, his brother Auguste, his wife, Julie Benoist Chopin, and their son Oscar from 1836 to 1865 offer valuable insight into the personality of the author's future in-laws and provide eyewitness accounts of plantation life in Natchitoches Parish before and during the Civil War.

Victor Marie Jean-Baptiste Chopin, Kate's father-in-law, was born in

1. The letters cited below were provided courtesy of Julie Chopin Cusachs, Baton Rouge, and Renee Antonia Chopin, Nangis, France. All translations are mine.

May, 1818, in Loupeignes, a small French village between Soissons and Rheims near the World War I battlefields of the Marne, some seventy miles northeast of Paris. His mother died when he was twelve, and at the age of eighteen he left the family farm to try his luck in Mexico, as he records in a letter he sent to his brother from Le Havre on March 30, 1836:

> My dear Lamy,
>
> I received your letter just as I was preparing to leave tomorrow. We have been waiting three days for a favorable wind; it has just come and we are quickly taking advantage of it.
>
> I am leaving for New Orleans on an American steamship; once I am there I shall board another ship that will take me to Vera Cruz. . . .
>
> I have a letter of recommendation to hand over to Doctor Antomarchie, who was Napoleon's physician on St. Helen's island, and who has settled in Mexico. This letter, given to me by one of his friends, and others I have for different people, may be very useful.
>
> P.S. I am sailing on the "Olympia." [2]

Victor Chopin's elder sister, Marie-Therese Eugenie, and two brothers, Lamy, twelve years older, and Auguste, three years younger, remained in Loupeignes. We have no direct information from Victor between 1836 and 1847. It is only through a letter from Auguste to Lamy, written in Fismes, near Reims, in 1838, that we learn that their brother had given up the idea of sailing to Mexico and that he stayed in New Orleans for at least two years after his arrival.

A family friend, M. de Bussiere, who had encouraged him to leave for the United States, provided Victor the financial assistance necessary to permit Auguste to join him in Louisiana. The two brothers first lived in New Orleans, and Auguste later followed Victor when he moved up to Natchitoches Parish. This and other very valuable information is found in Victor's letter to Lamy, dated in Cloutierville, May 10, 1847.

> My dear Lamy,
>
> I have just arrived from New Orleans, and I am taking advantage of one of our compatriots to hand over this letter to you, giving you news of Auguste and myself. It is now almost twelve years since I left France, and I

2. Jean-Baptiste Chopin to Lamy Chopin, Le Havre, March 30, 1836, in possession of Renee Antonia Chopin.

reproach myself for not having ever given you any news; do not think it is a question of indifference. I have been buffeted by contrary winds for so long that I hesitated to begin a letter which would be nothing but a long recital of sorrows and vexations. Now that I have a stable situation, without being very rich, I think of you all the time, and I shall be happy only when I have visited you. After having unsuccessfully tried various kinds of jobs, I applied myself to the study of medicine. I obtained my degree here and set myself up about 125 leagues in the interior of Louisiana.

I have every reason to be pleased with this decision. I have succeeded as well as possible. I settled down in this area seven years ago and married four years ago, I have two young sons, a good little wife; and with the revenue from my clients, I have bought a plantation with twenty or so negro workers, which gives an average annual income of about 3.000 piastres (or 15.000 francs). In addition, my doctor's fees amount to about 12.000 francs per year.

I spend approximately six thousand francs per year on domestic and plantation expenses.

In the country where I live we cultivate cotton, which is the main source of revenue, corn or "wheat from Turkey" (which is used to feed the negroes and the animals) and sugar cane. This year cotton sells at only 11 to 14 "sous" a pound, as the harvest has not been abundant. In an average year an acre of ground yields 400 pounds of cotton. Each negro cultivates about 8 acres of cotton in addition to the corn required for the plantation. In a well-managed estate capital invested can bring in 15 to 18 percent net. Auguste, who was not working in New Orleans, is with me. He manages my estate which is about two leagues from my home. He seems to be willing to buckle down to it and I shall do all I can to encourage him and help him.

P.S. You will notice that I have changed my Christian name from Victor to Jean-Baptiste, which is how I am known here; I think the former brought me bad luck.[3]

Thus, according to this letter, Victor Chopin, henceforth known as Dr. Jean-Baptiste Chopin, settled in Natchitoches Parish in 1840, married Julie Benoist in 1843, and apparently obtained his medical degree in Louisiana, not in Mexico as stated by biographers Daniel Rankin and Per Seyersted. The general tone of this letter, as well as the precise financial details it

3. Jean-Baptiste Chopin to Lamy Chopin, Cloutierville, May 10, 1847, in possession of Renee Antonia Chopin.

contains, enables us to accept the authenticity of Dr. Chopin's portrait as drawn by Daniel Rankin in his 1932 biography of Kate Chopin: "Victor Chopin came to America with an array of very narrow, very set ideas. These he never changed. After a brief residence in America he acquired the adamant conviction that nothing American was of permanent value except American money. One of his determinations was not to marry unless he could have a wife of genuine French lineage. When he met Julie Benoist he was satisfied. Her lineage was without reproach, entirely French; her inheritance too was worth his esteem" (*CS*, 84).

Julie was the daughter of Charles-François Benoist and Marie-Suzette Rachal. The first known ancestor of the Benoist family, a chamberlain of King Charles VI, can be traced back to 1437. This family includes the famous eighteenth-century "King's painter and wax sculptor" Antoine Benoist. He made a wax portrait of King Louis XIV, which can be seen today in the museum of French history in the château of Versailles. His grandson the knight Antoine Gabriel François Benoist moved to Canada in the eighteeth century. One of his sons settled in St. Louis where he married Marie-Catherine SanGuinette. One of their seven children, Louis Auguste, became a prominent banker in St. Louis and will be referred to later. Another son, Charles François, established himself in Natchitoches Parish, and fathered Julie Benoist.[4]

In 1848, Dr. Chopin's brother, Auguste, died of fever in Cloutierville, having failed to make a fortune, as indicated in a letter from Jean-Baptiste to Lamy, dated May 2, 1849; Jean-Baptiste complains, "All your revolutions prevent us from selling our cotton."[5]

In 1853 Dr. Chopin visited his relatives in France and returned to Louisiana in the fall just after a disastrous epidemic of yellow fever, which he describes in his letter to Lamy on November 28, 1853:

> The epidemic has spread from New Orleans inland and caused terrible havoc everywhere. In the small town where my family lives, more than one third of the population is now dead, and many more would have died if the

4. Further information concerning the Benoist family may be found in *Histoire des grandes familles françaises du Canada: Aperçu sur le chevalier Benoist et quelques familles contemporaines* (Montreal, 1867).

5. Jean-Baptiste Chopin to Lamy Chopin, Cloutierville, May 2, 1849, in possession of Renee Antonia Chopin.

others had not decided to seek shelter in the woods. In my family three persons were affected—my wife and two of my children. Thank God, they were saved after having been in a desperate condition for a few days, especially my wife and my little daughter. Unfortunately, my wife's family has not been so lucky. Four people died in a few days: my father-in-law, his twenty-year old son, his fourteen-year old daughter and their maternal grand-mother.

. . . All this anxiety and all the losses incurred here have made my wife disgusted with this country. She is quite ready to go and live in France: and so I have decided to return along with my family. As soon as I have settled my father-in-law's inheritance, which I am obliged to handle, we shall come to join you. Unfortunately, I fear that it cannot yet be for next spring.[6]

Dr. Chopin remained in Louisiana after having cleared his father-in-law's estate, and one year later he acquired a plantation of 4,367 acres with its buildings and ninety-four slaves. This domain, located a few miles from Cloutierville, had belonged to Robert McAlpin, whose cruel treatment of slaves allowed him to serve as a model for Harriett Beecher Stowe's character Simon Legree. Kate Chopin seems to have accepted the traditional tale about Robert McAlpin since she revived it in her first novel, *At Fault*, in a dialogue between Gregoire and Melicent, who pass by the grave of the former plantation owner, renamed McFarlane.

By a curious association of ideas, the reputation of Jean-Baptiste Chopin also suffered from his quite fortuitous relationship with Robert McAlpin. The excerpts quoted from his letters demonstrate that he had a particularly strong will and wanted to succeed at any price. The pursuit of profit and the desire to obtain the maximum yield from his agricultural production made it essential for him to treat his slaves with great severity. However, it seems exaggerated to give credence to a local legend contending that Oscar's father was a tyrant whose cruelty equaled that of Simon Legree. It would be reasonable to conclude with Daniel Rankin that "perhaps some of the odious traits that linger about the memory of Robert McAlpin have come forward to cloud the remembrance of Dr. Chopin. A strange confusion exists on both sides" (*CS*, 86).

Oscar Chopin was born in Cloutierville in 1845. He had two sisters,

6. Jean-Baptiste Chopin to Lamy Chopin, Cloutierville, November 28, 1853, in possession of Renee Antonia Chopin.

Eugenie and Marie, and a brother, Lamy, who was to remain close to his elder brother and his wife, Kate. Although documents evoking Oscar's early years are scant, we do know something about his life as an adolescent. His father made him work as an overseer to force the slaves to labor in the fields. Oscar rebelled by running away at the age of fourteen and for over a year lived in Cloutierville with his aunt. His mother had to resort to trickery to visit him, since her husband refused to provide her a means of transportation.

When the Civil War broke out, Dr. Chopin returned to France with his family and left his plantation under the care of a friend, Charles Bertrand. They settled in Château-Thierry, about twenty miles from the family estate where Lamy resided. In 1862 Jean-Baptiste decided to visit his Louisiana plantation and made an adventurous trip alone, as a letter written by his wife to her brother-in-law, dated at Château-Thierry, May 1, 1862, attests:

> My dear brother,
> I have just heard from Mr. Chopin and I hasten to let you know. He arrived in New York in good health after a fourteen-day crossing. He thinks it will be very difficult to reach the South. Perhaps he will find it impossible to cross before the capture of New Orleans, which the North is certain will happen. Yet I see from the latest news that one should not despair and that the Confederates still hold good positions and are more than ever determined to defend themselves.[7]

Dr. Chopin seems to have remained in Louisiana for over a year. Two letters from Oscar to his cousin Louis-Antoine, written in Château-Thierry in the autumn of 1863, suggest that his father was still abroad. He never mentions his father's name in the course of ten pages, and he thanks his uncle's family for taking care of his mother, who, quite evidently, was living alone with her children in Château-Thierry.

Oscar completed his secondary education at the College de la Madeleine, which numbered three hundred students divided into four classes. Oscar's scholastic records are missing because the school closed in 1880, and the archives were sent to the archbishopric in Reims, which was destroyed by fire during World War I. All we know is that Oscar took the

7. Julie Benoist Chopin to Lamy Chopin, Chateau-Thierry, May 1, 1862, in possession of Renee Antonia Chopin.

baccalaureate examination at the Sorbonne in 1863 and was unsuccessful. In a letter to his cousin dated November 21, he wrote: "My other colleagues were no luckier; six candidates for literature, six failed. . . . Poor Chateau-Thierry, it deplores its failed scholars this year. In Meaux, out of eight candidates, all met the same fate."[8]

In fact, the tone of his letter indicates that the young man seemed neither to regret nor repent. He spent the next day in the company of most welcoming girls in an establishment of ill repute known as "Le Boum Magenta." He admits himself that he deserved his fate in another passage from the same letter: "Oh, after all it is no setback: it is the most natural consequence of my former laziness. Like the hare, I was too late off the mark. . . . It is both a lesson and a warning." In spite of his failure to pass the baccalaureat, we must say that in tone and in style Oscar's letters reflect a very sound liberal education, a keen sense of humor, and a personal gift for narration. These qualities are evident in the following extract from another letter, dated October 18, 1863:

> Last Monday, we hastened to see Henri Monnier, a stage actor of the Odeon. He was making a fleeting visit here, to give the public of Chateau-Thierry a special performance of *Monsieur Prudhomme*. Everyone ran to see him. The "aristo . . . cracy" of the region, this noble aristocracy with its manners, its prudish ways . . . and its so subtle wit . . . but I was about to unleash all my fury with my words. I'll keep quiet. Let us leave aside this poor aristocracy, its erudition, its apish antics; for after all, these bony shoulders and white arms may be afraid to expose themselves to our eyes, profane menials that we are. And they can be witty without having to know their grammar. Every word that drops from their lips, I mean the women (for I can't stand those confounded prudes), must appear to be charming and evocative, even though they say the most stupid nonsense: it's normal, it's accepted. How much nicer are our working girls with their noisy and natural laughter and their bold looks which do not pretend to be stifled by shyness. Old stupid prudes of high society, be gone! . . . But I am letting myself go too far and I have almost forgotten the show."[9]

Dr. Chopin apparently returned to France in 1864 and then came back to Louisiana with Oscar in the summer of 1865. This is one of the numer-

8. Oscar Chopin to Louis-Antoine Chopin, Chateau-Thierry, November 21, 1863.
9. Oscar Chopin to Louis-Antoine Chopin, Chateau-Thierry, October 18, 1863, in possession of Julie Chopin Cusachs.

ous details included in a letter written to Lamy dated at New Orleans, December 27, 1865:

> My dear brother,
>
> I am taking advantage of a trip to New Orleans to send you this letter. Since postal communications have not yet been reestablished here, it is always difficult to send mail to France. Otherwise, I would have written to you earlier. When I came back, I found my home in the same condition as I had left it. The only thing is that there was no harvest last year, and the forecast for next year is not very good. We are short of labor. The countryside has been deserted, for the negroes have made the best of their freedom by dashing into the towns, where they have been fed until now, whenever they did not find work paid by the Government. However, we are beginning to grow tired of this state of things and are trying to send them back to their homes but, in general, they are little inclined to work. Next year the cotton harvest will be poor. Fortunately, I found a fair amount of cotton from previous years, and it sells at about three times its pre-war price.
>
> When I left, Oscar was in good health, and busy preparing cotton for dispatch.[10]

As we have already seen, Dr. Chopin's reputation in Natchitoches Parish prior to his sojourn in France was poor. Upon his return, it worsened. The other planters became even more jealous of this man who was wealthier after the war than before. Their rancor increased when he acquired a new plantation located on the opposite bank of the Cane River that had formerly belonged to a planter, John Garnahan, who had been ruined by the war. Oscar seems to have suffered from his father's poor reputation, for a short time after his mother's return from France in 1866, he decided to find a way to leave the region. Mme. Chopin wrote to her brother Louis Antoine Benoist beseeching him to find a position for her son in his St. Louis bank. This was quickly achieved, for a letter from Oscar to his cousin Louis dated September 12, 1866, informs us that he joined the Benoist family and enjoyed working for his uncle's company.

This letter, the last one by Oscar in our possession, gives some insight into the young Creole's personality when he was about to lead an independent life in St. Louis, four years before his meeting with his cousin Kath-

10. Jean Baptiste Chopin, New Orleans, December 27, 1865, in possession of Renee Antonia Chopin.

erine O'Flaherty. In general, he retained the carefree attitude of his joyful bachelor days in France:

> St. Louis is really a charming place and, to give you an idea, my dear Louis, I would say that its delights are as great as those of the Rivoli in Paris. It is charming. It is intoxicating. There is indeed a vast opportunity for love and I can assure you that the god of Eros is not forgotten here. But talking of love, I always remember my debut in this field and the first object of my affection. Do you recall that lovely blue-eyed blond of the railways? and also my other beloved brunette from the Faubourg Montmartre in Paris? These love affairs, however, have long since been replaced in my heart by many other more and more pleasant ones.[11]

Despite his apparently frivolous attitude, Oscar, now twenty-two, was seriously concerned about his future. Realistic in recognizing his own good fortune, he discouraged his cousin from coming to settle in the United States in the fear that he might not benefit from the same opportunities and connections (from the same letter):

> I promised to tell you about this country and what can be done here. Today Louisiana is literally ruined and those who can leave, do so. Young people are flocking westwards, here and to Cincinatti. In St. Louis, life is very good. For my first month I earned 50 piastres with the prospect, within a year, of obtaining annually 2.500 to 3.000 piastres. You can see that it is not bad for a good-for-nothing of my sort. But the big problem is that one must know English, which young Frenchmen here generally object to. I would be glad to have you here with me. We could certainly spend many happy moments together, but I know how difficult it would be for you to learn English, and I cannot incite you to come over here to stay and work. I hope, however, to see you one of these fine days, travelling about the country as a tourist and admiring our Western capital.

The son of a wealthy Louisiana planter, but above all a young man who basked in the excellent reputation of the Benoist family in St. Louis high society, Oscar Chopin could hope to establish himself by marrying a young lady of good lineage.

In 1869 his mother's health was suddenly impaired, and his father de-

11. Oscar Chopin to Louis-Antoine Chopin, St. Louis, September 12, 1866, in possession of Julie Chopin Cusachs.

cided to leave his plantation to resettle in New Orleans so that his wife could be closer to medical centers. But Oscar remained in St. Louis and did not see his mother again until a few days before her death, on April 15, 1870. By that time, he was already engaged to Katherine O'Flaherty.

After their June marriage and a European honeymoon, where the young couple witnessed the fall of the Second Empire on September 4, they returned to America at the end of that month. Upon their arrival in St. Louis, they found a moving letter from Oscar's father and decided to leave immediately for New Orleans. After his wife's death in April, Dr. Chopin had left his home in the Vieux Carré on Royale Street to move into a luxurious suite in the St. Louis Hotel (presently the Royal Orleans Hotel), a favorite rendezvous for French Creole society. During the few weeks that she knew him, Kate Chopin seems to have managed to charm her churlish father-in-law, whose presence she would evoke in *The Awakening* as "one of that old Creole race of Pontelliers that dry up and finally blow away" (*KCA*, 65). Dr. Chopin died on November 13 and was buried two days later next to his wife in the old St. Louis Cemetery in New Orleans. The tomb, still intact, was opened in 1982 by special permission of the bishopric to receive the mortal remains of Louis Cusachs. Julie Chopin Cusachs wanted to pay a last homage to her ancestors and, in a certain way, to rehabilitate the memory of her grandfather.

Although Kate Chopin lived exclusively in St. Louis at the time of her literary production, she made frequent trips to Louisiana to visit her husband's relatives. She often stayed with her brother and sister-in-law, Lamy Chopin and Frances Hertzog, who lived in the large plantation home at Derry near Cloutierville. This French Creole family played a key role in Kate Chopin's life, and echoes of her Louisiana in-laws pervade her work, mainly in her first novel, *At Fault,* and many short stories set in the Cane River region.

"What Are the Prospects for the Book?" : Rewriting a Woman's Life

HEATHER KIRK THOMAS

> Yet the woman was dead and could not deny,
> But women forever will whine and cry.
> So now I must listen the whole night through
> To the torment with which I had nothing to do—
> —Kate Chopin, "The Haunted Chamber"

In February, 1899, while awaiting the April publication of her novel *The Awakening*, Kate Chopin wrote the poem a portion of which appears above (*CW*, II, 734). Suggesting that Chopin composed it after at least one evening's heated discussion of her forthcoming manuscript, the poem records her burgeoning cynicism about the eventual reception of her novel and strongly suggests that she was not unprepared for its mixed reviews. Despite the predictable reservations of turn-of-the-century moralists and society editors to Chopin's overtly sexual treatment of the "woman problem" in *The Awakening,* the novel's importance has persisted and has been rediscovered by feminists and literary critics of recent decades. In fact, as a result of new textual, theoretical, and sociocultural reconsiderations nearly one hundred years after publication of *The Awakening,* we may safely state that Chopin's novel has successfully challenged the canon and won permanent recognition.

Unfortunately, the innovative literary theories that led to the recovery and investiture of Chopin's text have not always sufficiently focused on her biography, much of which remains enveloped in a Victorian shroud. In particular, the final five years of her life after the publication of her novel in 1899 have been substantially mythologized. Although her writing characteristically displays a supremely sardonic voice and her personal correspondence confirms a genuine literary ambition, Chopin is still described in modern anthology headnotes and critical studies as a defeated and demoralized woman who retired from literary and public life after unfavorable reviews of *The Awakening*.

I propose that this interpretation is a decidedly cavalier misreading of the author of so many lighthearted stories and southern sexual spoofs. Instead, there is strong circumstantial evidence that increasingly poor health prevented Chopin from maintaining her formerly prolific literary activities in the final years of her life. This alternative view calls into question the patriarchal notion that Chopin terminated her ten-year literary career in a fit of hurt feelings and is compatible with what we know of her writings and temperament.

In a recent discussion of Henry David Thoreau and *Walden*, Lawrence Buell remarks insightfully upon the bizarre literary custom of canonizing writers: "It is not just the texts that are canonized, but the figure, especially in the case of an autobiographical writer." [1] This is as true for Kate Chopin as for Thoreau. When *The Awakening* finally achieved canonical status, we canonized its author. But in Chopin's personal life several periods remain shadowy and controversial, probably the result of the current demise of biographical criticism. However, old myths die hard. This article is written in hopes of extinguishing what I believe to be one of the most crucial biographical myths about Chopin—that an emotional depression following harsh reviews of *The Awakening* silenced her pen and retired her from literary life. In fact, her portrayal as a nineteenth-century "weeping female" may have substantially affected her reputation as a serious artist in the literary marketplace of her time.

Daniel Rankin, who prepared the first comprehensive critical Chopin biography in 1932, endeavored to ameliorate the damage to her literary reputation by citing examples from publications he felt had unfairly represented her emotional situation after the publication of her novel. For instance, he cites Leonides Rutledge Whipple's statement in the 1907 *Library of Southern Literature* that "the unfriendly reception given [the novel] by certain narrow-minded critics struck deep at the author's heart, even killing her desire to write so that from about 1899 until her death . . . she produced nothing more" *(CS*, 185). Rankin also includes a statement

---

1. Lawrence Buell, "The Thoreauvean Pilgrimage: The Structure of an American Culture," *American Literature*, LXI (1989), 199.

by Chopin's daughter, Lelia Hattersley, Whipple's source for his note, on the effect of the novel's reviewers on her mother: "I know how deeply she was hurt by many facts, principally that she never wrote again" (*CS*, 185). And finally Rankin quotes from an entry in the 1930 *Dictionary of American Biography* that echoes the testimonies of Chopin's daughter and Whipple: "It is one of the tragedies of recent American literature that Mrs. Chopin . . . should have been so grievously hurt by the attacks of provincial critics as to lay aside her pen" (*CS*, 185–86).

A representative survey of recent articles, books, and anthology headnotes reveals an amazing similarity to the unfortunate early biographical sketches that Rankin strove (unsuccessfully) to correct. For instance, her most noted modern critic, Per Seyersted, states in the introduction to *The Complete Works of Kate Chopin* that she felt so much like a "literary outcast" that her writing, as a result, was "soon to cease altogether." (*CW*, 30). The *Columbia Literary History of the United States* (597) repeats the testimony of Chopin's peers that she was "crushed" by the rejection of her novel and "wrote very little in the remaining five years of her life." She felt "left by the wayside" as she herself wrote in the short sketch "A Reflection"—struck mute as Larzer Ziff has so accurately written. Helen Taylor, in a newly published comparative study of "gender, race, and region" in Chopin's fiction, reiterates the belief that the novelist was terribly "disheartened at the critical reception of *The Awakening* and wrote little more before her death in 1904."[2] And finally, even the *Norton Anthology of Literature by Women*, edited by noted feminists Sandra M. Gilbert and Susan Gubar, proposes that Chopin's decreased productivity in the final years of her life might have been "related to the failure of her book" (993).

Beginning with the nineteenth-century male gatekeepers and female moralists and continuing into recent times, the literary community has successfully propagated an unfortunate paradigm of histrionic female behavior in Chopin's reaction to a few bad reviews. In fact, these notices were widely mixed. Some praised the novel's structure and artistry, although objecting to the overt treatment of adultery and suicide. Like a faded

---

2. Helen Taylor, *Gender, Race, and Region in the Writings of Grace King, Ruth McEnery Stuart, and Kate Chopin* (Baton Rouge, 1989), 202.

family daguerrotype, this portrait of Chopin has been preserved and passed down by her critics, a curiously old-fashioned memento of a restrictive culture in which women were perceived as irrational and genetically inclined to attacks of "the vapors."

Yet to read Chopin's fiction and personal papers is to recognize that the facts portray a far different situation from the one accepted and reiterated for nearly a century by so many editors and critics. Such a revision will clarify Chopin's attitude toward her artistic career after the publication of *The Awakening* and suggest, before these previously mentioned misconceptions about her life are canonized along with her novel, that the reduced literary production of her final five years was the result of an increasingly debilitating physical illness, not a defeated, embittered decline into silence. If we examine the facts following Chopin's publication of her novel in April, 1899, it becomes readily apparent she was never severely depressed over the reception of *The Awakening*. Rather, during the summer of 1899 she experienced a serious illness from which she was never to recover completely and which probably contributed to her death in 1904 from a brain hemorrhage.

In "The Haunted Chamber," Chopin sardonically remarked upon the actual fate of a woman much like her protagonist in *The Awakening,* Edna Pontellier: "Yet the woman was dead and could not deny" (*CW*, 734). Chopin would undoubtedly find it ironic to see her literary reputation in analogous circumstances today. But since she cannot speak out to deny the unsubstantiated rumors attributed to the final years of her life, we shall attempt to combat them for her. This is a feasible and happy task, moreover, since the facts immediately subsequent to the publication of *The Awakening* do not substantially alter our understanding or perception of Chopin as the same ambitious writer who had pursued success in the literary marketplace throughout her career. If we assemble the testimony of her personal correspondence, literary compositions, financial transactions, real-estate dealings, and journal entries, we receive an increasingly clearer mental and physical picture of her after the April, 1899, publication of her novel. And in particular her two extant but unpublished logbooks (1888 to 1902), in which she recorded the titles, dates of composition, submissions, rejections, and sales of her essays, short stories, novels, poems, and a play, offer extremely credible evidence of her continued artistic commitment and ambitions.[3]

Having begun her work on *The Awakening* during the summer of 1897, Chopin sent the manuscript in January to Way and Williams, the publisher of her most recent collection of stories, *A Night in Acadie* (November, 1897). Although they accepted her novel (but no date is recorded in her logbook for this acceptance), it was eventually transferred to Herbert S. Stone, also of Chicago, in November, 1898. Further evidence of her continuing efforts to publicize herself as a writer, Chopin's logbook receipts show she earned twenty-five dollars for a reading in February at the local "St. George's Guild." She was complimented by an editor in the St. Louis *Star* of February 13, 1898, who called her "probably the most talented writer of Creole stories" in the nation (6). However, the *Star*'s reviewer went on to inquire why native Missouri authors like Chopin had previously failed to employ "Missouri and Missouri people as a subject." Since we can determine from her correspondence that Chopin was an avid reader of her notices, it seems no coincidence that in the month following this flattering mention in the *Star* she composed "Elizabeth Stock's One Story," a rare tale set in rural Missouri.

Chopin's logbook shows that in April, 1898, Way and Williams accepted a new collection of her short stories, tentatively titled *A Vocation and a Voice*. However, when the collection was later transferred to Herbert S. Stone along with *The Awakening*, the new publisher returned it to Chopin in February of 1900, a gesture probably less indicative of any critical flap over her novel than a publisher's conclusion that story collections were not selling well. Additional evidence of her continued perseverance in searching for a literary agent (again, confirmed by that year's correspondence), Chopin made a business trip to Chicago in mid-March. Throughout 1898 she continued her translations of tales by her acknowledged mentor, Guy de Maupassant, but she wrote more poetry than fiction that year, completing only "Elizabeth Stock's One Story," "A Horse Story," and "The Storm." Written on July 19 but never offered to a publisher in her

3. Logbooks in Kate Chopin Collection, courtesy of the Missouri Historical Society, St. Louis.

lifetime, the last story's depiction of a sensuous southern adulteress suggests a newly amoral reenvisioning of Edna Pontellier's situation in *The Awakening*. During the summer of 1898, Chopin probably vacationed at White Oaks, Wisconsin, since a topical poem written in August was given the title "White Oaks." And as noted previously, both *The Awakening* and *A Vocation and a Voice* were transferred to Herbert S. Stone that November.

In addition to her literary activities, Chopin continued the real estate dealings with which she apparently supported herself and her six children throughout 1898. In fact, one of her logbooks contains a detailed business memorandum written that year listing her loans and leases on four St. Louis properties. In December of 1898 Chopin made a brief trip to Natchitoches Parish, Louisiana, to complete the sale of the "Fontenot plantation" containing the small early Louisiana-style home and 135 arpents of land where she and her children had lived before her husband's death in December, 1882. Natchitoches courthouse records show that the power of attorney dictating the terms of this sale was completed in St. Louis before Chopin's visit to Louisiana. This formality enabled Chopin to make her trip to the South even briefer. In a very few days she concluded the sale of the plantation, renewed old friendships with relatives and others, and still managed to return to St. Louis in time to celebrate Christmas with her children. Her trip coincided with a sudden southern snowstorm that later inspired the impressionistic piece "A December Day in Dixie," and the poem "Old Natchitoches" may have been written during her stay in Louisiana. However, a more significant sign of her literary ambitions at the time is represented by the following notice in a local newspaper dated December 25: "Mrs. Kate Chopin, after a short stay of one week, has returned to her home in St. Louis, where she will remain during the Christmas holidays, then will spend the rest of the winter in New York."[4] As no evidence has been located that places her in New York during the early months of 1899, this information must have been wishful thinking on Chopin's part or might represent the zealous publicity efforts of a provincial society editor and admirer.

4. Unidentified newspaper clipping, in Scrapbook No. 69, Melrose Collection, Cammie G. Henry Research Center, Eugene P. Watson Memorial Library, Northwestern State Universtiy of Louisiana.

The year 1899 saw the April 22 publication of *The Awakening*, which had been accepted by Herbert S. Stone in January, one month before they returned Chopin's proposed collection, *A Vocation and a Voice*. According to her logbooks, she wrote only four stories in 1899 but completed numerous poems. Although the year 1899 has been too frequently characterized by scholars as defeating and depressing because of Chopin's disillusionment over reviews of her novel, by all indications those reviews were widely mixed.[5] If some notices disapproved of the novelist's treatment of adultery and female sexuality, others praised her skillful technique and use of locale. Nonetheless, amid a supposed literary brouhaha, Chopin sat optimistically for publicity photographs for the *Critic* and her publisher, Herbert Stone. Moreover, when she wrote Stone in June to inquire "What are the prospects for the book?" she self-confidently enclosed a local review of her novel that "seems so able and intelligent—by contrast with some of the drivel I have run across that I thought I should like to have you read it when you have the time"(*KCM*, 137). Finally, written May 28, Chopin's ultimate comic rebuttal to her critics appeared in the form of a good-natured but supremely sardonic "retraction" in the July *Book News* in which she claims, "I never dreamed of Mrs. Pontellier making such a mess of things and working out her own damnation as she did. If I had had the slightest intimation of such a thing I would have excluded her from the company. But when I found out what she was up to, the play was half over and it was then too late" (*KCM*, 137).

In general, reports of Chopin's severe depression over the novel's reception have been derived from posthumous interviews with her children or friends. Contrary to this hearsay evidence, her personal correspondence never suggests she was disheartened. What her letters do specifically mention, however, is a serious illness she sustained during the late summer or fall of 1899. On August 24, 1899, Chopin wrote from St. Louis to Richard B. Shepard in Salt Lake City to answer his query regarding her published works (*KCM*, 141). Written two and a half months later, however, her second letter to Shepard, dated November 8, 1899, and composed at her home in St. Louis, is more interesting:

---

5. See *CS*, 173–74, and *CB*, 173–78. See also selected excerpts from reviews in *KCA*, 145–55.

> *Since receiving and answering your letters last July I have had a severe*
> *spell of illness and am only now looking about and gathering up the scat-*
> *tered threads of a rather monotonous existence* [emphasis added]. Kindly
> let me know if you have procured my books or if it is still your desire that I
> send them to you. . . . Hoping you will pardon my unavoidable neglect in
> responding to your wishes.
>
> Yours very sincerely
> Kate Chopin[6]

Although no information links Chopin and Shepard beyond these two letters, hers of November 8 indicates that she experienced some confusion
about the passage of time during the summer months of 1899. Per Seyersted maintains that Chopin "was usually very clearheaded and exact. Are
there letters missing here, or has she become forgetful or a little muddled
when she speaks of letters (plural) and July (instead of August), and of
'my unavoidable neglect in responding to your wishes'? We can only
speculate."[7] Although Seyersted's final determination is that Chopin's
summer illness was most likely "of a psychological kind," I would argue
that her letter provides circumstantial evidence sufficient to associate the
summer of 1899 with the beginning of Chopin's gradual but observable
physical decline until her death.

The facts in her case are as follows: In October she spent time in Wisconsin, as the letters of the apparently apocryphal Lady Janet Scammon
Young and Dr. Dunrobin Thomson were forwarded to her the first of that
month by publisher Herbert S. Stone in care of "Mr. O. W. Meysenburg,
Lake Beulah Station, Wisconsin"(*KCM*, 142–47, 199*n*.46). Chopin's
youngest child, Lelia, was away at least during the month of August. The
society column of the August 3, 1899, St. Louis *Mirror* remarks that
"Miss Lelia Chopin, who is visiting . . . at Excelsior, Minn., won the
prize at a thimble bee last week, which was given there," and on September 14, the editor also comments upon her return: "Miss Lelia Chopin has
just returned from Lake Minnetonka, where she has spent the summer with
Mrs. E. C. Chase." Although a young lady who would make her debut in
the fall might well travel without her mother, her youngest child's absence

6. Per Seyersted, "Kate Chopin's Wound: Two New Letters," *American Literary Realism*, XX (1987), 71–75.

7. *Ibid.*, 74.

might also have been arranged to allow the novelist a quiet convalescence in St. Louis or Wisconsin.

Chopin's personal papers provide little mention of her experiences with ill health, but she is well known for her reluctance to discuss private matters in print. Several exceptions, however, suggest that her 1899 physical illness might have been related to a previous history of chronic health problems. For instance, in an August 13, 1870, honeymoon diary entry, she mentions a problem with recurrent headaches: "Had one of my fearful headaches, which took me directly to bed—knowing that sleep alone would come to my relief" (*KCM*, 82). Likewise, a February 20, 1897, essay, the second in a series of six written for the St. Louis *Criterion* that year, recounts Chopin's recent consultation with a doctor who treated her for eye "inflammation" (*CW*, 708). Characteristically, Chopin downplays this illness. Instructed by the doctor not to "read, write, nor sew," she humorously reports the results of her convalescence on her household: "Well, the newspapers remain unread; letters are lying unanswered, and the boys are sewing on their own buttons" (*CW*, 708).

In the summer of 1899 Chopin might have experienced a painful recurrence of the migraine headaches she documented in 1870 or a return of her 1897 problems with her eyes. Interestingly, loss of vision furnishes the central plot concern in several of her earlier short stories—for example, "The Recovery" (February, 1896) and "The Blind Man" (July, 1896)—as she similarly uses physical illness in her fiction after *The Awakening*. However, Chopin's letter to Shepard itself offers substantial circumstantial evidence for proposing that she suffered a real physical illness during the summer and fall of 1899. And this conclusion appears to be more in line with her literary opinions and lifework than the belief that she suffered from a disastrous emotional decline.

In addition to having raised six active children to adulthood, she successfully managed parcels of Louisiana and St. Louis real estate and ambitiously pursued a literary career involving a lively correspondence with editors and agents and requiring public appearances and readings at local guilds and literary clubs. Moreover, despite winning a national reputation in the early 1890s for her regional short stories, she experimented with other genres (poetry, drama, essay, and novel) throughout her career. Finally, in the comprehensive logbooks Chopin began in 1888, she continued to make regular entries of each completion, submission, rejection, and sale of her writings until December, 1902. These logbooks alone furnish substantial proof that a determined professional like Chopin did not abandon her artistic endeavors after one bout of unfavorable reviews.

In November, 1899, when she resumed her writing, she might have done so to quell rumors that she had experienced an emotional or creative decline after the publication of her novel. At the same time, she might have wished to reassure her local audience of the return of her health. Her informal essay, which appeared November 26, 1899, in the St. Louis *Post-Dispatch*, commences, "On certain brisk, bright days I like to walk from my home, near Thirty-fourth street, down to the shopping district" (*CW*, 721). The essay makes a strong case for her physical stamina and good humor.

In fact, perhaps attempting to dispel gossip that she had been seriously affected by critiques of her novel, she portrays herself as undisciplined, even lackadaisical, in her approach to writing: "Eight or nine years ago I began to write stories—short stories which appeared in the magazines, and I forthwith began to suspect I had the writing habit. The public shared this impression, and called me an author. Since then, though I have written many short stories and a novel or two, I am forced to admit that I have not the writing habit. But it is hard to make people with the questioning habit believe this" (*CW*, 721).

Despite Chopin's witty dismissal of herself to the ranks of "scribbling women," the deprecating tone of her mock persona is misleading. An indication of her more serious and professional side is her exclamation of unquestionable exasperation when people mistake her for a dilettante: "How hard it is for one's acquaintances and friends to realize that one's books are to be taken seriously, and that they are subject to the same laws which govern the existence of others' books!" (*CW*, 722). Another significant factor confirmed by Chopin's essay is that several of her children were absent from St. Louis at that time. Although the circumstances and duration of their absence have not been explained by her biographers, the children she mentions, who are "at a safe distance" in Kentucky, Colorado, and Louisiana, might have been shuttled to relatives or friends because she suffered an illness that summer (*CW*, 723). We know that her daughter, Lelia, spent the month of August in Minnesota.

Only a few days after the publication of this personal essay in the *Post-Dispatch*, Chopin appeared on November 29 by invitation of the elite Wednesday Club at their Reciprocity Day with local authors. According to her logbook, she received fifteen dollars to read her story "Ti Demon." (However, the sketch "A Horse Story" was originally given this same title in her logbook, so she might have read either one.) Among the other local talents invited to perform their works was her poet friend Robert E. Lee Gibson. On the following day, a recounting of the Wednesday Club activities printed in the *Post-Dispatch* displays no hint of chastisement over Chopin's latest novel. The complimentary description calls "Ti Demon" a "touching little story of creole life," and the editor specifically selects Chopin's splendid outfit of "black satin with white lace trimmings, jetted front and blue velvet toque" as representative of the "beautiful gowns" worn by the assembled guests. In addition, the November 30 issue of the St. Louis *Mirror* mentions Lelia Chopin (who would be twenty in December) as one of "this season's debutantes and the only daughter of Mrs. Kate Chopin, who stands now among the first writers of the day."

If the reader of Chopin's November 26, 1899, essay had no knowledge she had been the center of a local scandal over *The Awakening*, it would be impossible to discern any spitefulness or resignation in its author. Additional evidence that Chopin was never ostracized in St. Louis for her book is suggested by the aforementioned accounts in newspapers and magazines, whose editors continued to celebrate her talents and remark upon her social life in their columns as they had prior to the publication of her "shocking" novel. And since by November, 1899, Chopin resumed attendance at public social functions, returned to her writing, and immediately after the completion of "Ti Demon" sent the story in December to an editor at the *Century*, it seems safe to conclude that by winter she had recovered, at least temporarily, from that summer's illness and felt able to pursue her normal activities (*KCM*, 147–48).

Chopin's literary production after the publication of *The Awakening*, however, demonstrates a revealing preoccupation with illness that was probably provoked by hers. In thematic focus and leitmotif, Chopin's writings suggest a fascination with the effects of catastrophe, the onset of disease, and the loneliness of old age. In her November 26, 1899, essay Chopin had argued that interesting plots or eccentric characters offered by well-meaning friends or acquaintances were never useful to her. "I am completely at the mercy of unconscious selection" (*CW,* 722). If Chopin's creative imagination was indeed dependent upon a process of "unconscious selection," then her work from the year 1899 and immediately after should reveal at least some of her subliminal preoccupations. And Chopin's works from this time are characterized by repeated thematic treatments of illness, aging, and death, beginning with her meditative poem "A Life," dated and titled by manuscript May 10, 1899:

> A day with a splash of sunlight,
> Some mist and a little rain.
> A life with a dash of love-light,
> Some dreams and a touch of pain.
> *To love a little and then to die!*
> *To live a little and never know why!*
> (*CW,* 734; emphasis added)

Two other undated Chopin poems attributed to 1899 by Seyersted also evaluate the transitory nature of human existence. The first, "Because," contrasts the moral choices associated with free will to the predestined cycles of nature and the instinctual lives of animals (*CW,* 734). The second, "A Little Day," represents a telling evaluation of the poet's life expectancies:

> A little day is mine 'twixt night and night
> *So short 'tis nearly done—*
> There might have been more joy more light
> Yet do the shades come without the sun—
> I'll be no grumbler—take it all in all—
> 'Tis better than t'ave had no day at all.
> (*KCM,* 42; emphasis added)

The stories "The Godmother" and "A Little Country Girl," written in January and February, 1899, before the publication of her novel, were clearly inspired by Chopin's December, 1898, visit to Natchitoches Parish. After composing the poem "A Life" in May, she apparently wrote nothing during the summer she was ill. She resumed her writings in November, however, and completed the November 26 essay for the *Post-Dispatch,* a brief meditative piece, "A Reflection," and the story "Ti Demon."

"A Reflection" is decidedly not a work of fiction. Its autobiographical import suggests it was originally written as part of her essay for the *Post-Dispatch* but deleted by the author herself as too personally revealing. Without specifically naming her persona, Chopin describes her situation as a woman nearly fifty years old, and most likely having suffered a recent lengthy convalescence, as being left "by the wayside" out of the "moving procession of human energy" (*CW,* 622). Reminiscent of John Steinbeck's story "The Leader of the People," the overall tone of "A Reflection" is the dawning of loneliness, yielding to exhaustion, and finally caustic resignation. However, typically in Chopin's ironic outlook, she finally rationalizes that from where she sits by the wayside she can at least "hear the rhythm of the march," unlike the frenetic marchers who require neither leader nor cadence because they "do not need to apprehend the significance of things" (*CW,* 622).

Composed in November, the story "Ti Demon" is also revealing, considering Chopin's professed creative dependence on "unconscious selection." Baptized Plaisance, the central character, Ti Demon, was given his nickname as an infant by his mother because his incessant crying kept her awake at night. As the boy grew into manhood, however, the name became "almost a synonym for gentleness" because of the boy's well-known reputation for "bovine mildness" (*CW,* 623). Although the story has no overt focus on illness, sickness, or death, it is a violent tale of drunkenness and misguided jealousy that leads to an act of brutality by a normally gentle man. After Ti Demon mistakenly attacks what he sees as an interloper for his beloved Marianne, he loses both fiancée and reputation. Hence, "Ti Demon," is a tale with a moral, in its own way reminiscent of Hawthorne's "Young Goodman Brown" or "The Minister's Black Veil," in that a single evening's events, compounded by the altered attitudes of the villagers, forever change the direction of a man's life.

Chopin's correspondence shows that she was an avid reader of the reviews of *The Awakening,* and her statement in *Book News* indicates that she was well aware that some readers had strong objections to its content. Certainly her acquaintances must have informed her of local rumors that she had experienced a serious emotional decline in the wake of those reviews. Knowledge of this local gossip might have furnished part of the unconscious inspiration for Chopin's story "Ti Demon." Not unlike the isolated act of her central character (or in her case, as the result of one problematic novel), she might have feared she would later be "pointed out to strangers by those of a younger generation who had no distinctive idea of the nature of [her] crimes" (*CW*, 627). Ironically, even Chopin's attempts to place the story (and to save her maligned reputation) failed. The editors of the *Atlantic* rejected it on January 18, 1900, because of its "sombre" and "sad note" (*KCM*, 148).

The following year's literary production more overtly exhibits Chopin's unconscious preoccupation with illness, aging, and mortality, as four of the five stories she completed in 1900 dramatize these themes. The single exception, "A December Day in Dixie" ("One Day in Winter"), is a nostalgic account of her December, 1898, trip to sell her marital homestead in Natchitoches Parish, and Chopin had revised this piece off and on since first completing it in January, 1899. When the manuscript was finally shortened, she submitted it to *Youth's Companion* on February 15, 1900. Her logbook indicates they bought the story for ten dollars in March, but no publication has been located there. As evidenced by her logbook records, several of Chopin's stories written after 1899 and sold to *Youth's Companion* were apparently never published there. As the magazine's longtime editor Daniel S. Ford had been an early admirer and publisher of her work, in all likelihood these omissions are attributable to his death in 1899 and a resultant change in editorial policy rather than any blacklisting of Chopin. Nine months following the publication of *The Awakening*, on January 23, 1900, Chopin completed the story "Alexandre's Wonderful Experience," a tale of a New Orleans antique dealer's assistant who suffers temporary memory loss as a result of illness. Autobiographical details abound in the story, as the young dreamer Alexandre is constantly inventing new plot twists to resolve the lives of people he meets. Moreover, analogous to Chopin's own aspirations, Alexandre's "secret and consuming passion was an ambition to rise in the world, and if a lively imagination was to count for anything he would reach the heights in no time" (*KCM*, 22). The story turns upon his habit of daydreaming outrageously romantic solutions to his problems, and its New Comedy resolution reveals the marriage of his benefactors that will make those daydreams a reality.

However, the central climax of the tale lies ultimately not in this idyllic union but in Alexandre's sudden onset of unconsciousness, his subsequent period of hospitalization, and a related loss of memory. The Afro-American spiritual "Jordan Am a Hard Road to Trabble" is the only melody in Alexandre's mind for a long time until he is awakened by a "white-capped young woman" who mocks his oft-repeated refrain (*KCM*, 25). When Alexandre is finally released from the hospital, his first impressions curiously echo Chopin's own meditations about being "left by the wayside" in "A Reflection": "They told him he might go home: but he went out and sat on the warm stone coping in the sun. The flush of rushing spring tide was in the air and the people all seemed light-headed and glad. Alexandre, too, rejoiced to be alive and to feel himself again one of the multitude" (*KCM*, 26).

Apparently for Kate Chopin, as for Emily Dickinson, "Pain" could have an "Element of Blank." And nothing would be more terrifying to a professional writer than encountering a dark void where one was unconsciously accustomed to returning for literary inspiration. In Chopin's case, such a memory lapse would have been particularly fearful, as her success as a local-color writer had been achieved by continued creative employment of materials from her distant Louisiana past. As her letter to Richard B. Shepard seems to indicate, her illness that summer might have involved a short period of amnesia similar to Alexandre's. Additional evidence for a comparable experience may be linked to one of the two extant manuscripts of this story that has "many changes" in an unknown hand (*KCM*, 191*n*.5). If Chopin had difficulties with her vision or memory in the latter half of 1899, a friend might have served as her amanuensis.

After "Alexandre's Wonderful Experience," Chopin composed three more stories that year. The plot of "The Gentleman from New Orleans" (February 6, 1900) specifically turns upon a sick and aging mother's request to see her beloved daughter one last time before her death: " 'Her mother's failing pretty smart,' went on Parkins, caressing Mrs. Buddie's cheek but showing not half so much emotion now as Mr. Buddie who was frankly shedding tears. 'She couldn't stand the trip from Winn. . . . The last words she says was, 'Si Parkins you fetch my girl to me if you got to bring her across Bud Benoite's dead body; if we wait any longer it might be too late' " (*CW*, 637).

"Charlie" (April, 1900), a fairly predictable account of a southern tomboy tamed by puppy love, includes a darker subplot emanating from the accidental dismemberment of Charlie's beloved father, who loses his right hand. For a lighthearted, wry initiation tale, the narrative is surprisingly dark in its treatment of death and illness. When Charlie was a youngster, she believed that physical disease was only a state of mind and that even death might be avoided if one strong-mindedly willed it away. Thus, Charlie says when Tinette's baby dies, "If she had only thought she didn't have the measles instead of thinking so hard that she did, she wouldn't have died" (*CW*, 645). However, as Charlie approaches womanhood, she realizes that wishing away death is a naïvete professed by little girls. She finally comprehends that life is most valued after one has confronted first-hand the possibility of death. Hence, when Charlie and her sisters receive word that their father is out of danger, "the crushing pressure was lifted, and they rejoiced that it was to be life rather than death—life at any price" (*CW*, 664).

At the story's conclusion, Charlie devotes her life to serving as a "right hand" to her father, a happier and infinitely more androgynous resolution to father-daughter relationships than Chopin depicted in *The Awakening*. The story's open-endedness also optimistically suggests Charlie's possibilities as her future husband's "right hand." If Chopin suffered a temporary disability and needed physical assistance herself the previous year, her employment of this metaphor to suggest familial loyalties might reflect the unconscious natural selection of her own illness.

Finally, "The White Eagle," written May 9, 1900, is a deceptively simple and moving narrative of an independent spinster's childhood, middle age, and death. Its ironic tone exposes the euphemisms about death in favor of its realities—that "people die and children squabble over estates, large or small" (*CW*, 671)—but it also tells of a strong woman's devotion to the past, symbolized by an ornamental iron yard eagle. An ominously white symbol of her own approaching death, the eagle was always kept in a corner of the woman's room because it helped her "to remember; or, better, he never permitted her to forget" (*CW*, 672). At last succumbing to a "fierce fever," the crooked and grizzled old woman observes the eagle leave his corner and perch "pecking at her bosom" (*CW*, 672). Unlike the soaring bird imagery Chopin employed in *The Awakening* to depict the "artist with the courageous soul that dares and defies," in this story the iron eagle is weighted firmly on the ground, for after the death of the woman, he is placed on her grave as a monument (*KCA*, 63). With the passage of time, atop the "sinking grave the white eagle has dipped forward as if about to take his flight. But he never does. He gazes across the vast plain with an expression which in a human being would pass for wisdom" (*CW*, 673). Chopin's ironic commentary on the inevitability of death and even her choice of a suitably enigmatic grave monument for the old woman imply a kind of self-recognition.

If Chopin had more than metaphorically gazed at the ominous white eagle of death in the corners of her life, two poems she completed that year deserve attention. Seyersted has noted that the manuscript of the poem "Alone," dated July 6, is not in Chopin's handwriting, a peculiarity that might confirm some loss of manual dexterity. Secondly, the poem "To the Friend of My Youth: To Kitty" has been titled and given an August 24, 1900 (?), composition date by Daniel Rankin, based on evidence now lost. An August 24, 1870, entry in Chopin's honeymoon diary, however, confirms that the month and day allocated to the poem by Rankin correspond to Kitty Garesche's birthday (*KCM*, 85). After recovering from her illness, Chopin might have written the poem to memorialize her friendship at Sacred Heart Academy in St. Louis. Kitty Garesche took religious vows the year of Chopin's marriage.

The thematic concerns of Chopin's work from this period, as well as the existence of manuscripts prepared or edited by other hands, strongly suggest she was visually or physically incapacitated during the summer and fall of 1899. If she had recently confronted the possibility of encroaching death, her experience may have resulted in a parallel creative impulse to portray illness, aging, and death.

Definitive evidence for Chopin's temporary recovery from her summer's illness and her return to the literary community is represented by an essay-review unknown to most Chopin scholars. Reprinted in my " 'Development of the Literary West': An Undiscovered Kate Chopin Essay," this piece was probably completed about the time it was published—December 9, 1900—as the featured front-page article of the St. Louis *Republic*'s *Sunday Magazine* book section.[8] Chopin's essay is entitled the "Develop-

---

8. Heather Kirk Thomas, " 'Development of the Literary West': An Undiscovered Kate Chopin Essay," *American Literary Realism*, XXII (Winter, 1990), 69–75.

ment of the Literary West." Confirming Chopin's continued warmth for her local audience and exhibiting a confident critical voice, the omnibus essay sweepingly discusses the development of a western literary tradition, from its genesis in the early diaries of St. Louis's Father de Smet through the seminal realism of Bret Harte and Mark Twain to a localized discussion of St. Louis authors. As part of her survey, Chopin also mentions her personal aversion to the turn-of-the-century "Chicago school" (the literary naturalists) whom she considers too preoccupied with "unpleasant" themes.

A unique feature of this essay is the watercolor portrait that accompanies it, a bespectacled, white-haired Chopin, painted by her artist son, Oscar. As this portrait represents the only known image of Chopin wearing eyeglasses, it may furnish another circumstantial clue that her eyesight was affected by her 1899 illness. In addition, this issue of the *Republic* contains a separate article about Chopin as one of several St. Louis women who have "recently achieved considerable success" (10). The reviewer mentions that Chopin's "problem novel," *The Awakening,* was "severely criticized" but also notes that this was "not so much [because] of the workmanship as of the story; *but Mrs. Chopin says she does not mind that*" (emphasis mine).

Compared to her literary production immediately following *The Awakening,* Chopin's writing from 1901 until her death follows a decidedly new direction. Perhaps she felt a pressing need to convince her local and national audience that she had never been despondent over the book's reception or to demonstrate to those who knew she had been ill that she was now sufficiently recovered to resume her professional career. An examination of her writings in the final years permits several tentative conclusions. First, the work she completed then suggests she was garnering her limited physical strength to recapture her former place in the regional fiction market by completing pieces she knew from experience could be easily placed at eastern magazines like *Youth's Companion* and *Vogue.* For instance, in 1901 she wrote only three known stories, and those were apparently written (or at least entered in her logbook) in a three-day composition sequence. Only one of these, "The Wood-Choppers" (October 17, 1901), exists in manuscript. It was sold to *Youth's Companion* for forty dollars and published in 1902. The two other titles listed are "Millie's First Ball" (October 16, 1901) and "Toot's Nurses" (October 18, 1901). The first of these Chopin entered as sold for thirty dollars to *Youth's Companion*; the entry for "Toot's Nurses" was later crossed out in her log book, so she may have destroyed it.

Chopin's last known story was composed in 1902, two years before her death. "Polly," a superficial love story obviously created for a family audience, was quickly sold and published in *Youth's Companion* that summer. This was to be her final piece of fiction in print. Chopin began a story entitled "The Impossible Miss Meadows" (*ca.* 1902 to 1903) set in Wisconsin and obviously based upon her summer visits there, but it was never completed.

In addition to the evidence of her writing, we can draw other conclusions, based on fact, about Chopin's final years. Just as a radical change took place in her literary preoccupations after her health was first affected, when her illness became increasingly more debilitating, she made alterations to her schedule of duties and responsibilities. Chopin approached most of life as a pragmatic businesswoman. Echoing the earnestness she employed to salvage her damaged literary reputation before her death, her personal and financial life exhibits a similar pattern of tidying up loose ends.

In 1900 Chopin began the first of several real-estate transfers in Louisiana that would free her from the annual responsibility of managing her properties there. On November 10, 1900, Natchitoches courthouse records show she sold land to her brother-in-law Lamy Chopin, a sign that she was less able to manage her own properties personally and thus was simplifying the transfer of her estate to her future heirs. This trend of extrication from her Louisiana lands was to follow in 1902 and 1903. In addition, she might have also needed capital at that time for a wedding gift to her firstborn son, Jean, who was married in 1902.

If continuing ill health depressed Chopin throughout these years, she never spoke of it in her correspondence. Apparently she had expressed her own personal creed in the 1899 poem "A Little Day" when she wrote, "I'll be no grumbler" (*KCM*, 42). Nonetheless, after 1902, Chopin was never to recover her robust health. In all likelihood, increasingly serious and repetitive bouts of illness rather than any psychological depression gradually silenced her pen after that year. Documents filed in Natchitoches Parish in October, 1902, show that Lamy Chopin (her brother-in-law) and

Phanor Breazeale (the husband of Marie Chopin Breazeale, Oscar's sister) were granted power of attorney for Chopin and her heirs. And in December, 1902, according to St. Louis Probate Court records, Chopin formulated and signed her Last Will and Testament in the presence of two witnesses, almost two years before her death.

Even less is known of Chopin's activities in 1903 except that according to Natchitoches Parish records, land was sold on four occasions during November on behalf of Chopin and her heirs, and her sister-in-law Eugenie Chopin Henry may have died in Louisiana that year. An apologetic note written during July to a Mrs. Douglas in St. Louis indicates Chopin was keeping up an active social calendar and even planned to spend a week in "the country" that month. However, the year of the Douglas letter has not been confirmed (*KCM*, 150).

Chopin moved in late 1903 or early 1904 from her old home at 3317 Morgan Street, where she had completed most of her writing, to a new brick dwelling at 4232 McPherson Avenue. She might have benefited financially from the death of her maternal uncle Charles Faris in May of 1904; St. Louis Probate Court records indicate he left his niece an inheritance. However, Chopin's death on August 22 from "cerebral hemorrhage," attributed to exhaustion after a full day's outing at the St. Louis World's Fair, would come before she realized any gifts from Faris' estate.

Although scholars have attributed the year of Chopin's birth to both 1850 and 1851, the age of fifty-three that appears in her St. Louis obituaries would concur with her statement in a personal diary entry (*KCM*, 95). Following her death, this obituary from the August 22, 1904, evening edition of the St. Louis *Post-Dispatch* is representative of several local accounts that praised Chopin's last novel while announcing her plans for a forthcoming short-story collection: "[In] 1899 her novel, 'The Awakening,' was published in Chicago. This more sustained effort, while esteemed a success, did not overshadow the two preceding volumes, and it is still to the latter that the discriminating reader turns. . . . Since the publication of 'The Awakening' Mrs. Chopin had published no important work, but the announcement was made some time ago that another volume of short stories was to be issued this year" (1).

The facts of Chopin's life and her composition schedule from 1899 until her death in 1904 provide convincing evidence that once she began to write for publication in the late 1880s, she approached her literary life with ambition and energy. Her logbooks; her correspondence with publishers, agents, and newspapermen; and her relationship with the literary set in St. Louis and Chicago confirm that her voice was never silenced because of the disappointing reception of *The Awakening*. Furthermore, Chopin's active business interests are verified by real-estate records from the period and her 1902 will, which left to her children shares in a Kansas City coal company and various parcels of St. Louis real estate. It is interesting to note that she bequeathed to her youngest child and only daughter, Lelia, in addition to her personal jewelry and clothing, a parcel of real estate for her own use, "free from any debts or claims against her husband." The residue of Chopin's property was divided equally among her sons. Surely this feminist gesture, recognized by all daughters of Virginia Woolf, exhibits Chopin's characteristic touch. Lelia's inheritance is a symbol of her mother's experience: To be truly independent, a woman must have her own property and a personal income.

Both in life and in art, Chopin was levelheaded, ambitious, and practical. After her summer illness of 1899, when she returned to her writing and social activities in November, she must have become increasingly aware that at least some of the local editors and socialites had portrayed her in her absence as a bedroom recluse with a prototypical case of female hysterics. Realizing that her physical health was gradually failing (and she may also have suffered an accompanying loss of memory or vision), she must have apprehended her need to work rapidly if she was to recover her literary reputation before her death. If Edna Pontellier's nemesis in *The Awakening* was the refrain "remember the children," as a professional writer and capable mother of six, Chopin undoubtedly wanted her children to remember her, but not as an emotional weakling who collapsed under the pressure of a few hypocritical editors and gossips.

Because of her failing health and her anticipation of death, I would argue, Chopin's compositions written after her illness represent a final attempt to recapture her successful status, at least in St. Louis, as a woman of letters. Michael T. Gilmore has effectively demonstrated that in their later careers writers such as Hawthorne and Melville moved "toward authorial poses of distance and impersonality because of their estrangement from the market system."[9] Chopin appears to have wrestled similarly with the angel art in the elite as well as the popular literary marketplace. If she too altered her characteristically ironic, even cynical authorial voice in her later, more traditionally oriented fiction, she may have resumed her more marketable early style in an attempt to recover her reputation as a regional writer. If so, she was determined to be remembered as a writer, not simply as a wife, a friend, or a mother of children. As a result of her efforts and despite her failure to repair her critical reputation in her time, Chopin represents a model of perseverance for the serious ambitions of nineteenth-century women writers in the literary marketplace.

Even at her most ambitious, Chopin probably never dreamed of the fame her work has earned today. But in the darkly discouraging moments of their final years as writers, it is doubtful that Hawthorne, Melville, or Dickinson anticipated canonical status either. When her health permitted, Chopin appears to have spent her concluding years repairing the damage to her literary reputation. We honor her efforts by reconsidering the questions and commitments of her life. If feminists like Chopin have earned an honored place for *The Awakening* in an overwhelmingly patriarchal canon, and Lawrence Buell has correctly ascertained our tendency to canonize an author with his or her textwork, it is surely time to discard outdated Victorian interpretations of Chopin's life. As Carolyn Heilbrun has so forcefully argued in *Writing a Woman's Life*, we must responsibly retrieve "honest" biographies of writers who have successfully challenged the canon.

9. Michael T. Gilmore, *American Romanticism and the Marketplace* (Chicago, 1985), 152.

II Daring and Defying

Assent—and you are sane—
Demur—you're straightaway dangerous—
And handled with a Chain—
                              —Emily Dickinson

The Awakening of Female Artistry

DEBORAH E. BARKER

Charles Baudelaire, in his essay "The Painter of Modern Life" (1863), praises the role of the artist as a "man of the world," the "*flaneur*," the "passionate spectator," who can move through all aspects of the city observing the women he encounters. According to Baudelaire, the woman functions as

> that being towards or for whom all their [men's] efforts tend; that awe-inspiring being, incommunicable like God (with this difference that the infinite does not reveal itself because it would blind and crush the finite, whereas the being we are speaking about is incommunicable only, perhaps, because having nothing to communicate); that being . . . for whom, but especially by whom, artists and poets compose their most delicate jewels; . . . woman, in a word, is not for the artist . . . only the female of the human species. She is rather a divinity, a star, that presides over all the conceptions of the male brain . . . the object of the most intense admiration and interest that the spectacle of life can offer to man's contemplation.[1]

Baudelaire describes the male artist's appropriation of the female as a silent cipher into which men pour their desires and visions of beauty, thus exemplifying the argument put forth by recent feminist art and film critics that the visual representation of women by men reflects the power of the male gaze to appropriate the image of woman and objectify and "commodify" her. An example of this empowering is found in the following comments from a late-nineteenth-century essay in which the writer concedes that "modern literature as well as ancient courts women of genius, and modern education and freedom have opened the learned branches of letters to the sex with satisfactory results," but in the areas of painting and sculpture, where "execution is inextricably welded with invention," women "have been little more than parasites." The author, who goes by the initials

---

1. Charles Baudelaire, *Baudelaire: Selected Writings on Art and Artists,* trans. P. E. Charvet (Middlesex, 1972), 423.

D.S.M. only, deplores the existence of women artists' exhibitions and maintains that "this pastime of painting" should be "driven back to the Charity Bazaar" (D.S.M. 731). He also laments the waste of time, money, and energy spent in attempting to train women as artists because it "depends on the illusion that education can supply the place of a king of inventive gift, so rare among women that there are millions to one of odds against its occurrence." As Griselda Pollock has observed, "The sexual politics of looking functions around a regime which divides into binary positions, activity/passivity, looking/being seen, voyeur/exhibitionist, subject/object."[2]

With its traditional emphasis on the female form (particularly the female nude as an essential feature of art training), painting serves as a metaphor for the psychological and economic subjugation of women. The use of nude models (generally female), considered an essential feature of art training, was often prohibited to women artists until the late nineteenth century. Linda Nochlin cites an 1885 photograph of the women's modeling class at the Pennsylvania Academy that reveals the women art students using cows rather than nude models. And Germaine Greer argues that even among such women as Henrietta Rae, who ignored criticism and painted female nudes, "when one looks at her boneless, pink and hairless creations, lyrically swarthed with tulle and surrounded by roses, it is immediately obvious how the female artist has had to blinker herself."[3]

This phenomenon exemplifies the Freudian emphasis on a scopic sexual economy that, as Luce Irigaray has stated, is particularly inappropriate for representing female desire. And because painting has historically been produced by men for men, the exchange of the image of women is a corollary to Levi-Strauss' concept of the exchange of women as the basis of social organization, a concept expanded upon by Irigaray in her discussion of the traffic of women. As Pollock explains, "the *flaneur*-artist is articulated across the twin ideological formations of modern bourgeois society—the splitting of private and public with its double freedom for men in the public

2. D.S.M., "Women Artists," *The Living Age,* CCXX (1899), 730, 731; Griselda Pollock, *Vision and Difference: Femininity, Feminism and the Histories of Art* (New York, 1988), 87.

3. Linda Nochlin, "Why Are There No Great Women Artists?" in *Woman in Sexist Society,* ed. Vivian Gornick and Barbara Moran (New York, 1971), 495; Germaine Greer, *The Obstacle Race: The Fortunes of Women Painters and Their Work* (London, 1979), 320.

space and preeminence of a detached observing gaze whose possession and power is never questioned, as its basis in the hierarchy of the sexes is never acknowledged."[4] The male artists' appropriation of the female, as described by Baudelaire, also points to a tradition of depicting the female body as an object of male desire, which characteristically ignores the possibility of women desiring their own, or other women's bodies.

In *The Awakening* (1899) Kate Chopin explores the different facets of the appropriation of women, including its artistic, sexual, social, and religious manifestations. Chopin confronts these issues through her creation of a woman painter, Edna Pontellier, and her friend and model Adele Ratignolle. Edna's attempt to paint Adele brings to the foreground the problems she faces as a woman artist in attempting to paint her own desire without objectifying Adele. But it also brings to the forefront Edna's growing sensuality and her dissatisfaction with the social and religious restrictions placed on women as wives and mothers.

The painting scene is directly followed by Edna's moment of awakening in which she begins to "realize her position in the universe as a human being" (*KCA*, 17). Part of what makes the scene of Edna's painting radical is that her desire is directed toward Adele, not Robert.[5] Robert attempts to control the scene by placing himself in a position of authority and intimacy between the two women. Thus, he surveys Edna's work with "close attention" while "giving forth little expressions of appreciation in French, which he addressed to Madame Ratignolle" (*KCA*, 13). He even places his head on Edna's arm as she works, but his "oblivious" attentions are repulsed. Instead, Edna's attention is focused on Adele. Her sensuous assessment of Adele breaks through a male libidinal economy based on heterosexual genital sex. The sensuality of Edna's desire for Adele is palpable. She does not wish just "to try her hand" at "painting" but to "try *herself* on *Madame Ratignolle*. Never had that lady seemed a more tempting subject than at that moment, seated there like some sensuous Madonna, with the gleam of the fading day enriching her splendid color" (*KCA*, 13; emphasis added).

In addition to the complications faced by a female artist regarding her

4. Luce Irigary, *This Sex Which Is Not One*, trans. Catherine Porter and Carolyn Burke (Ithaca, N.Y., 1985); Pollock, *Vision and Difference*, 71.

5. See Chapters V and VI, *KCA*. See also Kathleen Lant, "The Siren of Grand Isle: Adele's Role in *The Awakening*," *Southern Studies*, XXIII (Summer, 1984), 167–76.

position and that of her model, Edna intensifies her situation by her conception of Adele as a Madonna. Significantly, this puts Edna in a tradition of religious iconography that has exalted the Madonna as the embodiment of an unobtainable model of womanly virtue: simultaneous chastity and motherhood based on submission and obedience. Edna's depiction of Adele as a Madonna refers to an earlier description of her as a mother-woman and the quasi-religious language that describes her. Mother-women "idolized their children, worshipped their husbands, and esteemed it a holy privilege to efface themselves as individuals and grow wings as ministering angels" (*KCA,* 10). The mother-women, like the Madonna, are in a position of adoring and of being adored as both worshiper and angelic figure, but in both positions they are effaced as individuals. The Madonna's power and worth come from her position as the silent bearer of the Word incarnate. Her value is strictly positional. It is not what she does but what is done to her for which she bears her fame and status in a patriarchal religion. She is almost literally a "vessel" of God.

The sensuous, romantic aspects of Adele and the religiously dutiful and sacrificial elements come together in the double function the Madonna serves in Christian iconography. The Madonna is fecund yet chaste, and she serves as an object of desire at the same time that she is safely out of reach of human contact. These conflicting images are exemplified by Edna's rapt admiration (she "liked to sit and gaze at her fair companion as she might look upon a faultless Madonna") and her desire to "try herself" on the tempting image of Adele, the "sensuous Madonna."

Julia Kristeva examines the cultural and psychological significance of the pictorial representations of the Madonna, focusing on the Madonnas of Leonardo da Vinci and Giovanni Bellini. Her insights into the artist's relation to the maternal body prove relevant to Edna's relationship to Adele, who is not only referred to as a Madonna but is also pregnant when Edna chooses to draw her. According to Kristeva, the Madonna serves as the supreme fiction of the unity of mother and child, "hypostatized by Christianity" in an attempt to establish "a subject at the point where the subject and its speech split apart, fragment, and vanish. Lay humanism took over the configuration of that subject through the cult of the mother; tenderness, love, and seat of social conservation." The maternal body therefore maintains the fiction that our coming into being is somehow tied to a subject, the mother, rather than realizing the more disquieting reality, as Kristeva stresses, that we come into existence from a void, a "subjectless biological program" that is instilled into a "symbolizing subject, this event called motherhood."[6]

Da Vinci with his emphasis on the fetishized figure of the Madonna and on representation, reinforces the concept of the unity of the subject. The Madonna's rapt attention to the child emphasizes the mother-child bond and the image of the maternal body as the subject through which our "being" originates. Bellini, on the other hand, goes through a series of phases. He begins with the rigid orthodox version, which allows for no space between mother and child. He proceeds to a Madonna who seems to find her pleasure beyond the child in the averted gaze, then to the sexual, hostile figure of the Madonna and child as antagonists, and finally to a depiction in which the Madonna's jouissance dissolves into the expanse of luminous color and space that knows no bounds. For Kristeva, Bellini's "predominance of luminous, chromatic differences" is "beyond and despite corporeal representation" and attempts to transcend the domain of the symbolic to the place where biology and society, symbolic and semiotic, the conscious and preconscious meet. The search for jouissance "appears wherever color, constructed volume, and light break away from the theme . . . implying that they are the real, objectless goal of the painting."[7]

The emphasis on an "impressionistic" use of color and light to create a subjective rendering of nature, as outlined by Kristeva, is similar to the qualities of Edna's vision of Adele and the "gleam of the fading day" that enriched "her splendid color." And Edna's "sensuous susceptibility to Beauty," which first attracted her to "the excessive physical charm of the Creole," reflects the "homosexual-maternal aspect" of motherhood that Kristeva describes, the realm of the semiotic, which consists of "a whirl of words, a complete absence of meaning and seeing; it is feelings, displacement, rhythm, sound, flashes and fantasied clinging to the maternal body." According to Kristeva, it is through an identification with the maternal body in its marginal position that the artist is able to reach "his own specific jouissance, thus traversing both sign and object."[8]

Understanding the maternal body and the work of art as a site of the

6. Julia Kristeva, *Desire in Language,* ed. Leon Roudiez, trans. Thomas Gora, Alice Jardine, and Leon Roudiez (New York, 1980), 237, 242.

7. *Ibid.,* 243, 248.

8. *Ibid.,* 239–40, 247.

unrepresentable clash of nature and culture, of an inexpressible "maternal jouissance," suggests at least a partial explanation for Edna's inability to render a realistic depiction of Adele, the pregnant "sensuous Madonna." As the narrator explains, "The picture completed bore no resemblance to Madame Ratignolle. She was greatly disappointed to find that it did not look like her. But it was a fair enough piece of work, and in many respects satisfying" (*KCA*, 13). On the one hand, given the emphasis on realistic art in the mid-nineteenth century, Adele is justified in assuming that the painting should resemble her.[9] In this light, Edna's ability as an artist is seriously in question, especially since the painting "bore no resemblance." Yet we cannot assume at this juncture that Edna lacks the ability to render Adele's likeness, for upon Edna's return to New Orleans after her summer at Grand Isle, we learn that she has a collection of "old sketches" that are a testimony to her realistic drawing skills. And Adele herself praises the sketches as realistic: " 'Surely, this Bavarian peasant is worthy of framing: and this basket of apples! never have I seen anything more lifelike. One might almost be tempted to reach out a hand and take one' " (*KCA*, 56). Nor can we assume that Adele's beauty is particularly difficult to capture, for we are told, "There was nothing subtle or hidden about her [Adele's] charms: her beauty was all there, flaming and apparent" (*KCA*, 10). The painting is also described as "satisfying in many respects," which further suggests that Edna has talent.

If Edna has the ability to render a realistic depiction of Adele, the question remains, why is it that she does not? The problem of depicting Adele as a sensuous Madonna lies in the contradictory position of the mother-woman, for precisely in her role as a type of Madonna, as a mother-woman, Adele becomes "efface[d] . . . as [an] individual." And to identify with the maternal body as represented by Adele would mean that Edna too would be effaced as an individual. In order to capture the sensuous essence of Adele, or what Kristeva would refer to as maternal jouissance, Edna must go beyond realistic representation. Mary Kelley suggests this as a strategy for dealing with the dilemma of woman as spectator.[10]

In assessing Edna's attempt to paint Adele, it is also important to ex-

9. Barbara Novak, *American Painting of the Nineteenth Century: Realism, Idealism, and the American Experience* (New York, 1979), 211–13.

10. Mary Kelley, "Desiring Images/Imaging Desire," *Wedge,* VI (1984), 9.

amine the tension between representational realism and an increased emphasis on color and light evident in the art world of the nineteenth century, especially as it developed in what Barbara Novak calls the "painterly mode," a combination of elements of both American luminism and French impressionism: "The painterly alternative . . . sought a visual realism based on a sensational response to light and color. . . . On the one hand it was crystallized to offer a more stable presentation of forms in space, relating to American realist traditions. On the other, it was diffused into an amorphousness that transcribed abstract 'essences' of feeling and emotion, becoming part of a sparse tradition of American romantic reverie." [11]

In America, the luminists, with their extended horizons, their use of radiant light and brooding shadow, attempted to solve the real-ideal split by using natural landscapes but taking them a step "beyond" realism. In France, the impressionists moved even further from realism in their use of vivid color and bold brushstrokes to create an overall image or mood rather than a technically realistic representation. As Michael Gilmore notes in his essay "Revolt Against Nature," the influence of impressionism in *The Awakening* is one of liberation. However, he maintains that neither Edna nor Chopin could achieve full freedom. "Edna never relinquishes a limiting Victorian notion of what constitutes a 'real' self. And Chopin, in her quest for escape from representation, reverts to nature as a pattern to be imitated" (*NEA*, 60–61). Another component in the real-ideal debate, which parallels Edna's artistic imagination, was the privileging of the painter's mental image over the natural object. The late-nineteenth-century American artist Albert Ryder, who was greatly influenced by European art, stressed the artist's imagination as the source and focus for painting, and stressed the importance of color over technical accuracy. Ryder often used his mental pictures as the source of his art. "I've often carried the idea for some of my pictures around in my mind for five years before I began to put them down on canvas." He felt free to create something "better than nature, for it was vibrating with the thrill of a new creation." [12]

Although we receive limited information about the content of Edna's painting, we have many instances of her mental "pictures." She has a

11. Novak, *American Painting*, 235, 248.
12. *Ibid.*, 211–12, 213.

habit of translating her impressions of nature, her memories, and her re-action to music into "pictures." For example, when listening to "musical strains, well rendered, [Edna] had a way of evoking pictures in her mind" (*KCA,* 26). And in describing her thoughts to Adele, she demonstrates her propensity to view nature as a picture: " 'First of all, the sight of the water stretching so far away, those motionless sails against the blue sky, made a delicious picture that I just wanted to sit and look at' " (*KCA,* 17).

This scene in particular mirrors the elements of the luminists, including an emphasis on an expanding horizon, a lack of a framing device, a sense of suspended time, and as Novak terms it, a "mode of expression through a subjectivity so powerful that the artist's feeling is transferred directly to the object, with no sense of the artist as intermediary." [13]

Both of these strategies, emphasis on color and light and privileging of the artist's mental image, suggest ways of looking at Edna's relationship to her art. And her attempt to paint Adele (Chapter V) suggests a transition, if still somewhat tentative, from the realistic "old sketches" to a more innovative style that Edna's art instructor, Laidpore, later describes as "growing in force and individuality."

Following a similar pattern, the painting scene in Chapter V serves as a transition in Chopin's writing style from the more realistic domestic scenes to the increased use of lyric, opulent, and vivid imagery in Edna and Adele's walk on the beach, the midnight swim, the trip to Cheniere Caminada, culminating in the radiance and sensuality of the farewell din-ner and Edna's final swim into the ocean. As Sandra Gilbert has noted, the opening scenes "seem determinedly realistic, low-key, landbound," and Chopin has "formally acknowledged Flaubert's influence" by "examining her heroine from a solid and stolid male perspective." But despite the fact that the opening chapters seem ordinary enough, they have, according to Gilbert, an "unrepresentative point of view" and an "air of almost impres-sionistic improvisation . . . or rather they seem as vividly literal as objects in a painting by Renoir or Seurat." [14]

The scene of Edna's painting in Chapter V demonstrates this unrepre-sented point of view. The word *evidently,* describing Edna's dissatisfac-

13. *Ibid.,* 96.
14. Sandra Gilbert, "The Second Coming of Aphrodite: Kate Chopin's Fantasy of De-sire," *Kenyon Review,* V (Summer, 1983), 42–66, 46.

tion with the painting of Adele, erodes the narrator's authority over the character's thoughts. Although the narrator often has omniscient knowledge of the characters, in this scene the narrator is in the same position as an observer who views the scene from the outside and then tries to draw conclusions. The distinctions between the characters' thoughts and speech are blurred. It is not clear if Adele's own dissatisfaction is stated aloud or she only thinks it. The narrator comments that the painting was "a fair enough piece of work and in many ways satisfying," but we do not know by what standards it is a fair work or who it is that finds it satisfying— Adele, Robert, or the narrator.

Again the reader is forced to evaluate the scene independently. This shift in point of view forces the reader to step in and draw self-constructed conclusions, a shift that allows for an alternative, more radical reading concerning Edna's relationships to Adele and her own artistic vision. As Gilbert explains, the events of the early scenes take on greater significance as the novel progresses: "It is only as one scene dissolves into another, as the narrative point of view gradually enters Edna's strengthening consciousness, and as objects and activities insistently recur, like elements of a protracted dream, that they begin to gain what eventually becomes an almost uncanny power." [15] The "uncanny power" of Chopin's skill and innovative technique as a writer are made apparent at the dinner party by the ironic statement of Miss Mayblunt. At the height of the party, young Victor Lebrun is garlanded in roses and draped in a white silken scarf. "As if a magician's wand had touched him, the garland of roses transformed him into a vision of Oriental beauty. His cheeks were the color of crushed grapes, and his dusky eyes glowed with a languishing fire" (*KCA*, 89). While "losing herself in a rhapsodic dream as she looked at him [Victor]," Miss Mayblunt exclaims, " 'Oh! to be able to paint in color rather than in words!' " (*KCA*, 89).

Chopin describes Miss Mayblunt somewhat satirically as a woman "no longer in her teens, who looked at the world through lorgnettes and with the keenest interest." She is also suspected of being an intellectual and a writer "under a *nom de guerre*." Mayblunt's statement suggests that words are not capable of rendering the splendid opulence of the scene before her.

15. *Ibid.*, 47.

Yet Chopin's ability to render the resplendence of the party scene (not only in terms of color, but also in terms of sound, scent, and touch) vividly belies Mayblunt's assumption. Mayblunt here represents not only a certain type of writing (that which apparently lacks color) but also a vision of the world that is limited by her nearsightedness and an unwillingness to enter fully the public sphere and use her own name for her writing. In contrast, Chopin, like Edna, demonstrates the growing "force and individuality" of her work.

The sensuous quality of the dinner scene, the "moral indeterminacy" of the novel, the creation of an adulterous heroine who pursues her painting and not her homemaking—all mark a break between Chopin and her predecessors, the literary domestics. By creating a heroine who refuses to sacrifice her art or her sensuality, Chopin distinguishes herself from the local colorists, as outlined by Ann Douglas, whose heroines are often socially and artistically isolated. Mary Kelley explains in *Private Woman, Public Stage* that the previous generation of women writers had dealt with the complexities of being private women on a public stage by emphasizing their domestic role as wives and mothers and downplaying their public notoriety and economic independence: "They published, but often under the cloak of anonymity. From their literary income they supported or contributed to the support of themselves and their families, yet felt compelled to justify that support on the domestic need. And, most significantly, they struggled in their tales to assess and place a value on women's lives while disparaging and dismissing their own literary efforts." [16]

This attitude is reflected in Fanny Fern's *Ruth Hall,* in which the young heroine is forced to adopt a literary career to support herself and her children. When her daughter Nettie asks if she will grow up to be a writer, Ruth answers, " 'God forbid, God forbid. . . . No happy woman ever writes.' " [17] Even when a woman works by choice, like Christie in Louisa May Alcott's *Work,* the emphasis is placed on her domestic skills, her compassion, and her ability to help others. Christie chastises herself for

16. Ann Douglas, "The Literature of Impoverishment: The Women Local Colorist in America 1865–1914," *Women's Studies,* I (1972), 3–54; Mary Kelley, *Private Woman, Public Stage* (New York, 1984), xi. For a discussion of Chopin's relationship to the literary domestics and the local colorists, see Elaine Showalter, "Tradition and the Female Talent: *The Awakening* as a Solitary Book" in *NEA,* 33–57.

17. Fanny Fern, *Ruth Hall* (New Brunswick, 1986), 175.

selfishly enjoying her fame as an actress. After a providential accident, she gives up the stage to pursue a more domestic situation that allows her to aid others. And in Alcott's *Little Women,* Jo, the lively and ambitious author, gives up her writing career to become a wife and mother. This is not to say the heroines were not courageous or assertive or that female authors did not have an immense effect on the publishing community. They created new markets for women's novels and brought a new emphasis to the importance of a woman's role in society, but it was accomplished within certain limits of behavior for both the author and her heroine.

Chopin, as a respectable widow who lived with her mother and her children, maintained the code of respectability for a woman artist, but her heroine, Edna, does not. By creating a heroine who participates in a male-dominated profession, Chopin recreates the struggle that her predecessors faced as they broke into a new field. As Ann Douglas points out, "One should say that it was a significantly less daring thing in America to be an authoress in 1880 than in 1840. . . . Women were breaking into other professions, most notably medicine, and it was in controversial areas like this, rather than in literature, that the battle for increased freedom for women was principally being fought." [18]

In many ways, Edna's life is the exact opposite of the heroines of the literary domestics. Although she is modest about her talent, she is willing to pursue it at the expense of her domestic duties. And not only does she not need the extra income to aid her family, she uses it to leave her husband and set up her own household where she is free to entertain other men. By selling her painting, Edna enters the economic sphere as an agent and not as an object of exchange. It is precisely her positional role as a woman that she insists on disregarding. Her "instinct" is to rid herself of Leonce's money and thereby cease to be a man's property. Edna's mother has left her money (although even in death her mother's "will" is not strong enough to allow for a direct inheritance from mother to daughter; it is mediated by her father, who sends it to her in "driblets"). And this money, in combination with her knowledge of the racetrack (learned from her father) and her income from her painting, is enough to allow her "freedom and independence."

Chopin takes a basic theme of the literary domestic novel—the woman

18. Douglas, "Literature of Impoverishment," 12.

on her own, struggling in a new field—and radicalizes it by stripping away all the sentiment of the home and presenting a heroine who pursues social, artistic, and sexual freedom.

The tension between the role of mother and the role of the artist is further emphasized through the contrary characters Mlle. Reisz and Mme. Ratignolle and their relation to their bodies. In many ways, the alternatives represented by Adele and Mlle. Reisz match the alternatives posed by the tradition of the literary domestics and the local colorists, respectively. As Douglas explains, for the sentimentalists the home was "an emblem of what they like to call female 'influence.' As such it was closely related to their vaunted sexual superiority: indeed, enclosed and private, it was symbol of their own inner space, into whose rich and warm atmosphere they . . . invited the privileged male exhausted from his debilitating conflict with the competitive world." In contrast, for the local colorist, the home represented "the womb in a new and destructive guise. It is no longer a garden of delights, but a bed of weeds; it is not rampantly fertile, but barren, and even poisonous." [19] Chopin demonstrates her ability to create both types of heroines, but she attempts to move beyond either alternative through her creation of Edna, a heroine who desires artistic and sensual pleasures.

Mme. Ratignolle, who is the picture of sensuous beauty, has given her body to her role as mother-woman by her biennial pregnancies. In contrast to the importance of color associated with the sensuous image of Adele, Edna describes Adele's domestic life as a "colorless existence which never uplifted its possessor beyond the region of blind contentment" (*KCA*, 56). For an artist who is concerned with color and expansive horizon, "colorless existence" and "blind contentment" provide no alternative: "Edna felt depressed rather than soothed after leaving them [the Ratignolles]. The little glimpse of domestic harmony which had been offered her, gave her no regret, no longing. It was not a condition of life which fitted her, and she could see in it but an appalling and hopeless ennui" (*KCA*, 56). Adele has given herself to her children "body and soul," something Edna is not willing to do for either her children or her art.

Mlle. Reisz, on the other hand, remains a childlike anorexic figure who has developed her art at the expense of her physical desires. Her cramped

19. *Ibid.*, 20.

apartment suggests the physical deprivation of her life. Edna feels "chilled and pinched" as she enters Mlle. Reisz's room, which "looked cheerless and dingy to Edna. . . . A bust of Beethoven, covered with a hood of dust, scowled at her from the mantelpiece." And although her music is moving to Edna, the price of her talent is suggested by "the lines of her body settled into ungraceful curves and angles that gave it an appearance of deformity" (*KCA,* 64).

Edna is not willing to accept Mlle. Reisz's belief that the artist must sacrifice the self for art. From the start, Edna has shown an unconventional attitude toward her work. In the reader's first encounter with Edna as a painter, Edna establishes her own criterion as an artist, which she maintains throughout the novel. She stresses the importance of process. "She felt in [painting] satisfaction of a kind which no other employment afforded her." After Edna has declared herself a painter and has begun to take lessons and to work with regularity, "with sureness and ease," she is still "devoid of ambition, and striving not toward accomplishment" but drawing "satisfaction from the work in itself." The "ease and freedom" with which she handles her brushes in Chapter V is reaffirmed in Chapter XXVI when she measures her growth as an artist by the "ease and confidence" that she has gained in her painting. Even if Edna does not live up to Mlle. Reisz's ideal of the "courageous soul" of the artist or the "bird that would soar above the level plain of tradition and prejudice [who] must have strong wings," these are not Edna's definitions and do not seem to reflect her conception of the artist. In recounting Reisz's pronouncement, Edna states, "I'm not thinking of any extraordinary flights. I only half comprehend her."

Although critics associate Edna's artistic endeavors with Mlle. Reisz, it is Adele to whom Edna first brings her sketches, and she is the first person to whom she confides her desire to paint. Adele's good opinion and faith in her friend's talent allow Edna "to put her heart into her venture." In a play on the concepts of "valueless" and "worth," Edna assesses Mme. Ratignolle's opinion as valueless. And from a position of traditional art criticism, it is valueless: Her pronouncement will not affect the marketability of the paintings (as Laidpore is able to do). However, the rare meaning of *valueless* is "beyond value" as in *priceless,* and Adele's intangible moral support has great worth.

Edna's sensual response to Adele's beauty inspires her to paint, and

Adele's openness inspires her to "loosen the mantle of her reserve." On the one hand, Edna's relationship with Adele represents an extension of what Carroll Smith-Rosenberg refers to as the "female world of love and ritual," which was a predominant part of women's lives from the eighteenth to the mid-nineteenth century.[20] Edna and her husband, Leonce, lead basically separate lives, and Edna demonstrates much greater intimacy with Adele than with Leonce. One could take the argument further and assert that Edna's unfulfilled desire for her "beloved" represents her love for Adele, not Robert, and that Robert is merely a poor substitute whose inclusion in Edna's list of unsustained lovers reflects the fact that men do not satisfy her sexually or emotionally. As previously discussed, the homosexual element corresponds to Kristeva's "homosexual-maternal aspect," an identification with the mother in which the semiotic prevails. In this light, Edna's longing for the "beloved" looks past even Adele to Edna's absent mother.

However, to interpret, as Cynthia Griffin Wolff has, Edna's discontent, oral impulses, and final desire to merge with the maternal ocean as a pre-oedipal desire for pure union is problematic when it explains away all the complexities of the novel by regarding Edna as a regressive, narcissistic personality.[21] Such a reading ignores the social and historical implications of the novel. Chopin has created a complex blend of social and psychological elements. The maternal body serves as an emblem for Edna's struggles precisely because it occurs at the union of the social and biological, the conscious and unconscious, the symbolic and semiotic.

Edna's painting allows her an active role in interpreting the world around her. It also allows her greater control over her life. Edna metaphorically and literally attempts to take herself out of the "traffic of women," as evidenced by her decision to move out of Leonce's house and her desire to walk through the streets of New Orleans alone rather than be escorted or chauffeured. "I always feel so sorry for women who don't like to walk; they miss so much—so many rare little glimpses of life: and we women learn so little of life on the whole" (*KCA,* 105). This freedom of move-

20. Carroll Smith-Rosenberg, *Disorderly Conduct: Visions of Gender in Victorian America* (New York, 1985).

21. Cynthia Griffin Wolff, "Thanatos and Eros: Kate Chopin's *The Awakening,*" *American Quarterly,* XXV (October, 1973), 449–71.

ment and observation is what Baudelaire celebrates in the artist as the *flaneur.*

Using the categories of locations and of types of women encountered in Baudelaire's imaginary tour of the city, Pollock has created a grid with which to examine the relationship of public versus private space in the work of two female impressionist painters, Berthe Morisot and Mary Cassatt, vis-à-vis their male counterparts. Pollock finds that although Morisot and Cassatt depict women in public places, there is a difference in the type of public space accessible to them. They inhabit the respectable world of the theatre or park, not the backstage of Degas, the cafés of Renoir, or the brothels of Manet. Morisot and Cassatt more often depict scenes in a private domestic sphere and frequently use their friends, family members, servants, and nannies as models (much like Edna). Through "proximity, intimacy and divided spaces [they] posit a different kind of viewing relation at the point of both production and consumption" in order to "develop alternative models for negotiating modernity and the spaces of femininity."[22]

Edna too seeks an alternative space of femininity. She desires the "little glimpses of life denied to most women," (not the "little glimpses" of "domestic harmony" at the Ratignolles'), but in her own version of the *flaneur,* she does not head for the backstages, cafés, and brothels of New Orleans. She seeks out a quiet garden in the suburbs, a place "too modest to attract the attention of people of fashion, and so quiet as to have escaped the notice of those in search of pleasure and dissipation." Edna desires the masculine privilege to travel unencumbered and to observe life, but she does not necessarily desire to frequent "masculine space"—the freedom to choose, not merely to imitate.

The key concept linking Edna's artistic growth and her growth as an individual is her progression from an obstructed view to a penetrating vision. In Edna's remembrance of traversing the field of grass as a young girl, her "sun-bonnet obstructed the view," and when she is a grown woman at the opening of the novel, the sunbonnet still serves as an encumbrance, a sign of her role as a valuable commodity. When we first "see" Edna, she is approaching beneath the "pink-lined shelter" of her sunshade,

22. Pollock, "Vision and Difference," 84–85, 90.

but the sunshade has not protected her white skin while she swam in the ocean. " 'You are burnt beyond recognition,' [Mr. Pontellier] added, looking at his wife as one looks at a valuable piece of personal property which has suffered some damage" (*KCA*, 4). And for him, Edna is a valuable piece of property; her leisure, her ability to remain untouched by the sun, her lack of need to work outdoors betoken her husband's affluence.

However, as Edna gradually takes control of her life, she increasingly expands her vision. The doctor is the first to notice the change: "There was no repression in her glance or gesture" (*KCA*, 70). And after securing the pigeon house for herself, she had "a sense of having descended in the social scale, with a corresponding sense of having risen in the spiritual. Every step which she took toward relieving herself from obligations added to her strength and expansion as an individual. She began to look with her own eyes; to see and to apprehend the deeper undercurrents of her own life" (*KCA*, 93).

Not until the final scene of the novel can Edna extend her vision without interruption; her ability to discard her clothing and the absence of the sunbonnet literally and figuratively allow a sense of new sight.[23] She is able to "cast the unpleasant, pricking garments from her, and for the first time in her life she stood naked in the open air, at the mercy of the sun, the breeze that beat upon her, and the waves that invited her. . . . How strange and awful it seemed to stand naked under the sky! how delicious! She felt like some new-born creature, opening its eyes in a familiar world that it has never known" (*KCA*, 113).

In the description of Edna's elation at standing exposed in the sun and her sense of a new and expanded vision, Chopin invokes Emerson's famous lines from *Nature*: "Standing on the bare ground,—my head bathed by the blithe air, and uplifted into infinite space,—all mean egotism vanishes. I become a transparent eye-ball. I am nothing. I see all. The currents of the Universal Being circulate through me; I am part or particle of God." [24]

Emerson's interest in light and vision has been so closely identified with the luminist painters that as Gayle Smith states, "It appears to be almost

23. Robert Collins, "The Dismantling of Edna Pontellier: Garment Imagery in Kate Chopin's *The Awakening*," *Southern Studies*, XXIII (Summer, 1984), 176–90.

24. Ralph Waldo Emerson, *Nature, Addresses and Lectures*, ed. Robert E. Spiller and Alfred R. Ferguson (Cambridge, Mass., 1971), 10, Vol. I of *The Collected Works of Ralph Waldo Emerson*, ed. Alfred R. Ferguson *et al.*

impossible to write about the luminist painters' attitudes toward nature and the role of the artist without citing Emerson's famous transparent eyeball passage from *Nature*." [25]

However, even as Edna's expanded vision is similar to Emerson's, it also differs in crucial ways that indicate Edna's resistance to the moral quality associated with the luminists and transcendentalism. Earlier in the novel Edna falls asleep while reading Emerson, and as Per Seyersted points out, "She may concur with the transcendentalists in their disregard for external authority, but she is not yet ready to wake up to the full light, or perhaps not interested in communion with their kind of divinity. Instead, she symbolically unites herself with the Gulf by taking a 'refreshing bath'" (*CB*, 156). Although I would argue that Edna does "wake up to the full light," it is a different revelation from that of the transcendentalists, and I would agree that she is not "interested in communion with their kind of divinity." For Emerson, nature is essentially moral, a means to understanding the infinite: "Every natural process is but a version of a moral sentence. The moral law lies at the centre of nature and radiates to the circumference. . . . Nor can it be doubted that this moral sentiment which thus scents the air, and grows in the grain, and impregnates the waters of the world, is caught by man and sinks into his soul." [26]

For Edna, nature, the sea, also speaks to the soul: "The voice of the sea is seductive; never ceasing, whispering, clamoring, murmuring, inviting the soul to wander for a spell in abysses of solitude; to lose itself in mazes of inward contemplation" (*KCA*, 15). But to Edna the sea is sensuous and maternal, not moral. Emerson's transformation into the transparent eyeball and his union with the Universal Being take place while he is in the woods, his feet squarely on the ground. Edna's merging with nature leads her to the ocean and ultimately to death. Her union is more sexual, more like Walt Whitman's description in "Out of the Cradle Endlessly Rocking." The phrase Chopin uses twice—first in Chapter VI, the original "awakening" chapter, and then as Edna takes her final swim—reflects Edna's sensuous response to the sea: "The touch of the sea is sensuous, enfolding the body in its soft, close embrace" (*KCA*, 113).

Edna's moment of awakening also differs profoundly from that of Em-

25. Gayle Smith, "Emerson and the Luminist Painters: A Study of Their Styles," *American Quarterly*, XXXVII (Summer, 1985), 193.

26. Emerson, *Nature, Addresses, and Lectures*, 26.

erson. As Emerson describes it, "The best, the happiest moments of life, are these delicious awakenings of the higher powers, and the reverential withdrawing of nature before its God."[27] Edna's awakening, however, demonstrates her ambivalent attitude toward God and religion: "In short, Mrs. Pontellier was beginning to realize her position in the universe as a human being, and to recognize her relations as an individual to the world within and about her. This may seem like a ponderous weight of wisdom to descend upon the soul of a young woman of twenty-eight—perhaps more wisdom than the Holy Ghost is usually pleased to vouchsafe to any woman" (*KCA,* 14–15).

The above passage ironically conflates the imagery of the Annunciation and Pentecost. Botticelli, in *Descent of the Holy Ghost,* places Mary in the center of the apostles at Pentecost. Although he depicts Mary as a matron, her breasts and rounded stomach are accentuated.[28] For Edna, the light of wisdom is not a flash of heavenly inspiration but a gradual understanding of her relations as an "individual to the world within and about her." The ponderous weight she carries is not the swelling of her belly but the weight of wisdom. Edna, like Mary, has been singled out among all women, but in Edna's case there appears to be a certain apprehension on the part of the deity in allowing such a gift to *any* woman.

Edna will not silently "bear" the Word made flesh, nor will she receive the gift of tongues, but she does learn to think and act for herself. Only after her "awakening" does Edna divulge to Adele that she is no longer religious. As a girl, Edna rejected the Protestant religion by "running away from prayers, from the Presbyterian service, read in a spirit of gloom by [her] father that chills [her] yet to think of" (*KCA,* 18). As an adult, she dissociates herself from the model of the Madonnalike "mother-women," and later she flees from the Mass at Our Lady of Lourdes (the site of an 1858 vision of the Virgin Mary).[29]

Although there is a sense of progression in the novel, of Edna's increasing mastery of her art and her vision, the ending is not wholly positive.

27. *Ibid.,* 30.

28. Marina Warner, *Alone of All Her Sex: The Myth and the Cult of the Virgin Mary* (New York, 1976), Fig. 14.

29. Michael Carroll, *The Cult of the Virgin Mary: Psychological Origins* (Princeton, 1986), 118–20.

She pays an extreme price for her "freedom." The ending, rather than signaling a regressive downfall or a joyous voyage, seems a sober indictment of the possibility for women's unencumbered artistic vision in the society of the novel. A woman's willingness to "bare all," to explore the reaches of her vision, is a dangerous enterprise and one, it would appear, that can be done only outside the confines of society. Edna must delve into the freedom of the "wild zone" of women's culture to achieve her vision fully.[30] But in the world of *The Awakening* the "wild zone" is also a danger zone and points to the precarious position of women artists attempting to transcend a male tradition.

30. Elaine Showalter, "Feminist Criticism in the Wilderness," in *The New Feminist Criticism: Essays on Women, Literature, and Theory*, ed. Elaine Showalter (New York, 1985), 259–61.

The Awakening: *A Recognition of Confinement*

DOROTHY H. JACOBS

Edna Pontellier's daring in asserting her will, striving to gain control over her life, and recognizing her relationship to the world would not be so remarkable were it not for the evidence throughout *The Awakening* of the multiple constraints that are part of her existence. In many ways, the novel chronicles Edna's growing awareness of the nature of those claims on her autonomy; hence, the title refers not only to the rousing of her erotic, individual, and spiritual impulses but to the entire series of awarenesses that culminate in her sleepless certitude about her position in the universe. Thus, *The Awakening* shares with the greatest dramatic art that most dramatic of themes, painful self-recognition. Although Chopin tells us that Edna "had abandoned herself to Fate, and awaited the consequences with indifference," nowhere does the author suggest the sort of omnipotent decree which determines Oedipus's destiny (*KCA,* 103). Neither does Edna suffer the humiliations and griefs of Lear. Nevertheless, she does come to a similar kind of knowledge; she finally perceives herself within a world that while apparently open to her potentialities, remains closed to her deepest wishes and her will.

At her farewell dinner, crowned with a diamond tiara, draped in the "golden shimmer" of a gown whose satin lacks the "myriad living tints" of her matching, "vibrant flesh," Edna suggests "the regal woman, the one who rules, who looks on, who stands alone" (*KCA,* 88). But this luxurious evocation of power offers no sustained sense of actual regality. Even as she glowingly offers an appearance of ruling glory, Edna hears the recurring, chilling whisper of hopelessness.

Indeed, she is not a queen. Unlike Oedipus and Lear, this protagonist is Mrs. Pontellier, wife and mother, defined by her relationship to husband and children. Oedipus and Lear begin by ruling and learn the limits of their power. Edna begins by discovering the urge to rule her own life. Only in that process does she, like her famous forebears, learn the limits of her power. Of the many differences, the essential radical one separating Mrs.

Pontellier from the great tragic heroes is precisely her nonregal status. She must begin her process of perception not from a position of power, but, quite basically, from a recognition, gained in a small instance of physical triumph, that she alone can accomplish something she thought impossible. Oedipus, confident because of his solving of the riddle, and Lear, sure of the affection of Cordelia, begin from thrones of authority. Edna starts hesitantly, fearfully, but increasingly resolved to act for herself.

For her homelier predicament the domestic dramas of Henrik Ibsen may provide more immediate analogues. That the struggle of a woman to recognize her confinement and to attempt to break free of it has inherent dramatic qualities is clear from the literature of the late nineteenth century. Nowhere is this drama so ably realized as in three of Ibsen's masterworks: *A Doll's House* (1879), *Ghosts* (1881), and *Hedda Gabler* (1890). Realistic, poetic, disturbing, these plays have inspired some of the terminology so frequently used in categorizing *The Awakening*. The essential quality for the purpose of this essay, though, is the focus upon woman as captive wife and her recognition of that bondage.

A Doll's House dramatically establishes primary sources of confinement, foremost among these insistence upon the duties of a wife and mother. Concurrent and supportive factors are authoritative males, societal reinforcements, and the solitude of the woman. With some variations, especially in intensity, Ibsen explores the impact of these restrictions upon his female protagonists. Kate Chopin also uses these major elements in *The Awakening*. How she develops them in narrative form can be appreciated by comparing her emphases and methods with those of her angry Norwegian predecessor.

The opening dialogue of *A Doll's House* immediately establishes Nora as an adorable and demeaned wife. Torvald calls her "my little squirrel" and "my little songbird," continually reiterating in the guise of affection his possession of her, his elevated perspective over her, and his use of her as a pet. Her suggestions he categorizes as "whims and fancies." Nora keeps secret her efforts to save her husband's life because "Torvald would never bear to think of owing anything to me! . . . . It would ruin everything between us."[1] The truth, she fears, would wreck the marriage.

Indeed a truth does upset this patriarchal ménage, but it is not what

1. Henrik Ibsen, *A Doll's House,* in *Eight Plays* (New York, 1951), 15.

Torvald discovers about her that destroys the marriage. It is Nora's recognition of Torvald's selfishness and her immaturity that causes her to slam the door on the doll's house. Recollecting her childhood, Nora realizes that her adoption of her father's opinions was a means of getting along, a way of maintaining a frictionless doll's house. With this conditioning, she moved effortlessly into the hands of her husband. Seeing herself as a doll, not a "real person," Nora abjures the role of mother, asserting that she is as unfit for the job as Torvald had angrily proclaimed, by reason of her duplicity. To Torvald's traditional appeals to her responsibilities as wife and mother Nora responds with a claim to a duty to herself, primarily to think for herself, clear of what Torvald says, of what "most people say—or what they write in books," and of what religion says.[2]

From the outset of *The Awakening,* Chopin presents her protagonist with significant advantages. Edna Pontellier has a personal dignity, a physical stateliness, and an abhorrence of coquetry that place her beyond the sort of trivialization practiced on Nora. Nevertheless, she too is bound by marriage. Our first view of her is from the perspective of her irritated husband. From his opening critical remarks, his looking at her as "at a valuable piece of property," his perfunctory return of her rings, and his inability to join in the jollity of Edna and Robert, Leonce Pontellier has the polished and distanced demeanor of a sophisticated proprietor. Introduced as framed between two aggravating caged birds, Mr. Pontellier soon again finds his wife remiss, this time because of what he calls her "habitual neglect of the children" (*KCA,* 7). Whereas Nora's idealism and naïvete combine to furnish a merry gloss to her marriage, Edna has initial recourse to inexplicable tears, more sustained dependence upon moods, a naturally dreamy disposition, and increasingly a determination to exercise her will. Yet despite these assets, it is her marital state that impedes her beloved Robert, and it is thoughts of her children that make her lose hope of freedom.

A conspicuous motif throughout the novel is the contrast between Mme. Ratignolle, the exemplary mother-woman, and Edna Pontellier. No specific reason accounts for Edna's apparent predisposition to be herself, a woman uncommitted to unremittent, relentlessly maternal efforts. Neither

2. *Ibid.,* 73–74.

is she revolted, like Hedda Gabler, by the mere suggestion of maternity. Ibsen's devoted mother-figure Mrs. Alving, in *Ghosts,* suffers deprivation to protect her son. She, like Nora, awakens late to a realization of the futility of her "saving" lies for preserving marriage. Edna is quite different. Early on, she admires the beauty of the wholly motherly woman just as she simultaneously acknowledges not a deficiency nor an abhorrence but simply a conviction about herself as not totally maternal. After dinner with the entwined Ratignolles, Edna feels no envy but pity for the "colorless existence" based upon Mme. Ratignolle's subsumption in husband and children. To Edna, "it was not a condition of life which fitted her, and she could see in it but an appalling and hopeless ennui" (*KCA,* 56).

What Edna savors in her private thoughts Hedda Gabler expresses in snide remarks, undisguised contempt, and destructive behavior. Hedda's rage to control a destiny takes a markedly masculine form in her reliance upon the pistols that are her paternal inheritance. Lacking the internal resources of Edna, Hedda reacts to boredom ferociously. She attempts to control and destroy other people; finally she shatters the cozy and hateful domesticity provided by her husband while forestalling any further limitations upon herself with a fatal shot from General Gabler's remaining pistol. Whatever the appraisal of Hedda's character and actions, there can be no doubt that wifehood and motherhood are as stultifying for Hedda as the middle-class trappings that purporting to be her domain, actually enclose and limit her.

Only once does Edna Pontellier exhibit any comparable violent reaction to her condition. Chastised again by her husband, this time for not being "at home" for her scheduled callers and failing to provide an agreeable dinner, Edna, in her room, paces, tears a handkerchief, smashes a vase, and more pointedly, tries to grind her wedding ring into the carpet. Even though everyone at Grand Isle appreciates the handfuls of bonbons sent by Mr. Pontellier enough to consider him "the best husband in the world," his wife "was forced to admit that she knew of none better" (*KCA,* 9). At least he is not the overseer of macaroons whom Nora must elude.

Occasionally Edna is defiant to her husband, sometimes evasive, but usually inventive in her escapes. What seems to Leonce Pontellier reckless neglect of her Tuesday receptions is an insignificant loss to Edna. She simply wanted to go out, and she did. This continues. Walking about New

Orleans, discovering simple and unknown hideaways, and reposing in Mlle. Reisz's attic room are favorite escapes. The lure of the outdoors manifests more than a Whitmanesque, transcendental urge. It is an eloquent expression of Mrs. Pontellier's urge to get out of the house and all that it entails. At Grand Isle she and Robert lounge and chat on the porch of the summer cottage. Edna retreats to the porch's hammock and mosquitoes rather than stay within the precincts of her authoritative husband; she leaves an indoor party to perch outside on the gallery; she abandons the "stuffy" and "close" cottage for the pleasure of swimming. In town she looks at the expansive view from Mlle. Reisz's always-open windows; she scurries to leave the house, which feels like "some forbidden temple in which a thousand muffled voices bade her begone" (*KCA*, 84); she is glad that Robert never knew her in her old home; and she sits on the porch of her pigeon house to sort out her thoughts after seeing Mme. Ratignolle through her confinement. Finally, off-season, she goes alone to the beach and its endless sea.

Dispossession of the husband's goods is a motif common to Ibsen's dramas and Chopin's novel. Hedda Gabler merely distances herself through hauteur, but Nora insists upon leaving Torvald with the few possessions that were hers before marriage. Mrs. Alving rids herself of the last of Captain Alving's money by building the doomed orphanage. Edna, because of her income from her own paintings and a maternal inheritance (parsimoniously doled out by her father), enjoys furnishing her own house. The new tiny dining room is the scene for a comfortable intimate dinner with Robert; thus it contrasts her preferred independent life with the large, elegantly glowing, ultimately boring Sevres dining table at Mr. Pontellier's. In emphasizing the small dimensions of Edna's pigeon house, Chopin allies Edna's personally selected place with Mlle. Reisz's for expressing the values of convenience, spiritual ascendancy, and most importantly, autonomy. Edna moves much further than Hedda Gabler, who retires to an adjacent room for a noisy suicide; than Mrs. Alving, who remains among the ashes of her plans; than Nora, who closes the door on the doll's house. Edna selects and establishes a home for herself.

By including such delicious details, Chopin indicates that Edna's move is not only economically feasible but also rewarding for the gratification that can be derived only from a realization of one's own capabilities. Another advantage is her sense of separation from her father. Only during his

visit does she elect to "minister to his wants" not because of Mr. Pontellier's mistaken notion of "a deep filial attachment" but merely for her own
amusement. When Edna's father insists that she attend sister Janet's wedding, reproaching her for lack of womanly and sisterly devotion, Edna still
refuses to comply, not even offering an excuse beyond what she had earlier
remarked to her discomfited husband, that "a wedding is one of the most
lamentable spectacles on earth" (*KCA*, 66). Weary of the argument and
the entire visit, Edna is "glad to be rid of her father when he finally took
himself off" (*KCA*, 71). Mr. Pontellier, suspecting its past deadly effect,
does not follow the advice so authoritatively given by his father-in-law
for managing and coercing a wife. He relies upon the untraditional counsel of wise Dr. Mandelet, who urges the troubled husband to leave his
wife alone.

With Ibsen too, patriarchal authority is a major indicator of female
confinement. So conditioned to please father and husband is Nora that she
can no longer discern which are her own and which the required tastes of
Torvald's wife. Hedda retains the symbols of male authority, General Gabler's pistols, for her deadly purposes. Mrs. Alving fabricates a life of lies
to protect the fiction of Captain Alving as a leading citizen. Insisting upon
this social duplicity is the spiritual leader of the Alvings' community, the
duped and duping Pastor Manders. Not until she recognizes the ghosts of
the past in her present predicament does Mrs. Alving question the direc-
tions and moral rules given to her by this male authority. By contrast, Nora
has the sympathetic ear of Dr. Rank, someone who listens to her and to
whom she can express her long-repressed "Goddamit!"

Likewise, Edna enjoys the benevolent concern of Dr. Mandelet. These
representatives of the medical profession offer alternatives to the otherwise
misguiding edicts of the Ibsenite clergy and revolutionary variations on the
otherwise oppressive demands of husbands and fathers. Outside marriage,
of course, men cannot be quite so authoritative, for they lack the patriarch's prerogatives. Therefore, Edna's lover, Alcee Arobin, is gracefully
accommodating yet skillfully exciting, and he is never demanding. With
Robert, the ease of unacknowledged love gives way to agonies of yearning
as soon as Edna recognizes the depth of her attachment. Robert's capitu-
lation to the rules of Creole deportment, his insistence upon leaving her,
denies Edna the dominance of her passion.

Limitations on Edna's determination to do as she likes come, then, not exclusively from the house. Societal norms operate unceasingly despite Edna's daring in leaving her home, her "unwomanly" candor with Robert, and her confidence that she has awakened from a "life-long, stupid dream." In the flush of declared love with Robert, Edna asserts that they alone will be "everything to each other. Nothing else in the world is of any consequence" (*KCA,* 107). But the loved one she expects to wait for her adheres to his native gentlemanly code, one that seeks the husband's release of a wife, not a radical adoption, not even an understanding of Edna's bold claim to self-giving.

The leniency of Creole society, especially its tolerance for the attendant gallantry of a bachelor, actually indicates the confidence of its patriarchs. By her reactions to Creole ease in sexual topics, Edna reveals her prudish upbringing, reinforced by her father's tedious prayers. Faintness in the church at Cheniere Caminada occurs because of Edna's feelings of "oppression" during the service. Happy and refreshing escape takes place in the sea-whispering air and the restful cottage of Mme. Antoine. In this woman's comfortable and magical place, a restorative physical communion takes place as Edna notices her own fine flesh, sleeps, eats, and revives.

Traditional religion and society sustain her no more than they do Ibsen's hapless Mrs. Alving. Rather, church and social gatherings consistently weary and depress Mrs. Pontellier. Whether soirees, days at the races, or elegant dinners, these occasions offer none of the pleasure Edna experiences in solitary walks and swims, Robert's frequently silent companionship, reveries at Mlle. Reisz's rooms, and mystic imaginings and tales of romantic escape. Details and intensity of mood in Edna's story of the lovers who paddled away, never to return, are vibrant for her attentive audience, most notably for Dr. Mandelet, who observes in her a creature "palpitant with the forces of life . . . warm and energetic," displaying no signs whatsoever of an earlier noticed listlessness or any repression (*KCA,* 70). Out of her musings come Edna's transformations from lassitude to energy, from passivity to assertiveness.

Edna Pontellier's boldness in moving out of the confinement of marriage, defying patriarchal authority, eschewing the tyranny of housewifery, and neglecting obligations to societal functions would seem to be the narrative evocation of what Bernard Shaw jauntily prescribed in 1892 for the emancipation of women in "The Womanly Woman":

The sum of the matter is that unless Woman repudiates her womanliness, her duty to her husband, to her children, to society, to the law, and to everyone but herself, she cannot emancipate herself. But her duty to herself is no duty at all, since a debt is cancelled when the debtor and creditor are the same person. Its payment is simply a fulfillment of the individual will, upon which all duty is a restriction, founded on the conception of the will as naturally malign and devilish. Therefore Woman has to repudiate duty altogether. In that repudiation lies her freedom.[3]

While Shaw's checklist summarizes fairly accurately the major antagonists to Nora, Hedda, and Mrs. Alving, it neglects to include an essential quality these Ibsenite protagonists share with Edna Pontellier. Dramatically poised against traditional entrapments for women in the late nineteenth century, these heroines certainly do question and defy these male-ordained duties. Nora disdains the law that labels her altruistic effort a forgery; Hedda bypasses moral laws; and Mrs. Alving challenges the wisdom of lying for maintaining reputation and a false ideal. But they all do so within a confine apparently unsuspected by the champion of Ibsen: their solitude. In this they predate, they anticipate, the figure first entitled as Chopin's *A Solitary Life*.

Other heroines have shared this quality of solitude. Recently Carolyn Heilbrun has summed up their situation: "The heroines of most novels by women have either no mothers, or mothers who are ineffectual and unsatisfactory. Think of George Eliot; think of Jane Austen; think of the Brontës. As a rule, the women in these novels are very lonely; they have no women friends, though they sometimes have a sister who is a friend." The mothers of Nora and Hedda are so inconsequential to the drama that they are never even alluded to. Mrs. Alving's aunts, her counselors for an economically and socially advantageous marriage, receive a one-line mention. Edna's mother does not figure in the narration either, except as the victim of husbandly coercion. As for sisters Janet and Margaret, they are already distanced by geography and play no part in Edna's life once she decides to boycott Janet's wedding. The threat of their alienation does not disturb Edna. According to Heilbrun, the mother's function is to prepare her daughter "to take her place in the patriarchal succession." Lacking

3. George Bernard Shaw, *The Quintessence of Ibsenism* (New York, 1957), 56.

effective mothers, then, daughters might well be ill prepared for roles as wives. Furthermore, Heilbrun continues, "for many women . . . there moved in their imaginations dreams of some other life . . . above all, the dream of taking control of one's life without the intrusion of a mother's patriarchal wishes."[4]

One of Edna's dominant characteristics is her capacity to dream of a life of her own. This seeking of her own direction, her indulgence of whims and moods, has as one of its sources the absence of maternal guidance. So thoroughly a mother-woman is Adele Ratignolle that she takes on the role of reminding Edna of her duties as wife and mother. For most of the novel Mme. Ratignolle serves as the model, even in Edna's painting of her, the self-sacrificing woman constantly aware of her "condition." Rather than inspiring Edna to emulation, though, Adele helps to sharpen Edna's awareness of her distinction from the type. Despite Adele's attempts at chumminess, Edna rarely confides in this hovering friend.

At the other extreme of social desirability is Mlle. Reisz, the woman whose unattractive physical appearance coincides with her frequently rude contempt for society. Mutual respect, however, links the pianist and the painter, both "different from the others." Spare dialogue, passionate music, and recognition of the truth about Edna's feelings mark their easy and honest communication. But neither does Edna follow this model of alternative womanliness, skewed as severely from traditional ideals as her decrepit violet corsage.

At the very core of Edna's personal awareness of confinement is the fact that "at a very early period she had apprehended instinctively the dual life—that outward existence which conforms, the inward life which questions." Essentially, then, Edna in childhood "had lived her own small life all within herself" (*KCA*, 15). This mode of living continues into her adulthood where her dreaminess and reserve are conspicuous indicators of her foreignness among the more voluble Creoles.

More significant even than her motherlessness and her alien origins in Presbyterian Kentucky is Edna's cultivation of aloneness. After her first triumphant swim, she walks away from the other members of the party; she does not welcome even Robert when he overtakes her. With an aston-

4. Carolyn Heilbrun, *Writing a Woman's Life* (New York, 1988), 118, 119.

ishing sense of privacy, she keeps her thoughts and emotions to herself as "a right." To the wondering Adele, Edna explains that she would give money and her life but not herself for her children. As tension between husband and wife increases, she says to him, "Let me alone; you bother me" (*KCA*, 57). Alone, she recollects the previous summer night's sail. She wanders to solitary and unfamiliar places. Chopin brilliantly concludes a description of Edna's happy and dreamy integration with nature thus: "And she found it good to dream and to be alone and unmolested" (*KCA*, 58). When her husband leaves for New York and her children go to their grandmother's, "a radiant peace settle[s] upon her," and she breathes "a big, genuine sigh of relief" (*KCA*, 72). At the closure of her first exultantly alone day, Edna feels a restfulness "such as she had not known before" (*KCA*, 73).

Because of her cultivation of a separate life, Edna is able to grow stronger as an individual, for she does what the Ibsenite protagonists merely began to do, "to look with her own eyes; to see and to apprehend the deeper undercurrents of life" (*KCA*, 93). Her spiritual intentions make the pigeon house pleasing to her, the escape from opinion and duty elevating to the soul. In Mlle. Reisz's housetop room with its magnificent view, she finds refuge from tiresome people and "a kind of repose" as she sits alone in "the shabby, unpretentious little room" (*KCA*, 95). Her lover offers "a walk or a drive or anything," but Edna chooses solitude. In the quiet of her reverie she recollects her recent meeting with Robert and speculates on the future. Another day, Edna sits in a remote modest garden-restaurant because "she found the place deserted" (*KCA*, 104). Never expecting to meet anyone she knows, she savors the quiet of this little retreat. In like manner she keeps within herself those concerns which trouble her. She excuses herself from Dr. Mandelet's invitation to confide in him. When she finds instead of Robert his note of good-bye waiting for her, she stretches out on the sofa, "never uttering a sound" (*KCA*, 111). Alone, claiming simple needs for any corner of rest and fish for dinner, Edna arrives at Grand Isle and insists upon a swim. As recollections, thoughts, and feelings mesh, her final conviction of a solitary life continues until her strength is gone.

Throughout these multiple revelations of Edna's solitude there is bountiful evidence of a tragic paradox. What distinguishes Edna as a modern heroine is her insistence upon development and realization of her self. That she takes no interest in her husband's formulas for making money or his elaborate architectural coverup of their separation; that she turns from the material comforts of a gracious society; that she instead looks inward, realizing that "the street, the children, the fruit vendor, the flowers . . . were all part and parcel of an alien world which had suddenly become antagonistic" (*KCA*, 54), identifies her as a noble protagonist. In her indulgence of moods and feelings she daily becomes more herself, "casting aside that fictitious self which we assume like a garment with which to appear before the world" (*KCA*, 57). Her daring, her pain, and her recognitions anticipate the existentialists.

Yet, admirable as she is, Edna suffers a limitation in this cultivated sense of the self. The lack that she can only temporarily fill is a direction. She wants something, at times anything, to happen. Returning from a visit to her children, she is "again alone" (*KCA*, 94), the melody of their presence losing its echo. So too, she eventually realizes, would the lovesong of Robert someday be mute. Her painting, while occasionally satisfying, is neither emotionally nor spiritually sustaining. Without the "old marriage plot," Edna needs what Carolyn Heilbrun says so many heroines seek, "another story for women, a quest plot" (121). When she extols walking, Edna explains that it allows her "so many rare little glimpses of life"; and she adds, "We women learn so little of life on the whole" (*KCA*, 105). Like Shakespeare's imagined sister, Edna strides into a world not eager to receive her, not ready with new scenarios.

This absence of exemplary texts is itself a stricture placed upon the solitary woman trying to live a life free of the old stories of love culminating and ending in marriage. Because her married life has been a "grotesque" dream, because Robert will not fulfill her romantic expectations, because she knows she is neither a mother-woman nor a great artist, she has nowhere to go so buoyant as the waters of the sea. Thus the existential paradox of self-realization, which includes painful awareness of the limitations of the self, has a particularly feminine definition in Kate Chopin's narration of Edna Pontellier's awakening.

Cognizance of another uniquely feminine barrier to freedom exists in Edna's conclusive recognition of her confinement. Here the novel is both explicit and suggestive as it unites the twin themes of nature and motherhood. From Chopin's first intonation of its seductiveness, the sea takes on ambiguous qualities of allurement. When Robert urges Edna to bathe, not his voice so much as the "sonorous murmur" of the Gulf reaches her "like a loving but imperative entreaty" (*KCA,* 14). To these recurring sensuous enticements Chopin adds the transcendental, ceaseless invitation to the soul "to wander for a spell in abysses of solitude; to lose itself in mazes of inward contemplation" (*KCA,* 15).

The language itself hints at the dangers of enchantment: *abysses, mazes,* and a *spell* suggest difficulties for the enticed soul. When recalling her wandering in the Kentucky meadow, Edna says she cannot remember whether she was frightened or pleased. From the beginning of her immersions in the apparently limitless world of nature, a duality of effects has been inherent. Escaping the gloom of Sunday prayers, young Edna must acknowledge the terror of being lost in an endless expanse. During her first joyful swim, "a quick vision of death" intrudes, momentarily appalling her and forcing her to look to the shore. Only when sailing across the bay to the Cheniere Caminada does she experience an unmitigated sense of escape, "as if she were borne away from some anchorage which had held her fast, whose chains had been loosening—had snapped the night before when the mystic spirit was abroad, leaving her free to drift whithersoever she chose" (*KCA,* 35).

But this crossing is not an actual immersion in a boundless and dangerous nature. Therefore, it becomes the prototype for Edna's romantic tale of lost never-returning lovers. At another time she hears jeering, mournful, hopeless voices from dark tortuously outlined foliage and an enormous sky. Finally, conclusively, the recitative of the sensuous sea again sounds as Edna walks to the shore. The repeated words of seduction lure her "on and on," despite recollections of the old terror, in a sort of synchronized harmony of sea and swimmer. Even in this luxuriance of sensuality, Edna cannot forget people and scenes—most of all, their voices.

Awash in the fecundity of the final images and implicit in the action of Edna's long, exhausting swim is the reminder of that enormous natural claim upon Edna, her children.[5] As a part of her life, she can accept,

5. See Robert White, "Inner and Outer Space in *The Awakening,*" *Mosaic,* XVII (1984), 108, for a discussion of the final images in *The Awakening.*

indeed delight in them, but she will not sacrifice herself for them. Nevertheless, despite her spoken convictions on this matter and regardless of her differentiation from the mother-woman, Edna is forced to accept maternity as an undeniable limitation upon her determination to give herself only where she chooses. She does not succumb to the importunities of the quasi-religious model of the "mother-woman." Edna is quite able to enter into the interests of her children and to treasure their voices and chubby embraces. For "a whole week long" she gives them "all of herself," while reciprocally "gathering and filling herself with their young existence" (*KCA*, 93). But the visit is not extendable to an entire sustained devotion of the self to them. How her children emerge as "antagonists who had overcome her, who had sought to drag her into the soul's slavery for the rest of her days" (*KCA*, 113) depends largely on the impact of that natural event, Adele's confinement.

The timing of Old Celestine's knock at the door is at least as important as the famous knocking at the gate in *Macbeth*. Interrupting the long-awaited declarations of Robert and Edna is the too-early request of Mme. Ratignolle for Edna's company. Edna's confidence about being no one's possession and a romantic future for her and Robert disappears in the urgency of her response to the exaggerated but nevertheless compelling entreaty of her female friend. Like Oedipus eager to help the Thebans by vowing to find the murderer of Laius, Edna undertakes to fulfill her promise to see Adele through the throes of childbirth, all the short while reassuring Robert of her love and imminent return. For both characters, the assumption of a noble task results in devastating personal revelations. An unpredictable voice of nature, Adele's womanly call disrupts, even destroys, the romance for which Edna has had such extravagant hopes. Insistent as the sea, this voice too begs a response even as it intimates danger. "Think of the children" becomes the refrain that summons Edna to her death.

In his critical biography of Chopin, Per Seyersted pointed out a significant difference between Edna Pontellier and her novelistic predecessors. According to Seyersted, Chopin presents a character who has an almost cavalier attitude, compared with the heroines of de Stael and Sand, toward wifely duties. Chopin appears to consider "these aspects of woman's emancipation too elementary for further comment and wants to move on to the really fundamental—and more taboo—factor which her predecessors had shied away from: the children" (*CB*, 145). Some of this paper argues against that easy dismissal of the "too elementary" nature of wifely duties, but I would agree that in her attention to the claims of children Chopin writes with a new daring. In his dramatizations of wives' emancipation Ibsen nowhere introduces the sensitive issue of maternal bondage. Kate Chopin does, in an astoundingly poetic fusion of all aspects in the theme of confinement.

Edna's dread at the agonizing childbirth deepens to extreme distress as "with a flaming, outspoken revolt against the ways of Nature, she witnessed the scene of torture" (*KCA*, 109). So harrowing is this scene that she is emotionally stunned, speechless, dazed as she leaves the exhausted woman, yet unable to leave behind her the haunting whisper of the mother. Edna's first words to Dr. Mandelet deny the cruelty he sees in Adele's insistence upon Edna's presence, although avowing the necessity that she think of the children. Her brave assertion of her right to be let alone falls into incoherence as she acknowledges the overwhelming exception to her autonomy, the children. Dr. Mandelet, somewhat like the wise Doctor of Morality or sermonizer in medieval morality plays, articulates his philosophy on the siren ways of nature. This nature, according to the sympathetic doctor, uses illusions as "a decoy to secure mothers for the race" (*KCA*, 110).

Assenting to this interpretation of her troubled spirit, Edna, in a remarkably succinct scene of self-recognition, characteristically admits to a lifelong stupor of illusions. Now she perceives the conflict between her desire for her own way and the rights of "the little lives." Even as she rehearses her reunion with Robert, the whisper of Adele's injunction intrudes. Hoping that she can put off the thought until tomorrow, Edna knows that "that determination had driven into her soul like a death wound" (*KCA*, 110). But there is no reprieve, not even for one night. Robert's ultimately romantic rejection—because he loves her—leaves Edna in the awful solitude of awakened motherhood.

The intrinsic link between her maternity and nature is realized in Edna's final act, her merging with the waters of the Gulf. Return to Grand Isle is necessary for the woman who sees herself as newly roused from a lifetime of illusions. No longer the dupe, now fully awake to her condition, she follows a sort of symbolic logic akin to Oedipus' blinding the eyes that failed to see who he was. Baring herself to air, wind, and sea, Edna feels the "delicious" sense of being a "new-born creature, opening its eyes in a familiar world that it had never known" (*KCA*, 113). Chill water is no barrier, for she is returning to the elements of which she is an undeniable part.

Of all the voices she hears as she walks to the beach, none is so powerful as her own, the voice usually so still but now recalled as having repeated "over and over to herself" the names of the only persons who matter, Raoul and Etienne. She has found a way to elude them and at the same time to rid herself of all the "unpleasant, prickling garments" that inhibit self-realization. Naked, "at the mercy of the sun, the breeze that beat upon her, and the waves that invited her" (*KCA*, 113), she knows the mercilessness of that nature that has drawn her by illusions to her final recognition.

Like the tragic hero, Edna fully engages her own yearning, her strengths, and her destruction. There is a magnificent calm, almost a stoicism, in Edna's acceptance of the limitations in her life. In full knowledge and recollection of her hopes, stripped of illusions, she swims in the milieu that expresses most openly a quintessence of her confinement.

The Quintessence of Chopinism

MARTHA FODASKI BLACK

At the 1988 Modern Language Association conference, Elizabeth Fox-Genovese asserted that Kate Chopin had "little patience with the woman question." In underscoring this argument by writing that Chopin had "scant interest in social problems," she misleads us. Her argument that Chopin tried "to treat sexuality independent of gender relations" overlooks the texual evidence in *The Awakening*.[1] Close analysis of the novel reveals that Chopin examines the interdependence of female sexuality and gender roles to challenge cultural assumptions about women. Even though she was not an advocate or unequivocal reformer, *The Awakening* reveals the influence of late-nineteenth-century feminists and their search for a new kind of heroine on whom women could model their lives.

Internal evidence and references in Chopin's other writings reveal that she was well aware of writers such as Henrik Ibsen, George Bernard Shaw, and Elizabeth Cady Stanton. Although her biographers—even her most recent, Emily Toth—have found no direct evidence of her having read Shaw, Chopin's symbolic framework and conception of her main characters were probably influenced by Shaw's essay "The Womanly Woman" in *The Quintessence of Ibsenism*. In the 1890s, when Chopin's novel was germinating, Shaw's controversial essays in defense of Ibsen were circulating. The essay in which he defined and defended the feminist heroine by wryly comparing married women to caged parrots could hardly have escaped Chopin's attention.

The Awakening opens with a description of a parrot and a mocking-bird—as Per Seyersted notes in his critical biography, "caged imitators," one of whom is "repeating its master's words, the other echoing the voice of other species" (*CB*, 159). This initial scene has, however, even more

---

1. Elizabeth Fox-Genovese, "Edna's Suicide," paper delivered at MLA convention, New Orleans, December 27, 1988; Elizabeth Fox-Genovese, "*The Awakening* in the Context of the Experience, Culture, and Values of Southern Women," in *ATA*, 34, 39.

importance than Seyersted attributes to it. The parrot screams, " '*Allez vous-en! Allez vous-en! Sapristi!*' " The talking birds annoy Mr. Pontellier, who can do exactly what the parrot advises—go away. He has the "privilege of quitting their society when they cease to be entertaining" (*KCA*, 3). This opening is integral to Chopin's novel, whose descriptive details imply her theme. Without stating a message, the carefully self-effacing author suggests through strategically selected particulars the domestic relationships that her novel will explore. Her references to birds become a commentary on the action. The colorful, noisy imitators, like women, entertain men until they depart for spheres of more compelling interest—business and entertainment in a man's world.

In the opening episode, Edna Pontellier's husband, who is spending a summer weekend at Grand Isle where his wife and two small sons are vacationing, displays his male prerogative. When his wife's chatter with Robert Lebrun—resident swain, a Creole version of the courtly lover, and son of the resort's proprietress—becomes as annoying and boring as the birds' prattle, Leonce "yawns, stretches," and leaves for the local hotel to play billiards with his male friends. His freedom is so complete that his wife does not even require an answer to her perfunctory question whether he will return for dinner, and he does not feel obligated to give one. Nor does he come home until he feels like it.

The source of the opening description with its combative tone is probably Shaw, in spite of the fact that he did not originate the comparison of wives to caged birds. In 1772 Mary Wollstonecraft wrote of women: "Confined then in cages like the feathered race, they have nothing to do but to plume themselves, and walk from perch to perch. It is true they are provided with food and raiment, for which they neither toil nor spin; but health, liberty and virtue, are given in exchange." Nearly a century later, Nietzsche wrote, "Men have so far treated women like birds who had strayed to them from some height; as something more refined and vulnerable, wilder, stranger, sweeter, and more soulful—but as something one has to lock up lest it fly away." [2] Whereas Nietzsche asserted that the cage was the right place for woman, the feminist Shaw insisted that woman had

2. Mary Wollstonecraft, *A Vindication of the Rights of Women*, Scott Library edition (N.p., 1891), 70; Friedrich Nietzsche, *Beyond Good and Evil*, trans. Walter Kaufman (New York, 1966), 235.

the right to be free. Others, such as George Eliot in *Middlemarch*, had taken Wollstonecraft's cue to liken wives to pet birds, but Shaw's comparison directly anticipates Chopin's treatment of women in *The Awakening*.

Although what Richard Ohmann terms Shaw's "pugilistic stance" was not congenial to Chopin, in her novel she deliberately set out to enlarge upon Shaw's analogy to test it. Woman's freedom is one of Chopin's persistent themes. As Joan Zlotnick has pointed out, her women, "young and old, are often faced with rejecting or fleeing from marriage." Chopin's latest biographer, Emily Toth, confirms that Chopin "drew on real life for most of her inspirations." Whereas Toth has found no written indication of Chopin's interest in Shaw, evidence of her reading is implicit in *The Awakening*. Even the fact that Chopin's father, Thomas O'Flaherty, was, like Shaw, an Irish expatriate would have piqued Chopin's interest. Her literary and cultural interests—interests, according to Nancy Walker, not stifled among women in the New Orleans subculture—would have spurred her. In St. Louis her home was a meeting place for intellectuals who surely would have buzzed about Shaw's stinging defense of Ibsen. As the central figure of a "vigorous intellectual" circle, Chopin, who delighted in attending "concerts and plays," would surely have been in on the great Shavian debate.[3] A literate, cultured woman aware of the intellectual temper of her times, Chopin had read and probably attended Ibsen plays and could hardly have overlooked Shaw's controversial work on Ibsen; after all, by the 1890s, it had created a stir in literary and intellectual circles all over the western world.

Nevertheless, in reviewing Hamlin Garland's *Crumbling Idols* (1894), Chopin dissociated herself from writers whose avowed aim was social reform (even though Garland's Ida Wilbur could be a model for Edna Pontellier; both rejected the conventional and arbitrarily restricted roles society prescribed for women). Impressed by Garland's "veritism," a style she emulated, Chopin defended fiction as a craft. Without anticipating late-twentieth-century reassessments, she wrote of Ibsen that he "will not be

---

3. Richard M. Ohmann, *G. B. Shaw, the Style and the Man* (Middletown, Conn., 1965), 235; Joan Zlotnick, "A Woman's Will: Kate Chopin on Selfhood, Wifehood, and Motherhood," *Markham Review*, III (1968), 2; Emily Toth, "A New Biographical Approach," in *ATA*, 60. Nancy Walker, "The Historical and Cultural Setting," in *ATA*, 67; Peggy Skaggs, *Kate Chopin* (Boston, 1985), 23.

true in some remote tomorrow, however forcible and representative he may be for the hour, because he takes as his themes social problems which by their very nature are mutable" (*CW,* 693).

Chopin's heroines are nonetheless drawn in marital settings like Ibsen's, even though the bleak Norwegian atmosphere differs sharply from the lush New Orleans region that lulls or awakens her women. In her story "A Shameful Affair," the heroine is indeed reading Ibsen (*CW,* 131). Readers can assume, therefore, that in spite of her objection to a writer like Zola who communicates "the disagreeable fact that his design is to instruct us," Chopin was well aware of Ibsen's domestic dramas and of the two so salient for her inspiration—*Hedda Gabler* (1890) and *A Doll's House* (1879), the latter of which, after its first performance in English with Shaw in the role of the blackmailer, played in almost every Western country (*CW,* 698). William P. Warnken has examined the parallels between *The Awakening* and *A Doll's House,* whose ideas about the "infantilization of women in marriage provoked extensive discussion and analysis in print." Among the most important contributions to the controversy was *The Quintessence of Ibsenism,* whose section on women presages Chopin's central fictional theme.[4]

Thus, despite her objection to "zeal for reform," the St. Louis Creole no doubt co-opted the parrot for the purposes of her art (*CW,* 24). Her novel about the womanly woman and female alternatives is diagnostic, treating characters within the fictive system that the realistic story demands. Although she first wants to tell her tale plausibly and effectively, the story is nonetheless a "problem" in the same way that Ibsen's plays are, despite the pronouncements of critics like Edmund Wilson and Lewis Leary, who prefer to consider *The Awakening*'s aesthetic apart from its social merits, or Fox-Genovese, who argues that Chopin "viewed woman's independence as a personal more than a social matter."[5] Firmly locating the personal in a social milieu that implies the relationship between the two, *The Awakening* is as much "problem" literature as an Ibsen play or a

4. Warnken quotation from Miriam Schneir, ed., Preface to *A Doll's House,* in *Feminism: The Essential Historical Writings* (New York, 1972), 179; George Bernard Shaw, *The Quintessence of Ibsenism* (New York, 1958).

5. Edmund Wilson, *Patriotic Gore* (New York, 1962), 591; Lewis Leary, Introduction to *The Awakening and Other Stories by Kate Chopin* (New York, 1970); *ATA,* 35.

Shaw polemic. Readers at the time of *The Awakening* were so aware of its challenge to middle-class mores that it was damned by critics for its immoral subject matter (but praised for its style) and banned in St. Louis, Mrs. Chopin's hometown. Outraged moralists wanted to make its supposedly wicked author suffer for her heroine's shocking sexuality and her suicide, almost vindicated as ecstatic release.

Puritanical Americans were even more offended in the age of Comstockery than the French in 1857 when Flaubert was tried for alleged obscenity in *Madame Bovary*. Whereas conventional French Catholics were scandalized by Emma, driven by lust and greed to subvert the conventional role of wife and mother, her gruesome death saved Flaubert from persecution because the hysterical adultress got what moralists thought she deserved. Chopin's heroine, a sensuous, intelligent American refinement on Emma, was perhaps even more disturbing because she more clearly chose her fate, thus raising the issue of a person's right to control her own life and even choose her own death.

Chopin's novel is therefore clearly a "problem" work whose reception prompted Chopin to write a tongue-in-cheek apologia: "Having a group of people at my disposal, I thought it might be entertaining (to myself) to throw them together and see what would happen. I never dreamed of Mrs. Pontellier making such a mess of things and working out her own damnation as she did. If I had had the slightest intimation of such a thing I would have excluded her from the company. But when I found out what she was up to, the play was half over and it was then too late."[6] Significantly comparing her novel to a drama and arguing that her realistic characters have their own rationale, Chopin tried to dismiss her indignant critics.

Shaw's witty attack on Philistine hypocrisy would have struck a responsive chord in Chopin, who was, even as a young woman in St. Louis, noted for her sharp, cynical social observations.[7] Shaw's description of the caged wife states Chopin's fears of bondage, fears expressed in an early "fable" she called "Emancipation," a parable that celebrates the animal instinct for freedom. Chopin describes a captive animal escaping its cage in spite of "limbs . . . weighted" to reach "the water that is good to his thirsting

6. *Book News*, XVII (July, 1899), 612.
7. Toth, "New Biographical Approach," 62.

throat. . . . So does he live, seeking, finding, joying, suffering. The door which accident had opened is open still, but the cage remains empty forever!" (*CW,* 38–39). It seems no mere coincidence that the self-conscious artist (who had been forced into freedom by her husband's premature death) drew on her own parable, using the water symbol for sexual freedom and fruition in conjunction with the bird motif of Shaw, with whose parrot she begins her novel.

Shaw compares the self-sacrificing "womanly-woman" to a pet whose natural sphere is thought to be a cage because it has never been seen anywhere else. Man, for his own advantage, relegates woman to the role of pretty entertainer and breeder, and then concludes that her unnatural confinement is natural. Shaw's extension of the analogy is a good gloss of the sort of woman Chopin depicts as the main foil for her heroine. Adele Ratignolle, the beautiful matron, is like Shaw's "idealistic parrots who persuade themselves that the mission of a parrot is to minister to the happiness of a private family by whistling and saying Pretty Polly, and that it is in the sacrifice of its liberty to this altruistic pursuit that a true parrot finds the supreme satisfaction of its soul." [8] Shaw's analysis could be a summary of Adele's raison d'être, for she accepts the role of wife-mother and complacently enjoys her conventional, comfortable marriage. She accedes to the adage that women often take as a prescription rather than description—woman's place is in the home. [9] She is what Betty Friedan later called a happy-housewife heroine, dependent upon her husband and children for definition. [10]

Kate Chopin describes Adele as a "faultless Madonna" (*KCA,* 12), confident, as her name suggests, in her noble role. Only slightly plumper than Petrarch's Laura, she has the standard features of the beloved of the love-sonnet tradition—golden hair, blue eyes, and rosy lips. Echoing Shaw, Chopin calls her a "mother-woman." From her maternal pedestal, she makes herself the central figure in the bourgeois drama of domesticity—a nurturing, selfless, self-sacrificing mother-goddess par excellence, exacting from her exalted position the adoration of others.

8. Shaw, *Ibsenism,* 23.

9. See Elizabeth Janeway, *Man's World, Woman's Place* (New York, 1971), for a discussion of this phenomenon.

10. Betty Friedan, *The Feminine Mystique* (New York, 1963).

Chopin's initial description is, however, somewhat ironic, for this "heroine of romance and the fair lady of our dreams . . . sewed away on the little night-drawers or fashioned a bodice or a bib," anticipating her children's winter needs and advertising her maternal care. She draws attention to herself by "always talking about her 'condition,' " even though her pregnancy isn't apparent early in the novel (*KCA,* 10–11). Enjoying the role of a weak, helpless dependent who faints easily and must be pampered because of her delicate condition, she is the epitome of the womanly women who "seemed to prevail that summer at Grand Isle. It was easy to know them, fluttering about with extended wings when any harm, real or imaginary, threatened their precious brood" (*KCA,* 10).

This not so rara avis makes the most of her position as decorative but fragile mother-Madonna. Because of her vested interest in the holy bonds of matrimony and maternity, she basks in the privileges of a mother hen who idealizes her domestic captivity. She smother-loves her children, although everyone knows that "the doctor had forbidden her to lift so much as a pin!" (*KCA,* 14). In dramatizing her dependence, she seeks masculine applause and support, achieving power through weakness. After complaining of various minor ailments, Adele "begged Robert to accompany her to the house" and "leaned draggingly upon his arm as they walked" (*KCA,* 20).

To prove her total devotion to the ideal that she represents, Adele rationalizes all of her behavior as good for her husband and children. Unlike Edna, she has, as Peggy Skaggs has noted, a "lack of aesthetic sensitivity . . . another limitation of her total immersion in her role." [11] Chopin writes, "She was keeping up her music on account of the children, she said; because she and her husband both considered it a means of brightening the home and making it attractive" (*KCA,* 25). Her husband's wish is her command. When Edna returns from a day at the Cheniere Caminada with Robert, Adele will not stay with her (although Leonce has gone to Klein's to look up a cotton broker to discuss business) because M. Ratignolle "detested above all things to be left alone" (*KCA,* 40). Although Edna pities "that colorless existence which never uplifted its possessor beyond the region of blind contentment," Adele and her husband, understanding

11. Skaggs, *Chopin,* 92.

"each other perfectly," are united in "domestic harmony" (*KCA*, 56), for
Adele sings her husband's song. They represent the social majority, which
according to Shaw accepts illusions about the beauty of the family as a
"holy natural institution." [12]

To live up to this bourgeois ideal, Adele remains confined at home.
Entertainments are house music or "a languid walk around the block with
her husband after nightfall" (*KCA*, 76). Nevertheless, although she is a
carefully realized portrait of Shaw's colorful musical pet in a cage, grati-
fied by the attention she gets and living her life for others, reality muddles
the pretty picture: The price of Adele's life is the scene of "torture" near
the end of the novel when her role is vividly clarified. While she is
in labor—the "work" expected of proper Victorian women—the wife-
mother who depends on the attention of others cries, " 'This is too
much! . . . Where is Alphonse? Is it possible that I am to be abandoned like this—neglected by everyone?!' " (*KCA*, 108). Her entrapment,
clear in this scene, is counterpointed by Edna's final solitary act of self-
assertion. The action of the novel is paralleled by Adele's pregnancy.
While yearning for new life quickens in Edna, the new life in Adele results
in her literal confinement, for she remains deaf to the angry voice of the
parrot whose refrain, like an inner voice for Edna, is a command to "Go
away! Leave!"

The parrot belongs to Mme. Lebrun, whose husband is departed, whose
sons are expected to go away to seek their fortunes and fulfillment. Even
the imprimatur of patriarchal tradition that sanctions Leonce's behavior is
obliquely suggested in the parrot's epithet " 'By Jove' ('*Sapristi*')." For
Edna, an outsider in Creole society who takes its badinage seriously, the
bird's imperative becomes a directive to escape from the restrictions of
motherhood and marriage. She discovers that she wants to be the sort of
bird that Shaw describes as the only kind "a free souled person can sympathize with . . . the one that insists on being let out of the cage as the first
condition of making itself agreeable. A selfish bird, you may say: one that
puts its own gratification before that of the family which is so fond of
it—before even the greatest happiness of the greatest number; one, that in

12. Shaw, *Ibsenism*, 56.

aping the independent spirit of a man, has unparroted itself and become a creature that has neither the home-loving nature of a bird nor the strength and enterprise of a mastiff." [13]

In her quest to be a free-souled person, Edna tries to achieve emancipation in the manner Shaw prescribed: "The sum of the matter is that unless Woman repudiates her womanliness, her duty to her husband, to her children, to society, to the law, and to everyone but herself, she cannot emancipate herself. . . . Woman has to repudiate duty altogether. In that repudiation lies her freedom; for it is false to say that Woman is now directly the slave of Man: she is the immediate slave of duty; and as man's path to freedom is strewn with the wreckage of the duties and ideals he has trampled on, so must hers be." [14] Although Edna does not admit to herself that she is a slave to man, she resolves "never again to belong to another than herself," knowing that the world will think her selfish.

The most severe test of her freedom, however, is her sense of duty to her children. Even though Adele's accouchement is to Edna a scene of horror, she cannot escape, except through death, Adele's admonition to remember her obligations to her sons. During the summer at Grand Isle, Edna tells Adele, " 'I would give up the unessential; I would give my money, I would give my life for my children; but I wouldn't give myself' " (*KCA*, 80). Before her suicide, Edna's children appear to her as "antagonists" seeking to enslave her soul forever (*KCA*, 113).

Her husband assumes that she should dedicate her life to serving her sons. Her failure to watch over them in the night while he is out enjoying himself is disquieting to him. After a week of agreeable freedom in New Orleans, the model husband expects to buy favor and forgiveness from his wife and children with bonbons. From the start, he regards Edna as "a valuable piece of property" (*KCA*, 4). As Shaw put it in outlining the position of women in marriage, Edna "finds that her husband is neglecting her for business" and that his real life "lies away from home" where he is "thinking of stocks and shares." Even down to his professional interests, Leonce is the type of husband Shaw depicts. And Edna had as a girl the

13. *Ibid.*
14. *Ibid.*, 53–54.

same idealistic illusions that Shaw says "youthful imagination weaves so wonderfully under the stimulus of desire" to delude women into accepting, indeed relishing, a submissive, nurturing role.[15]

But when Edna learns to swim and recognizes her desire for a man other than her husband, she awakens to the fact that she married only to comply with society's expectations. After her awakening, Edna yearns for the liberation sought by insurgent females of Chopin's time. As she begins to take pleasure in self-reliance, she turns to books and, significantly, chooses Emerson. Like that other transcendentalist Margaret Fuller, she determines to throw down "every arbitrary barrier to development" and to isolate herself to meditate on the meaning of her life.[16] Personal experience raises Edna's consciousness of her entrapment and her servitude as a woman of the nineteenth century.

Her declaration of independence to choose whom she will love suggests the influence of the outspoken Victoria Woodhull (née Claflin), who in 1873 broadcast her belief in free love and the need for women to revolt against sexual slavery in marriage. On her wedding trip, Kate Chopin had met one of the infamous Claflin sisters, probably Victoria, who shocked Americans by insisting, like Edna, on woman's sexual freedom (*CB*, 33–34). However, Edna's decent but paternalistic husband is perhaps not so blatantly sexist as the stereotype Elizabeth Cady Stanton described in an address on "Womanliness"—the male who prefers a woman "quiet, deferential, submissive, approaching him as a subject does a master." [17] Stanton considered marriage a tyranny in which "women have simply echoed" (like parrots?) male thought.

In *The Awakening* Adele parrots patriarchal attitudes, whereas Edna rebels against them. Although her husband is not overtly despotic, Edna's Creole lover, Arobin, surmises that for Edna, marriage is nevertheless a despotism to be overthrown. When she gives her farewell dinner before moving out of the family house, Edna, having ironically exchanged male for female monarchy, is now "the regal woman," who in her obvious su-

15. *Ibid.*, 52.

16. Margaret (Ossoli) Fuller, *Woman in the Nineteenth Century* (Boston, 1855), 36.

17. Elizabeth Cady Stanton, " 'Womanliness,' an Address to the N.Y. State Legislature, 1880," in *History of Woman's Suffrage*, ed. Mari Jo and Paul Buhle (Urbana, 1978), 25.

periority "stands alone" (*KCA,* 88). In playfully calling the dinner party her *"coup d'état,"* Arobin is partially right, for she is symbolically over-throwing the institution of marriage. Earlier she took off her wedding ring, having recognized it as a miniature fetter. She threw it on the carpet and stamped on it, "striving to crush it. But her small boot heel did not make an indenture, not a mark upon the little glittering circle" (*KCA,* 53).

Her attempt to destroy the sign of her bondage foreshadows her ineffec-tual struggle for freedom. She refuses to attend her sister's wedding, an occasion that she derides as "most lamentable" (*KCA,* 66), thus thwarting her authoritarian father, a former colonel in the Confederate army. Having "coerced" his wife into the grave, this rigid gentleman gravely advises Leonce to rule Edna, if necessary, through male compulsion (*KCA,* 71). In rejecting paternalistic dominance, Edna becomes without knowing it an isolated Shavian rebel trying to fly the coop society built for her.

Ironically, she moves to what her maid calls "the pigeon house." As a revolutionary act, such a move is indeed tame, for the pigeon is a domestic bird, usually monogamous, that we associate with a coop or wobbling parasitically on the ground, hoping to be fed. Even pigeons capable of sustained flight are called homing pigeons. Thus when Edna nests in the little house, the reader, wondering whether it is merely a microcosm of the family mansion, cannot feel reassured that she will have the strength to soar and fly away. Nevertheless, having "escaped" and accepted Arobin as her lover, Edna feels briefly some of the power that Shaw believed the free woman would experience. Chopin writes, "Every step which she took toward relieving herself from obligations added to her strength and expan-sion as an individual. She began to look with her own eyes, to see and to apprehend the deeper undercurrents of life. No longer was she content to 'feed upon opinion' when her soul invited her" (*KCA,* 93).

During the summer at Grand Isle, Edna had heard Adele playing a piece on the piano that Edna named "Solitude." When she heard it, she imag-ined the figure of a naked man standing beside a desolate rock on the seashore in an attitude of "hopeless resignation as he looked toward a distant bird winging its flight away from him" (*KCA,* 26–27). Although, as Larzer Ziff suggests, the fantasy may be erotic, this Whitmanesque day-dream embodies Edna's frustrated desire for masculine freedom and autonomy and presages the tragic denouement of the novel.[18] Divested of the raiments of sexual stereotyping, Edna longs for a heightened experience that would transcend sex roles.

Edna's longing for solitude reflects attitudes that Chopin no doubt found in Elizabeth Cady Stanton's 1890 address, "Solitude of Self." Indeed, Chopin's first choice of a title for her novel alludes to Stanton's feminist tract; she called *The Awakening* "A Solitary Soul." Stanton had argued that "self-sovereignty" is a prerequisite for individual fulfillment, a prescription that Shaw, a year later, advocated for women. Stanton stressed that "the isolation of every human soul and the necessity of self-dependence must give each individual the right to choose his own surroundings." But a Presbyterian with strong fatalistic tendencies who reads Emerson and demonstrates self-reliance by moving around the corner with a servant is no doubt being treated with tolerant irony. Edna clearly wants, however, to be the kind of person Stanton describes as "an individual, in a world of her own, the arbiter of her own destiny, an imaginary Robinson Crusoe with her woman Friday on a solitary island." [19]

Twice Edna goes to a solitary island, once to a real one and once to her pigeon house (not to mention her crucial summmer vacation and final trip to Grand Isle) where she is tended by a "woman Friday" while she experiences an awakening. At the Cheniere, all of her dreams of erotic fulfillment are aroused, and in the pigeon house her illusions are shattered. Edna's trip to the island with Robert makes her feel that she has escaped an "anchor" and become her own navigator. As Stanton wrote, "No matter how much women prefer to lean, to be protected and supported, nor how much men desire to have them do so, they must make the voyage of life alone and for safety in emergency they must know something of the laws of navigation." [20] Although Edna feels that she is gaining control, ironically she relies heavily on Robert. In playfully saying that she'll give him the pirate's gold and treasure they might find together, she innocently suggests the illicit love and sexuality she may offer him. Although she sleeps

18. Larzer Ziff, *The American 1890's: Life and Times of a Lost Generation* (New York, 1966), 302.

19. Elizabeth Cady Stanton, " 'Solitude of Self,' an Address Before the U. S. Senate Committee on Woman's Suffrage, 1892," in *History of Woman's Suffrage*, 326, 325.

20. *Ibid.*, 327.

and awakens on the island, like Rip Van Winkle, into a brave new world, it is not, despite her assertions, one for which she is fully prepared.

At the pigeon house, romance encounters reality, for Edna discovers that Robert is not the dashing romantic lover created by her overactive imagination, stimulated as it had been by the colors and textures of Grand Isle whose sensuous promises created a grand illusion. A charming but superfluous young man, Robert nevertheless shares Leonce's assumptions about women. Edna wakes to the fact that Robert assumes that Leonce owns her, that he must ask her husband's permission to love her. An impecunious variant of the male stereotype and an ineffectual Tristan to Edna's Isolde, he smokes cigarettes, whereas the wealthy, successful Leonce smokes cigars, denoting his masculine power and status. In light of Sara deSaussure Davis' theory that Edna is seeking the "delirium" associated with cigarettes laced with narcotics, Robert's switch from cigarettes to cigars might have provided another rude awakening for Edna.[21] It establishes him as the Philistine male who encages women. Edna realizes that Robert, who has finally indulged himself with a box of cigars, is as much a conformist as her husband. As if to confirm her discovery, her beloved makes a cowardly exit, destroying her dream of love.

Her awakening to the fact that she cannot consummate her romance with him fatally wounds her. Her friend Mlle. Reisz had warned her, " 'The bird that would soar above the level plain of tradition and prejudice must have strong wings. It is a sad spectacle to see the weaklings, bruised, exhausted, fluttering back to earth' " (*KCA*, 82). Edna's failure with Robert brings her back to earth and to her limited options. She can, but will not, return to domestic captivity, or she can suffer social and self-castigation if she denies her duty to her children and becomes a free-lover.

Edna's repressive Protestant training and romantic illusions create a dilemma that leads to her tragic death, a final act of existential independence that is also an act of desperation. Like the uncaged domesticated bird unfit for survival alone, Edna must be recaptured if she is not to be killed. Aroused by her newly found animal instincts, she has not developed the

21. Sara deSaussure Davis, "Chopin's *A Vocation and a Voice*: Its Relevance to *The Awakening*," paper delivered at MLA convention, New Orleans, December 28, 1988.

"strength and enterprise" of Shaw's mastiff. The exigencies of art and character portrayal demand that Chopin "kill" Edna, whose swim into the sea's sensuous embrace is nonetheless ecstatic and courageously defiant. Her death by water is a declaration of both freedom and despair.

Among the last images that flash through her mind as she is swimming out to drown are her military father, her married sister, and the young officer whom she desired from a fanciful distance. Even in death she cannot escape reminders of the cultural patterns that formed her—patriarchy, marriage, and promises of romantic love—illusions Shaw targeted in *The Quintessence of Ibsenism*. Although Edna is suited neither for marriage nor for the role of mother-woman, she is unprepared for freedom. The bird that she had fantasized earlier as winging away and about which Mlle. Reisz had warned her is, when she finally stands alone on the beach, wounded, "with a broken wing . . . reeling, fluttering, circling disabled down, down to the water" (*KCA,* 113).

In *The Sanity of Art* (1891) Shaw wrote that life is "not the fulfillment of a moral law or of the deductions of reason but the satisfaction of a passion in us of which we can give no account whatsoever." Edna wants to satisfy the unaccountable passion, the life force within her that longs for aesthetic and sensual fulfillment. Like Shaw (and Ibsen as Shaw interprets him), Chopin's heroine comes to believe in the individualism of obeying her senses, even though passions are dangerous. But in spite of her liberation, at bottom she has not fully forgone the notion, which Shaw disavows, that love is self-surrender or self-abandonment. "Love," he writes, "loses its charm when it is not free." Shaw would urge "a young woman in a mood of strong reaction against the preaching of duty and self-sacrifice . . . not to murder her own instincts and throw away her life in obedience to a mouthful of empty phrases." Although Edna's last interview with Robert would seem to illustrate her agreement, she commits suicide in literal self-abandonment and surrender to the sea. Chopin's description of her death, however, can be construed, like Shaw's feminist writings, as an attack on "the compulsory character of the legalized conjugal relation."[22]

22. George Bernard Shaw, *The Sanity of Art* (New York, 1908), 50; Shaw, *Ibsenism*, 39, 40.

Shaw distinguishes love as we idealize it from "the practical factor in society that is still more appetite." In her infatuation with Robert and her affair with Arobin, Edna learns the difference between romantic love and sexual appetite, and before her final dilemma decides that she will love without concern for society's demands. Nonetheless, having absorbed all too well her repressive Protestant training, she feels guilty for desires that do not conform to her notions of romantic love. Her confusion of "romance and passion" is a disorder that Shaw blamed on the social milieu of the times.[23] In trying to talk to Edna about things she "never dreamt of before" (*KCA,* 110), Dr. Mandelet voices Shavian ideas. A surrogate for Shaw (and Ibsen) who exposed the life lies upon which phallocentric culture depended in socializing women, the doctor tries to cure Edna by explaining the romantic "illusions" of youth that nature provides to serve as "a decoy to secure mothers for the race" (*KCA,* 109–110). He is too late to save her from electing a fate that demonstrates rebellion against two of Shaw's *bêtes noire*—the majority view that "the domestic career" is natural for all women and the "idealist illusion" that deludes women into accepting the marriage cage.

Whereas womanly-women gain self-esteem in motherhood and foster "the idealist illusion that a vocation for domestic management and the care of children is natural for women," the idealists, according to Shaw, attack women who lack the domestic vocation, calling them "not women at all, but members of the third, or Bashkirtseff sex." Shaw's essay on the womanly-woman was inspired by male response to this type of female—Marie Bashkirtseff, the literary sensation of 1890 whose diary was criticized by the editor of the *Review of Reviews* for being the shameless revelations of an " 'artist, musician, wit, philosopher, student, anything you like but a natural woman with a heart to love, and a soul to find its supreme satisfaction in sacrifice for lover or for child.' "[24] Finding this attitude "pestiferous," Shaw assailed the editor for insisting upon the feminine ideal. Chopin created Mlle. Reisz to represent the Bashkirtseff sex and a social microcosm to reveal the conventional response to such an emancipated woman.

Most of the vacationers at Grand Isle consider the eccentric pianist self-

23. Shaw, *Ibsenism,* 50. See Barbara C. Ewell, *Kate Chopin* (New York, 1986), 140, for a discussion of Edna's confusion.

24. Shaw, *Ibsenism,* 51, 50.

absorbed, arrogant, and unpleasant. Edna's initial response to her is mixed, but as she grows in self-awareness and in desire to love where she chooses and develop as she will, she is drawn to Mlle. Reisz, who lives alone in bohemian squalor and devotes herself to the high calling of her art. Her wizened ugliness may, however, have more than a little to do with her biological destiny, just as Adele's conventional beauty may have much to do with hers. The pianist warns Edna that " 'to succeed, the artist must possess the courageous soul . . . The soul that dares and defies' " (*KCA,* 63). Apparently having sacrificed much in her quest for artistic success, she has defied society's rules by remaining single. In contrast to the womanly women, the New Woman cares nothing for children. She tells Edna that the summer would have been " 'rather pleasant, if it hadn't been for the mosquitoes and the Farival twins' " (*KCA,* 49), who play kitsch piano duets that perhaps offend her more than their childhood.

However, Chopin treats Mlle. Reisz with the same indulgent irony she uses in depicting Adele. The emancipated woman who has cut herself off (or been cut off?) from romantic fulfillment enjoys Edna's visit somewhat voyeuristically. No matter what the season, Mlle. Reisz wears the same "shabby lace" and artificial bunch of violets on the side of her head" (*KCA,* 62), tokens of frustrated and blighted erotic fantasy. She titillates Edna with amorous music that moves the younger woman to tears. In describing Mlle. Reisz playing Chopin, Chopin is no doubt wryly reminding her educated readers of writer George Sand, Frederic Chopin's lover, a woman who successfully combined all three of the female roles examined in *The Awakening.* Identifying Edna as a femme fatale by referring to Keats's "La Belle Dame Sans Merci," Mlle. Reisz plays Isolde's song from Wagner's *Tristan and Isolde,* associating Edna with romantic agony and Wagner's tragic love-death motif. In spite of Mlle. Reisz's snobbish but serious preoccupation with her art, she gets a sterile emotional satisfaction vicariously, as Lynda Boren has indicated, through manipulating and sharing Edna's turbulent, newly awakened emotions. Like Shaw, whose *The Perfect Wagnerite* (1898) Chopin could have read while writing *The Awakening,* the pianist no doubt admires Wagner's artistic daring.[25]

25. Lynda S. Boren, "The Music of Passion: Kate Chopin's Experimental Keyboard," paper delivered at MLA convention, New Orleans, December 28, 1988; George Bernard Shaw, *The Perfect Wagnerite* (London, 1923).

She has wings to defy convention, but she lacks the sensuality that is even more a threat to society than her "third" sex.

Although aroused by the older woman's music and envious of her freedom to pursue her artistic interests, Edna does not want to emulate Mlle. Reisz's lonely life any more than she wants to accept a life like Adele's as a brood hen. Wishing for full self-realization, Edna longs to design herself as a New Woman without being condemned to the role of the Victorian feminine. As Per Seyersted notes, Chopin's stories deal with "what we might call the three main types of women: the 'feminine,' the 'emancipated,' and the 'modern' (to use the terminology of Simone de Beauvoir's *The Second Sex*)," types that Shaw anticipated, without emphasizing erotic satisfaction as an end in itself.[26] Chopin's Edna is aware of all three claims—the subservient role that she tries to escape, the "active taker" who puts "flesh above the spirit," and the "modern" woman who "prides herself on thinking, taking action, working, creating."[27] Edna rejects her subjugation as wife and mother, but having been socialized by a rigid puritan ethic, she cannot with impunity and without guilt achieve full emancipation and sexual liberation.

Because romantic ideals deluded her into desiring "the acme of bliss" that equates love with sexual desires, and because reality taught her that erotic satisfaction can be divorced from love, Edna is trapped by her delusion that without a man, she is incomplete. She wants Robert but knows that she will have to content herself with Arobin. Despite her talent as a painter, she recognizes that in her time and place the third option—what Shaw calls "emancipated" and de Beauvoir "modern"—is an inadequate model for her longings for completeness, for Mlle. Reisz's narrow life belies her brave talk of artistic daring. Aware of all of her choices, Edna realizes that none will satisfy her unaccountable passion for life. Having discovered the desire but not the sufficient will for self-actualization, Edna is ensnared by her romantic yearnings and the preset springs of polite society.[28]

To underscore her treatment of the three pigeonholes available to Edna,

26. *CB*, 103; see also Simone de Beauvoir, *The Second Sex* (1952; rpr. New York, 1974).

27. De Beauvoir, *Second Sex*, 798.

28. See Jo Ellen Jacobs, "*The Awakening* in a Course on Philosophical Ideas in Literature," in *ATA*, for a discussion of this dilemma.

Chopin creates variations on her theme. Adele, the womanly woman, is paralleled by the widow Mme. Lebrun, who dominates one son and dotes on the other, still living through her offspring. Mlle. Reisz, the unsexed voyeuristic woman with a profession, is paralleled ironically by the woman in black, probably a nun saying her beads, who is following a pair of young lovers. Edna, the sensuous woman who would fly from the cage of her conditioning, is confronted with representatives of her three sexual options—the young lovers, who exemplify romantic escape; the barefoot Spanish girl Mariequita, who stands for direct, earthy sexuality; and Mrs. Highcamp, who represents the possibility of sophisticated extramarital affairs. Edna dreams of lovers escaping the world in a pirogue; she frankly recognizes that she shares Mariequita's bold sensuality; and she fears that she could become a Mrs. Highcamp involved in a succession of affairs with younger men. She rejects the role of Adele and because of her aroused sensuality cannot, despite artistic talent, accept or aspire to the sterile independence of Reisz. When she faces the sea alone, she has run out of choices.

Thus with sensuous imagination, irony, and acute sensitivity to the climate of thought about women in her time, Chopin patterns a medium fully appropriate to her realistic, insightful message. She does not warn women to conform, but implicit in her imagery and her story is the idea that without fulfilling work and the collaboration of men, female freedom may be destined to frustration. Edna's broken wing is caused by the snare of her illusions and by the winds of social expectations. Although, as Leonce says, she does have "some sort of notion in her head concerning the eternal rights of women" (*KCA,* 65), she falls short of daring Shavian liberation. A diagnostic and a cautionary tale, Chopin's narrative subjects Shavian argument and feminist thought to the corrective of her imagination. Without compromising her aesthetic principles, Chopin created a work of "destruction," like Ibsen's problem plays, one that exposes the domestic lies people live by. According to Shaw, "Every step in morals is made by challenging the validity of the existing concept of perfect propriety of conduct." [29]

Chopin's novel is such a challenge. It illustrates Shaw's belief in works

29. Shaw, *The Sanity of Art,* 44.

of "destruction," for "the advantage of the work of destruction is that every new ideal is less of an illusion than the one it has supplanted; so that the destroyer of ideals, though denounced as an enemy of society, is in fact sweeping the world clear of lies." [30] In questioning the conventional lies about women, *The Awakening* is quintessential Chopinism. With uncompromising realism, wry irony that exposes the gulf between the illusions and realities of her characters, and sensuous symbolic detail that communicates theme without presenting it, the novel tests society's assumptions about women. It effectively gives Shavian argument fictional form.

30. Shaw, *Ibsenism*, 57.

III Earning the Right

She owns the fine house by the rise of the bank,
She hides handsome and richly drest aft the blinds of the window.
—Walt Whitman, Song of Myself

The Economics of the Body in Kate Chopin's The Awakening

JOHN CARLOS ROWE

> In families that I know, some little girls like to saw wood, others to use carpenters' tools. Where these tastes are indulged, cheerfulness and good-humor are promoted. Where they are forbidden, because "such things are not proper for girls," they grow sullen and mischievous.
>
> Fourier had observed these wants of women, as no one can fail to do who watches the desires of little girls, or knows the ennui that haunts grown women, except where they make to themselves a serene little world by art of some kind.
>
> —Margaret Fuller, *Woman in the Nineteenth Century*

Of the many awakenings Edna Pontellier experiences in Chopin's novel, each involves centrally her sense of her body. In the little side room of Mme. Antoine's cottage on Cheniere Caminada, Edna touches and looks at her body with a sense of self-discovery: "She ran her fingers through her loosened hair for a while. She looked at her round arms as she held them straight up and rubbed them one after the other, observing closely, as if it were something she saw for the first time, the fine firm quality and texture of her flesh. She clasped her hands easily above her, and it was thus she fell asleep" (*KCA*, 37). This is only one among many moments in which Edna seems to recognize herself by feeling the texture, form, and complexity of her body. Utterly unlike Dreiser's Carrie Meeber, whose body is defined by her clothes or by the gazes of others in which she assumes form, Edna experiences her body in scenes remarkable for their refusal of the reader's gaze. As many critics have noted, Edna's special experience of the materiality of her body occurs in moments of intense privacy, whether indoors or out. In public, her husband and her lovers possess her body, treating it as "a valuable piece of personal property," the intentional object of masculine desire.

It thus appears that the mere sentience of Edna's body is a site of rebellion against such possession, a refusal of the gaze or touch of the masculine *other* that so defines this closed Creole world. Significantly, the surfaces of Edna's body suggest most powerfully to her some inner, private, governing self. Her act of shedding her bathing suit as she heads for her concluding swim in the Gulf is foreshadowed repeatedly in the novel. Not only does she strip away the confining clothing in the little side room at Mme. Antoine's, she repeatedly loosens her clothing or replaces a stiff costume with a looser peignoir just before her most significant moments of self-recognition. Hidden within the fabric is another surface, alive to touch and its own sentience.

Apart from its construction by the masculine gaze and independent of the roles Edna is expected to assume (most often figured in her clothing), the stylistic postulation of Edna's body, rescues Edna's claims for some essential, still indefinable self from evaporating into transcendentalist sentiment and cliche: "Edna had once told Madame Ratignolle that she would never sacrifice herself for her children, or for any one. . . . 'I would give up the unessential; I would give my money, I would give my life for my children; but I wouldn't give myself. I can't make it more clear; it's only something which I am beginning to comprehend, which is revealing itself to me' " (*KCA*, 48). From beginning to end, this essential self is associated not only with Edna's physical body but also with the submersion of that body in the ocean, the medium in which the wholeness of the body can be sensed. As Chopin writes on the verge of Edna's final swim: "The touch of the sea is sensuous, enfolding the body in its soft, close embrace" (*KCA*, 113).

Sandra Gilbert's important reading of *The Awakening* as a modern retelling of the "second coming" of Aphrodite, to develop a feminine mythology for the otherwise alienated Edna (and her women readers), depends crucially on the mythic body of Aphrodite as an incarnation of the oceanic medium.[1] In Greek, *aphros* means "sea foam," making Aphrodite's associations with generative power explicit. The magic in Ovid or Hesiod derives from such extreme transformations—the formlessness of

1. Sandra Gilbert, Introduction to *"The Awakening" and Selected Stories*, ed. Sandra M. Gilbert (New York, 1984), 19–33.

the sea into animated, individualized form of a divine being, in this case the personification of natural energy in the erotics of the goddess's body. And ancient conventions of the human being carrying within its bodily form "traces" of its primal origins—the "oceanic" circulation of the blood, as well as a woman's body as microcosm for the ocean's vital fluid—support Gilbert's reading of the fantastic, mythic metamorphosis that Chopin effects in an otherwise quotidian subject of an ostensibly naturalist narrative. If the myth of Aphrodite works in *The Awakening*, however, it does so only by incorporating into our thinking about the body its essential power of transformation. Just this sense of the body as an act, as unthinkable apart from what it can do, however, including the most elementary recognition of the body as such, escapes Edna, even as Chopin uses this knowledge to explore woman's problematic relation to the new economics of speculative capitalism, the concept of the New Woman.

It is a transcendentalist convention still—from Thoreau wishing to stand neck-deep in a swamp to the "oceanic" sublime of Whitman. For Chopin, however, the moment of total immersion, in which the body experiences itself at once as self and natural other, marks the distance separating her narrative from those of the great romantics. For Edna, her body can be experienced only in its profound alienation from any natural context, denying absurdly the self-evidence of the natural health and vitality of this twenty-eight-year-old woman's body. The body as such, free from what is done to it or what it is capable of doing, is simply unpresentable, cannot be made to appear in its own self-evidence in any way that will provide Edna with the confidence to leave her tedious husband, trivial lovers, bonbon-hungry children.

Listening to Mlle. Reisz play in Mme. Lebrun's parlor, Edna imagines "the figure of a man standing beside a desolate rock on the seashore. He was naked. His attitude was one of hopeless resignation as he looked toward a distant bird winging its flight away from him" (*KCA*, 26–27). The imaginary figure is erotically charged with Robert Lebrun's presence, and as such it is the best image Edna can give to her own body, at once naked and resigned yet full of desire. In sum, even at the moment of imagining a body for "Solitude" (the name she gives the musical piece), a rather conventional imaginary object, this metaphoric body is already marked by its distance from the free activity of "a distant bird winging its flight away from him." Erotically charged as the naked figure is, it is psychically barred by Edna from the desire that ought to inspire it. His "hopeless resignation" is quite the opposite of desire, and it is the taboo on erotic desire that is strangely bound up with Edna's unformulated sense that she has been forbidden the sheer experience of the whole and natural body figured in "a distant bird winging its flight."

What does it mean to have a body? For Edna, and for Mme. Ratignolle, it is always someone else who *possesses* your body, and such "possession" already signifies something other than your body: a "wife," a "lover," a white sunshade, a sunbonnet, children, heirs. In short, the body is exchangeable for something else, has been transformed into something else, has entered an *economy* in which it can be so changed. What troubles Edna so profoundly is that it no longer belongs to her, but what she is can find no natural ground, no utterly transcendental experience of herself as a body. Even in that apparently primal moment of naked submersion in the sea, the body experiences itself as such only by means of an activity, a making, that may be as simple as the motions of the body to swim, either in a Kentucky meadow or off Grand Isle, she must understand her body as an activity rather than some thing, natural or social.

I do not mean to be metaphysical, to offer some fundamental phenomenology of the body as its own activity of transformation, but to attach these sentiments to the late-nineteenth-century context of Kate Chopin's novel. Swimming in the sea, even standing naked by a rock to gaze longingly after the spiritual token of the natural scene, that soulful bird, might have sufficed for Emerson, Thoreau, or even Whitman. For Chopin, the "swimming" motions of the child in her father's meadow in Kentucky disguise just what Edna would like to but can never genuinely do: cut and harvest, till the soil, grow and make something that would be a proper expression of her own bodily activity. Sharing with Edna that significant recollection of her childhood in Kentucky, Adele asks, " 'Where were you going that day in Kentucky, walking through the grass?' " Edna answers, " 'I don't remember now. I was just walking diagonally across a big field. My sunbonnet obstructed the view. I could see only the stretch of green before me, and I felt as I must walk on forever, without coming to the end of it. . . . Likely as not it was Sunday, . . . and I was running away from prayers, from the Presbyterian service, read in a spirit of gloom by my father that chills me yet to think of' " (*KCA*, 17–18).

The romantic promise of that meadow's grasses and the wind in her face will give Edna some sense of her independent body as she passes, as a scythe passes, diagonally across the meadow is quickly barred from her as she recalls that " 'my sun-bonnet obstructed the view' " and then that " 'I was running away from prayers' " and the gloom of her stern Presbyterian, military, cocktail-mixing father. Only a few pages earlier, at the end of Chapter V, as Robert urges Edna to come down to the shore for her bath with " 'the water must be delicious; it will not hurt you. Come,' " he reaches "up for her big, rough straw hat that hung on a peg outside the door, and put it on her head" (*KCA*, 14). Much as we would like to read this earlier scene as an invitation to the sea, the erotic passion with Robert, and thus a certain liberation, Edna's "memory" reminds us that the "sun-bonnet" of Kentucky or Grand Isle always belongs to the father, to the world of feminine decoration, to the masculine lover, and thus to a certain blindness, an incapacity to see as a woman. It is, after all, Robert who teaches Edna to swim and the "spurs of the cavalary officer" on the "porch" that she remembers in her final swim (*KCA*, 114). The rough straw hat and Edna's rejected bathing suit in her final swim both hang from a phallic "peg." She has "learned" something at least at the very last in her rejection of the bathing suit, whereas here she allows Robert to place that hat on her head. Even so, a woman's rebellion will involve much more for Chopin than merely the assertion of her naked self; that rebellion will require a thorough transvaluation of the modes of production that govern both the psyche and the economy of late-nineteenth-century capitalism.

But for the body to experience itself as such, it must feel itself making some thing in the particular process of making that allows the body to recognize itself in and through an *other*. In *The Body in Pain*, Elaine Scarry reads with care Marx's philosophical conception of human labor as the fundamental act of self-consciousness, which makes the alienation of the laborer from her product as psychically as it is materially impoverishing under capitalism. Focusing on "making," rather than "thinking" and "seeing," Marx and Engels' specific motives in focusing on bodily labor as the site of human self-consciousness are clear enough in *The German*

Ideology (1846), and Chopin seems to agree with them insofar as she too stresses Edna's physical body, especially its arms and hands and legs, rather than her eyes, head, or even speech.[2] As Scarry argues:

> That sentient beings move around in an external space where their sentience is objectified means their bodies themselves are changed. . . . Perhaps the single most striking formulation occurs in Frederick Engels's essay, "The Part Played by Labour in the Transition from Ape to Man." . . . Engels's speculation that the crucial location of the transition from ape to man had been in the hand, the organ of making, rather than in the skull, the attendant organ of thinking, has after many years been confirmed by the discoveries of anthropologists. . . . Engels also introduces into the essay the idea that the hand is itself an artifact, gradually altered by its own activity of altering the external world.[3]

Engels' principal examples of the hand as the agent of human self-making, paintings and lacemaking, are both conventional enough indications of how the hand produces design out of materials (paint and thread), lacking any inherent disposition to such designs. As Scarry demonstrates, Engels' point is that the complex anatomy of the hand—the "intricate weave of tendons, ligaments, muscles, and bones"—is quite literally transferred to the painting or the lace: "It is this interior disposition that is made visible and celebrated in the paintings or the lace: whatever the specific subject matter of a particular canvas (the sea breaking on the shore, flowers opening in a vase), part of its subject matter, part of what makes it available to the viewer, is the shape of the interior complexities and precisions of the sentient tissue that held the brush."[4]

The "remaking of the human body" is at once the ultimate philosophical aim of human labor—and thus of society—for Marx and Engels, even as this phrase carries with it all the horror of the late-nineteenth-century intellectual before the increasingly palpable threat that industrialism would transform nature, including the human body, into the "artifices" of commodity capitalism.

2. Elaine Scarry, *The Body in Pain: The Making and Unmaking of the World* (New York, 1985), 243–77; Karl Marx and Frederick Engels, *Capital* (New York, 1977).

3. Scarry, *Body in Pain*, 252–53.

4. *Ibid.*, 253.

Leonce Pontellier represents much more than the conventional dangers of industrial capitalism to factory and domestic workers. In *The Awakening* we have moved a step beyond the reflection of capitalist values in family relations (*i.e.*, gender relations determined by class and property) that Engels develops in *The Origin of the Family, Private Property and the State* (1884).[5] Leonce is not a "cotton broker" in the old sense but a commodities broker who deals primarily in futures. Reversing one of the sexist conventions of the domestic romance, Chopin stresses Edna's concern regarding her husband's extravagances. But Leonce reminds her of the basic law of the speculator: " 'The way to become rich is to make money, my dear Edna, not to save it' " (*KCA*, 53).

Leonce places his emphasis on the making of money as if it were an organic product, like the cotton he undoubtedly never sees. He refers to a kind of making that occurs apart from any expenditure of bodily energy and that has only the most illusory relation to the substance of the actual object or product to which it refers (cotton, for example). As Walter Michaels has pointed out, successful dealing in futures depends in large part on *not* owning the actual goods.[6] The recurrent nightmare of the commodities speculator is that he might have to take delivery of all those soybeans for which he has purchased futures contracts. By deferring ownership to some future and finally fictional date of delivery, the speculator concentrates on the increasingly independent game (or fictional story) of money (risk capital) that appears to grow without any labor on the part of the investor.

This Wall Street magic was a matter of considerable concern to agrarian interests in the later nineteenth century, since the farmer's production depended absolutely on the size of the crop, whereas the knowledgeable speculator could profit from either abundance or scarcity of the actual product. The fact is that this speculative economy and its fantastic narrative of money growing without human labor has come to define our postindustrial age, to the extent that farm subsidies and other efforts to control natu-

5. Frederick Engels, *The Origin of the Family, Private Property, and the State* (1884; rpr. New York, 1985).

6. Walter Michaels, *The Gold Standard and the Logic of Naturalism* (Berkeley, 1987), 67.

ral growth according to the conditions of the market are now accepted, even necessary practices.

Thus for Edna's domestic relations with her husband and her relation to her body as a productive agency, the very property that Engels insisted was the sole determinant of family (and thus sexual) relations has changed dramatically from the accumulated capital of the middle-class industrialist to the power to sustain the illusion of this new "commodity form" that is the speculator's crucial fiction. As Engels stresses, "The supremacy of the man in marriage is the simple consequence of his economic supremacy, and with the abolition of the latter will disappear of itself. The indissolubility of marriage is partly a consequence of the economic situation in which monogamy arose, partly tradition from the period when the connection between this economic situation and monogamy was not yet fully understood and was carried to extremes under religious form." [7]

I need hardly add that the scenes of gambling—Leonce at Klein's Hotel, Edna winning big at the Jockey Club in New Orleans—are meant to refer to this new speculative economy, which substitutes the entertainment (even the romantic adventure) of the game, its chance and risk, for the productivity of the farmer, wife, or industrial laborer. Leonce's patronizing tone toward Edna as he explains patiently the way to become rich is supposed to remind us how thoroughly unfamiliar Edna is with any of these changes in the commodity from a manufactured object to money that may grow fantastically on its own.

Thus our initial claim that Edna's body can be known only in and through its own activity, its own "self-making," is complicated by the fact that bodies in this new speculative economy may be nothing more than the effects (rather than causes) of certain economic practices that have dispensed quite neatly with the need for any particular product or any particular labor. The perverse beauty of a speculative economy is that it virtually liberates itself from the domain of bodily labor, both on the part of the speculator and the workers he nominally employs. The labor of the farmer (or manufacturer) in producing the object of speculation has little significance for the speculator as long as that speculator has reliable information

7. Engels, *Origin of the Family,* 113.

regarding that labor. Good horses or bad, the experienced gambler knows how to wager and win.

The crucial difference between Marx and Engels's lingering Hegelian conception of the human being as a maker of his or her self-image, and thus of his or her conception of the body as visible and familiar, and the relentless capitalist production of a fantastic world of consumer commodities radically detached from their means of production identifies Edna Pontellier's ambivalence regarding her body. Much of this depends on the complex processes Georg Lukacs analyzes in *History and Class Consciousness* (1923) under the heading of *reification,* a term that draws significantly on ideas in one of Chopin's most relevant contemporaries, Thorstein Veblen, whose *Theory of the Leisure Class* is generally considered a crucial piece of intellectual history in the reading of *The Awakening.*[8] Veblen and Lukacs expanded Marx's "commodity fetishism" as the alienation of the worker from the meaning of his own labor power to include what Carolyn Porter has termed "the consciousness of everyone living in a society driven by capitalist growth." Reification "generates, on the one hand, a 'new objectivity,' a 'second nature,' in which people's own productive activity is obscured, so that what they have made appears to them as a given, an external and objective reality, operating according to its own immutable laws." On the other hand, according to Porter, it generates people who assume a passive and "contemplative" stance in the face of that objectified and rationalized reality, people who seem to themselves to stand outside that reality because their participation in producing it is mystified.[9]

The speculator, of course, *works* that "second nature," which itself is constituted exclusively by the disembodied circulation of exchange values that we call the "market." I say "disembodied" because the market's definition in and through exchange value subordinates the discreteness of the commodity to its variable rate of exchange. The only sentience involved in such a market economy is the simulated excitement or thrill that the investor experiences when he risks his capital. Such excitement is, I think, often

8. Georg Lukacs, *History and Class Consciousness,* trans. Rodney Livingston (Cambridge, Eng., 1985); Thorstein Veblen, *Theory of the Leisure Class* (New York, 1899).

9. Carolyn Porter, "Reification and American Literature," in *Ideology and Classic American Literature,* ed. Sacvan Bercovitch and Myra Jehlen (Cambridge, Eng., 1986), 189.

conflated with the sort of erotic titillation that Edna experiences with Robert and Alcee, mere doubles of her husband, and that provides her with an illusory sense of the erotics—that is, the productivity—of her body.

The "passive" and "contemplative" stance of the alienated worker is analogous to the oppressive "languor" and "torpor" that so often overcomes Edna and is the objective correlative of her imaginary figure's "hopeless resignation." These moments of physical exhaustion are worth analyzing in some detail because they appear to have a certain structural regularity, despite their manifestly different dramatic contexts.

Before analyzing some of these moments, however, let me suggest their importance in terms of the Marxian thesis that the human body is presentable only in and through its productive labor, in terms of some representation that is the product of that labor. I want to begin, then, by drawing an analogy between the physical exhaustion of the laborer—the using up of the body and even the shortening of life—and the psychic torpor of Edna Pontellier. For Marx and Engels this exhaustion of the laborer has practical consequences in their arguments, especially in *Capital* where careful economic analyses demonstrate the inefficiency of capitalism insofar as it fails to provide for its workers' basic needs sufficient to renew their abilities to produce the product. Poor working conditions are extended in *Capital* to include inadequate living conditions and inadequate salaries to provide adequate nourishment for the human body performing the task required. But these practical arguments are equally philosophical since the "theft" that constitutes the capitalist's surplus value is quite literally stolen from the body the worker—its capacity to live. Taken too literally, of course, the concept of the human body employed in *Capital* could be termed narrowly mechanistic since not all labor wears away the body. Physical exercise strengthens the body, extends the life cycle, and so forth.

But Marx and Engels are equally concerned with the quality of life in psychic terms, and the exclusively *physical* exhaustion of the worker's body is more accurately understood as a psychical despair and resignation before the futility of labor. What is produced by such labor never returns to the worker as such, especially in assembly-line production where the finished product may never be seen by the worker. Such alienation of labor, is what makes possible the more "developed" practices of the speculator,

because industrial capitalism enacted a literal diminution of the significance of the worker's body. The next phase, often hopefully termed "late
capitalism" by optimistic Marxians, is part of that industrial logic: capitalism's ability to dispense completely with the human body as a meaningful
agent, a productive subjectivity.

Edna's moments of "exhaustion" express a certain despair regarding
the value and integrity of her labor, which helps align her anxieties regarding the reproductive powers of a woman with the comparable frustration
of the industrial worker. This futility, however, is rendered even more
problematic when we consider how the new speculative economy represented by Leonce, Robert Lebrun, and Alcee Arobin has transformed even
that physical labor into a sort of phantom of the speculative game. In its
furthest reach, *The Awakening* aligns the exhaustion of the body in labor
with the absolute extinction of the body enacted in this new speculative
economy. Along with the death of the body, then, goes any concept of self
as the making of a representation of the body. In the place of such material
selfhood, which is just what Edna desires throughout the narrative, the new
economy offers us nothing but roles or personas. Thus Edna's final swim
may be read in two contradictory ways that nonetheless describe quite adequately the two economies that Chopin wants to represent.

In one sense, Edna's final swim enacts the ultimate extinction of the
body as its own activity, its own labor. Reduced to nothing more than roles
assigned to her by male others—her father, her husband, her lovers—Edna
moves like some automaton to the Gulf and symbolically drowns the body
that no longer has any use value. Its skeleton goes to join the submarine
world that figures the unconscious of speculative capitalism, that watery
grave in which the stolen booty of pirates like Jean Laffite lies buried. In
another reading, compatible with Gilbert's, Edna rejects the roles of this
economy of simulation by stripping herself naked, exposing the phallic
peg that has kept her discarded swimsuit "ready" for her all along, and
heads for the Gulf to discover the value of her active body. In this context,
Edna's final swim is a rebellion against this fantastic world of speculation
for the sake of the undeniable productivity of the body itself, not simply
as a biology ("Remember the children!") but as the organ of self-represen-
tation. In this latter reading, the myth of Aphrodite is quite relevant since
a symbolic renewal is performed by Edna, a rebirth of those values of

productivity that industrial and then speculative capitalism have caused us to repress.

Edna's first experience of physical torpor occurs at the center of Chapter III, just after Leonce has returned late from gambling at Klein's Hotel and awakened her to attend to Raoul, who the father is certain has "a high fever" and needs "looking after" (*KCA*, 7). When Edna answers sleepily that she is quite sure Raoul has no fever, Leonce reproaches "his wife with her inattention, her habitual neglect of the children" and lectures her on the domestic duties she has assumed as a wife. It is a scene of patriarchal authority that will be repeated again in New Orleans when Leonce complains about the cook's scorched fish, and in this instance it clearly identifies Edna as her husband's servant.

Although she obeys his command in this instance, Edna finds herself crying as her husband sleeps soundly: "An indescribable oppression, which seems to generate in some unfamiliar part of her consciousness, filled her whole being with a vague anguish. It was like a shadow, like a mist passing across her soul's summer day. It was strange and unfamiliar; it was a mood. . . . The mosquitoes made merry over her, biting her firm, round arms and nipping at her bare insteps" (*KCA*, 8). This scene hardly requires much analysis since it self-evidently expresses the dependence of the wife's labor on her husband's command. Awakened to her duties by her husband, she is oppressed by an anguish that virtually immobilizes her were it not for the mosquitoes recalling her to her body: "The little stinging, buzzing imps succeeded in dispelling a mood which might have held her there in the darkness half a night longer" (*KCA*, 8).

Just as Edna refuses "to answer her husband when he questioned her," so Chopin refuses to tell the reader anything about the health or sickness of Raoul. In fact, the sleeping children exist in this scene only in Leonce's words, just as Edna's body is subject to his commands (quite literally, the sleeping body is ironically awakened by the patriarchal command). Only a few pages later, at the end of Chapter XI, Edna withholds her body from Leonce's desire in a scene explicitly designed to echo that in Chapter III. Leonce tries to convince her to come into the cottage and his bed by arguing, " 'The mosquitoes will devour you' " (*KCA*, 32). From her reply, " 'There are no mosquitoes,' " to her command, " 'Leonce, go to bed,' " and her refusal to be bullied, " 'Don't speak to me like that again; I shall not answer you,' " Edna finds strength and voice in denial (*KCA*, 32).

Both scenes are necessary stages in Edna's awareness of her own body, but both turn upon the denial of what the body can do, on the limited labor available to Edna at these stages in the narrative: childbirth and the satisfaction of her husband's sexual desire. In this scene too the work of denial, of rebellion, provokes a sort of languor: "The physical need for sleep began to overtake her; the exuberance which had sustained and exalted her spirit left her helpless and yielding to the conditions which crowded her in" (*KCA*, 32). In these two scenes Edna's frustration and rebellion are analogous to the industrial worker's recognition of the alienation of her labor power, an alienation by means of which the capitalist affirms his power to rule.

Dale Bauer and Andrew Lakritz have argued that "Edna's alienation is necessary to her awakening because it forces her to confront the values of her culture and to articulate her own. . . . Only by articulating her own stance, by bringing into the open what is her own ambivalence toward her culture, can she overcome both her self-imposed isolation and the repressive demands made on her by society. Edna's gradual awareness of her voice, her burgeoning consciousness, is crucial to her resistance. . . . Edna awakens to her cultural alienation rather than to sexual passion." [10] Bauer and Lakritz distinguish significantly between Edna's cultural and sexual awakenings, perhaps because previous critics have placed so much stress on the erotics of her body to the neglect of the political imperatives of her awakenings.

As much as I agree with Bauer and Lakritz that the fundamental question for Chopin is a woman's awareness of her cultural situation, her participation for better or worse with the modes of production that extend from factory and brokerage to bedroom and parlor, I think that Chopin wants for these very reasons to entangle Edna's erotic sense of her body with more general economic questions of human production. For women in the United States at the end of the nineteenth century, Chopin argues, these domains cannot be easily distinguished. Sexual ennui, like the fatigue of the industrial laborer, is not exclusively a physical consequence of exertion but a psychical effect of frustrated erotic and economic energies. As Engels reminds us, sexual production follows the same laws as industrial produc-

---

10. Dale Marie Bauer and Andrew M. Lakritz, "*The Awakening* and the Woman Question," in *ATA*, 51.

tion under capitalism: the alienation of the mother and children to the patriarch's theft of surplus value in the form of his heirs and the servitude of both mother and children to the patriarch's domestic law, including public laws against divorce and carefully regulating inheritance. This point is made explicit by Engels in such ancient customs as the Athenian father's legal right to sell his children.[11]

Edna's status as her husband's property involves the translation of her body into a masculine fetish. In the opening scene of the *The Awakening*, Edna appears quite literally through the haze of Mr. Pontellier's cigar smoke, figured in a succession of phallic metonymies that define decisively the masculine gaze: "Mr. Pontellier finally lit a cigar and began to smoke, letting the [newspaper] drag idly from his hand. He fixed his gaze upon a white sunshade that was advancing at a snail's pace from the beach. . . . Beneath its pink-lined shelter were his wife, Mrs. Pontellier, and young Robert Lebrun. When they reached the cottage, the two seated themselves with some appearance of fatigue upon the upper step of the porch, facing each other, each leaning against a supporting post" (*KCA*, 4). In Chapter XI, when Edna finally rises, full of physical exhaustion, to enter the cottage, she "tottered up the steps, clutching feebly at the post before passing into the house," asking, " 'Are you coming in Leonce?' " (*KCA*, 33). Leonce has been smoking cigars and drinking wine to dull his sexual desire, frustrated by Edna's refusal of his overtures. We hardly need Freud to read the transference from cigar to sunshade to post in the opening scene, cigar to post in Chapter XI. In the opening chapter, Leonce reproaches Edna, " 'What folly! to bathe at such an hour in such heat!' " and concludes, " 'You are burnt beyond recognition,' looking at his wife as one looks at valuable piece of personal property which has suffered some damage" (*KCA*, 4). The burning of the cigar, its transference from the hand of Leonce to the body of Edna, is brilliantly accomplished by Chopin, for it makes possible the first bodily representation of Edna that we have in the novel: "She held up her hands, strong, shapely hands, and surveyed them critically, drawing up her lawn sleeves above the wrists. Looking at them reminded her of her rings, which she had given to her husband before leaving for the beach. She silently reached out to him, and he, understand-

11. Engels, *Origin of the Family,* 145.

ing, took the rings from his vest pocket and dropped them into her open palm" (*KCA,* 4).

In this moment, the capitalist's gaze and law come together. We see Leonce looking, whereas what we see of Edna is just what signifies her capacity to work: her hands. Under the masculine gaze of the husband-capitalist, Edna's hands become "ugly" and "damaged" rather than "strong, shapely" implements of production. Dalliance with Robert Lebrun, as if granting such flirtation, belongs to the holiday behavior of a rich Creole's wife.

When Edna attempts to carry her rebellion further by way of Robert Lebrun and later Alcee Arobin, she merely encounters again and again the patriarchal structure of domination that binds her very conception of her body to the law of a masculine gaze that by the end of the narrative encompasses not only the various "arts" of society but its economics. In these episodes physical exhaustion follows her failed efforts to represent her self beyond the mode of psychical production that governs social and economic patriarchy. In Chapter XII, just after she has withheld her body from Leonce in Chapter XI, she sends Robert the command to join her on the excursion to the Cheniere: "She had never sent for him before. She had never asked for him. She had never seemed to want him before" (*KCA,* 33). But the romantic voyage that she performatively commands turns out to be little more than a journey into her unconscious alienation; a retelling of the masculine narrative in which she is nothing but a disembodied character.

Even if we disregard the wharf crowded with the two lovers, the lady in black, old M. Farival, and one of Robert's other dalliances, the Spanish girl Mariequita, we cannot ignore the conventionality of the romance that Robert and Edna compose as they sail away. Robert proposes an excursion on the following day to Grande Terre where they will "climb up the hill to the old fort and look at the wriggling gold snakes, and watch the lizards sun themselves," and Edna "thought she would like to be alone there with Robert." Even more conventionally, Robert suggests, " 'I'll take you some night in the pirogue when the moon shines. Maybe your Gulf spirit will whisper to you in which of these islands the treasures are hidden' " (*KCA,* 35). The history of Spanish colonialism—itself a version of its romantic other, the piracy and smuggling that flourished in the Gulf in the first decades of the nineteenth century—is merely a fantastic landscape for these lovers. Later, Mme. Antoine will tell Edna and Robert "legends of the Baratarians and the sea" she had been "gathering" "all her years" on the island (*KCA*, 39).

The legends of Jean Laffite are part of Gulf legend and history, especially in Barataria Bay where he and his brother Pierre created a community of pirates and smugglers between 1809 and 1817. It is not simply that piracy is capitalism's secret law; for Marx, piracy is one of capitalism's origins, as he makes clear in his efforts to account for the "primitive accumulation of capital" in *Capital:* "In actual history, it is a notorious fact that conquest, enslavement, robbery, murder, in short, force, play the greatest part [in the so-called primitive accumulation of capital]" (874). Just as Robert's flirtation with and combat with his brother, Victor, over the Spanish girl Mariequita is strangely bound up with his neocolonial business in Mexico, so sexual and economic politics are entangled in his otherwise trivial romance of the Baratarian pirates and their spoils.

If the legendary hideout of the Laffites offers Edna a romantic glimpse into the idea of an alternative community that might wage war against the proprieties and conventions of lawful governments, she was certain to know the rest of Laffite's story. Invited to join the English in their attack of New Orleans during the War of 1812, Laffite notified Louisiana officials of the impending attack. Despite Laffite's patriotism, Louisiana ordered an expedition to destroy the Baratarian community and capture the outlaws. Having escaped capture, Laffite offered the services of his imprisoned company in defense of New Orleans, an offer accepted by Governor William Charles Coles Claiborne in his proclamation of December 17, 1814. For their patriotism in defense of New Orleans, President Madison pardoned the Baratarians of all previous crimes on February 16, 1815.

The legends of Laffite seem to suggest for Chopin how easily rebellion may be co-opted. It is, after all, Robert who begins to tell these stories as just another part of his superficial flirtation, another effort to make his own pathetic bravura appear grander than it is. President Madison's pardon didn't do much to reform Jean Laffite, who subsequently set up a variety of other smuggling communities on the eastern coast of Mexico, which is also Robert Lebrun's destination when he leaves Grand Isle. By the same token, I can't claim Chopin could have known of Jean Laffite's reputed interests in European communism and his trip to Europe to meet Karl

Marx. This still-contested argument regarding Laffite's revolutionary purposes and interests was not made until 1952 in Stanley Clisby Arthur's *Jean Laffite, Gentleman Rover.*[12]

These stories of pirates and buried treasure frame Edna's next great moment of "oppression and drowsiness," which occurs predictably in the little "Gothic Church of Our Lady of Lourdes." Like conventional tales of romance, the church offers little relief to Edna, who must find reminders there of the strict Catholic taboos against adultery and divorce in Creole culture. It is not just the religious superego at work in this episode, however; it is the distance separating Edna's creative power from that figured in the miracle of Our Lady of Lourdes. The reference to Lourdes certainly connects the water imagery in *The Awakening* with the miraculous healing powers of the waters in the grotto where the Virgin Mary appeared to Bernadette Soubirous (1844 to 1879) in February of 1858. Chopin was familiar with the various accounts of Bernadette's visions from Zola's 1894 novel *Lourdes,* which she reviewed for *St. Louis Life,* on November 17, 1894 (*CW,* 697–99).

Given the mythic associations of women's creative powers with water and its powers of birth and miraculous revival, the allusion seems to give special credibility to Gilbert's argument that *The Awakening* promises a second coming of the Aphrodite myth. It remains, however, a profoundly ironic allusion since it refers Edna and the reader only to the means by which the history of the Catholic Church reinforces patriarchal authority. The peasant shepherd girl Bernadette Soubirous, who has her vision while tending her sheep, is utterly subordinated to the spiritual ineffability of the Virgin Mary, who becomes the church's proper Lady of Lourdes. Between 1858, the year of Bernadette's first visions, and 1901, when Pope Leo XIII consecrated the Church of the Rosary on the site of her visions, Bernadette of Lourdes was often an item in the Catholic news. Bernadette would not be canonized until 1933, however, a testament to the magical powers of Catholic patriarchy in virgin birth, of which the church's miracles are simply lesser and historical repetitions. The humble but honest labor of Bernadette is nothing in contrast with the magic of the church, virgin birth, miraculous cures.

12. Stanley Clisby Arthur, *Jean Laffite, Gentleman Rover* (London, 1952).

The buried treasure of Gulf pirates and the secret powers of the church share the same power to alienate Edna, just as later in New Orleans she will "drowse" over Emerson's essays. None of these idealist lures has any productive relation to her body; each is as alien as the wedding ring she vainly stamps with her boot heel in New Orleans. And yet Edna misses the shepherd girl Bernadette Soubirous in her flight from the church, fails to recognize how the relation of one's body to nature depends upon the labor of that body, perhaps because she knows the apparent freedom of the Gulf is haunted by the ghostly treasures of pirates, the submerged depths of the sea filled with the psychic traces of culture.

Throughout the narrative, Chopin gives us several modern versions of Bernadette Soubirous, modest instances of working women whose labor might perform miracles if it were dedicated to their ultimate social representation. Each is a servant: the black girl who "with her hands worked the treadle" of Madame Lebrun's sewing machine (*KCA,* 22) and later delivers Edna's invitation to the Cheniere to Robert; Mariequita, the Spanish girl over whom Robert and Victor Lebrun have fought, who carries her bamboo basket of shrimps "covered with Spanish moss" on the boat trip Robert and Edna take to the Cheniere (*KCA,* 34); the cook in New Orleans whose soup Leonce finds "impossible," whose scorched fish he pronounces inedible (*KCA,* 51–52). Edna recognized the black girl as merely a servant, Mariequita as a rival. Only with the cook does she have some passing empathy since she is responsible for the domestic servants. With some conviction, however, we may conclude that she never directly addresses her sisterhood with these exploited women from other classes, races, and economic conditions. Similar as the oppressive conditions of their labor are to her own, they never constitute an alternative community even fantastically glimpsed by Edna whose "awakenings" remain specific to the class and thus psychic profile of her own confinement.

Thus her torpor and sense of oppression are understandable. Edna successively experiences the inadequacy of the modes of production available to her to express her body, to offer her any substantial and self-sufficient being. It is, of course, naïve to forget the eroticism of these languors, the sexual reference of virtually every moment in which she encounters her ennui. We cannot speak as categorically as I have of the mere inadequacy of Edna's roles as wife, romantic lover, wife of a Catholic, since each of these moments is charged with sexual excitement, the affective tensions of desire withheld (from Leonce) or anticipated (with Robert). Each alternative for Edna to this point—wife, romantic, Catholic—betrays explicitly its failure to sublimate her vital sexual energy. This unrepresentable vitality exhausts her. At times, it is virtually postorgasmic, as when she emerges from her fitful nap at Mme. Antoine's ravenously hungry, tosses an orange at Robert, as if to parody some more dramatic Christian moment of sin, and experiences momentary euphoria.

Inextricable as such uncanny psychic awakenings are from sexuality, their very inadequacy, compounded by the successive references to Edna's natural will as an effect of her body, returns us with a certain perverse determinism to a woman's biological labor in birth. Thrown back endlessly on this alternative for a woman's social productivity, Edna is understandably horrified by the "torture" of Adele's birthing and by her friend's misguided advice, "Remember the children." The child is at once a living sign of the undeniable productivity of a woman's body, but Edna's children belong only to a patriarchal legal system that governs both the market and the home. No wonder that Edna experiences such ambivalence regarding her children and that those same children are the ultimate "antagonists who had overcome her; who had overpowered and sought to drag her into the soul's slavery for the rest of her days" (*KCA,* 113). In a novel celebrated for its authenticity regarding a woman's "natural" sensations and affections, *The Awakening* represents a woman's nature in extraordinarily ambivalent ways. In fact, as Edna only dimly recognizes at the very end of the narrative but Chopin knows all too well, there can be *no* nature for a woman that is not always already shaped and determined, inscribed and charted, by the laws of the social order.

No wonder, then, that Edna turns to art as her only defense against such a contrived world in which her body is nothing but a character in the dramatic fiction of patriarchy. In this regard, Chopin remorselessly denies Edna such consolations, as if to warn subsequent moderns that art is not always a way out. Chopin decisively represents Edna as lacking any distinctive artistic or intellectual talents. Mlle. Reisz's music stirs Edna's desire no more than an ordinary listener might be moved. Edna's drawings are either failed efforts at realism of the most obvious autobiographical sort—sketches of Adele, of Edna's father, the Kentucky Colonel—or of banal genre themes. " 'Surely, this Bavarian peasant is worthy of framing; and this basket of apples! never have I seen anything more lifelike. One might almost be tempted to reach out a hand and take one,' " Mme. Ratignolle praises her work, " 'Your talent is immense, dear!' " (*KCA,* 56, 55).

If I were to venture any reading of these subjects beyond the sheer conventionality of Edna's art, I would suggest that both again refer us to the problematic qualities of this new economy of speculation. The peasant's labor and the use value of the apples have been reduced by art to decorative images, such as one finds in the genre portrait or the still life. Edna's drawings express nothing more than the listless yearning of the leisure-class wife. The moderns from Henry James to T. S. Eliot, from Virginia Woolf to Gertrude Stein, who variously offered woman her identity in and through the self-making of art ought to have been required to read Chopin's *Awakening*. Clarissa Dalloway may someday grow up to become Virginia Woolf, Isabel Archer aspire to the self-consciousness of Henry James. But what of the Edna Pontelliers, who have little more than their common sense, human sensitivity, health, and longing for a body, a being, of their own? What of those who write no books, paint no pictures, have only recourse to faculties and affections that they possess in no greater degree than their servants and their friends?

When she does move out of Leonce's house, it is thanks only to a curious combination of resources: her winnings at the horse races with Alcee; income from her sketches, which she claims she is "beginning to sell"; and "a little money of my own from my mother's estate, which my father sends me by driblets" (*KCA,* 79). If they are selling, Chopin suggests, then those sketches are as bad as we are meant to think them, given the dilettantism of Edna's social companions. More significantly, these proceeds from her labor have the same status as her winnings at the track and her mother's small bequest. Each source of income, even as it helps Edna escape her husband's economic domination, derives from the patriarchy she flees. What connects the cotton speculator Leonce with the pirates in the Gulf is just what attracts him to gambling. The bonus of Edna's winnings at the Jockey Club is as sexually charged as the money Leonce divides with Edna the night after his late night of gambling at Klein's Hotel and his command that she attend the feverish Raoul. And her mother's bequest, itself the promise of some free transmission of property rights from mother to daughter, merely serves to sustain her father's authority over her since he sends it to her "by driblets."

Thus even before she bids farewell to her husband's grand house, long before Alcee and his flowers invade the private world of her pigeon house, Edna's room of her own already belongs to another, can be named by her servant, Ellen, as just that which represents a site of domestication, the confinement of a yearning spirit.

At Edna's farewell birthday party, Chopin employs the same irony to suggest how Edna's best gestures at freedom merely betray their patriarchal animation. Sandra Gilbert argues that the dinner party Edna "gives in chapter 30 is her most authentic act of self-definition. Here, she actually plays the part of the person she has metaphorically become: 'the regal woman, the one who rules, who looks on, who stands alone.' . . . Edna's dinner party is in a sense a Last Supper, a final transformation of will and desire into bread and wine, flesh and blood, before the 'regal woman's' inevitable betrayal by a culture in which a regenerated Aphrodite has no meaningful role." [13]

Gilbert is unquestionably right in claiming a certain serious drama, a decisive will to mythic truth, on the part of Edna in this episode. Certainly, her desire to constitute a pleasant and comfortable company, to create a meaningful, albeit microcosmic, social relation in which she might be said to have played a productive, even emancipatory role is essentially mythic. There can be no myth, after all, without culture, and it is just this mytho-poetic role that both Chopin and Marx imagine every worker ought to assume in his or her everyday labors, at home or in the factory. Yet from the outset of this party, the absent patriarchs, Edna's father and her husband, continue to direct the play. Although earlier she had refused to accompany her husband to select "new library fixtures," Edna is dressed here splendidly to match the table settings: "The pale yellow satin under strips of lace-work" of the tablecloth matches "the golden shimmer of Edna's satin gown" covered by a "soft fall of lace encircling her shoulders" (*KCA,* 87–88). Is Edna's lace (and that of the tablecloth) Chopin's ironic reference to the legend that Aphrodite's husband, Hephaestus, catching her in bed with her lover, Ares, threw a delicate golden net of his own

---

13. Gilbert, Introduction to "*The Awakening,*" 30.

making over them and displayed their embarrassment to the other gods? If Edna's diamonds and lace are simply updated versions of Hephaestus' "net," her figuration of Aphrodite deflates the power of at least that myth to save women from the masculine conflation of erotic love, marriage, and phallic making. The crystal on the table "glittered like the gems which the women wore," in Edna's case arranged as a crown, "a magnificent cluster of diamonds that sparkled, almost sputtered, in Edna's hair," a birthday present from her absent husband. " 'I shall ask you to begin with this cocktail, composed . . . by my father in honor of Sister Janet's wedding' " (*KCA*, 86).

Edna's party cannot live up to her dramatic, her mythic expectations, not simply because Chopin indulges the realist's propensity for mock epic and the fine art of sinking, or bathos, but because the quotidian realities of this frivolous evening are even more fantastic than myth. What is utterly fantastic, even phantasmagoric, about this dinner party is the manner in which the father and husband speak, even in their absences, dictate by a kind of perverse table turning the very terms of Edna's rebellion: "But as she sat there amid her guests, she felt the old ennui overtaking her; the hopelessness which so often assailed her, which came upon her like an obsession, like something extraneous, independent of volition. It was something which announced itself; a chill breath that seemed to issue from some vast cavern wherein discords wailed" (*KCA*, 88). It is desire for "the unattainable," but it appears, as desire most often does, in the absence of its object of satisfaction. Perhaps it is just his desire that a husband wants to encourage in his wife in accord with the inflationary laws of this new speculative economy.

Edna's desire is finally quite ordinary, simply realistic—*natural*, if that term could still carry meaning in the fin de siècle. She wants to experience her body in the world around her, not simply in the private moments when she touches herself as if to confirm an existence so tenuous in public but in the labor of socialization itself. As Scarry writes:

> The socialization of sentience—which is itself as profound a change as if one were to open the body physically and redirect the path of neuronal flow, rearrange the small bones into a new pattern, remodel the ear drum—is one of Marx's major emphases. Sense organs, skin, and body tissue have themselves been recreated to experience themselves in terms of their own objec-

tification. It is this now essentially altered biological being that, in going on to remake himself or herself in other ways, enters into that act of remaking as one whose sentience is socialized, fundamentally restructured to be relieved of its privacy."

Because these modes of objectification can be shared by others, they enable us to extend our "bodies," amplify our "privacy" (and thus our mortality) to encompass "society" (and thus an enduring history). In Scarry's reading of Marx's philosophy of the social commodity as an extension and amplification of the individual body, that commodity is not fetishized but endlessly productive: "For Marx, the more extended and sublimated sites of making should extend this attribute of shareability: the interaction made possible by a freestanding object is amplified as that object now becomes a 'commodity' interacting with other objects and so increasing the number of persons who are in contact with one another; the socialization of sentience should continue to be amplified as one moves to more extended economic (money, capital) and political artifacts." [14] Under capitalism such a socialist economy is detoured into the peculiar economy by which the amplification of a fabricated body (the capitalist's capital) depends upon the diminution of the natural body (the worker's physical body).

Put a simpler way, Edna's problem is also that of Chopin the writer: how to make the body *other*—an object, an artifact, a child, a novel— without losing that body. I have made Kate Chopin sound like a committed Marxist, which she was decidedly not, but she nevertheless understood her activity as a writer to involve a problematic sort of labor. As she writes in "In the Confidence of a Story-Writer," "The story completed, I was very, very weary; but I had the satisfaction of feeling that for once in my life I had worked hard, I had achieved something great, I had taken pains" (*CW,* 704). It seems simple enough to claim this painful satisfaction for literary creation until we recognize as Chopin does that such labor is meaningless without its circulation, without entrance into a market: "But the story failed to arouse enthusiasm among the editors. It is at present lying in my desk. Even my best friend declined to listen to it, when I offered to read it to her" (*CW,* 704). Scarry suggests that Marx's ideal socialist economy would depend upon commodities that serve functionally

14. Scarry, *Body in Pain,* 255, 256.

as verbal signs, that is, as points of contact between labor of sender and receiver rather than products belonging either to author or reader, capitalist or worker.

Perhaps Chopin's formal innovations in *The Awakening* demonstrate the utopian transformation of capitalist reification into a sharable social discourse. What begins as a naturalist novel concludes, as Gilbert argues, as a series of symbolic enactments subject to a wide range of interpretations. In reading the conclusion in terms of Edna's fate—does she sink or swim?—the reader merely affirms the laws of capitalism and their conventional reproduction in the naturalist novel. By observing the destiny of a fictional character intended to represent a class or group in an explicit social situation, the implied reader of the naturalist novel tacitly accepts the idea of sociohistorical determinism. To image a new history and economy in which the New Woman (and the New Man) might share in the coordinated labor of social production requires a new literary form.

Chopin's turn from naturalism to symbolism, from dreary realism to suggestive parable, offers the reader just such a gift. But we must be careful not to privilege any literary text lest we forget literature's conditions of production, its history. *The Awakening* marks the threshold between naturalism and modernism. Insofar as it offers its own symbolism as an alternative to the reification of capitalism, it is potentially a narrative of emancipation. But to the extent that this symbolism is produced only by sophisticated (and profoundly private) authors and readers, the novel merely anticipates the aesthetic utopias offered by the literary moderns. Symbols are, after all, an acquired taste and not very nourishing. As long as Chopin's literary economy excludes the labor of the young black woman (and thus the oppression of African Americans at the end of the century) or of the Spanish girl Mariequita, *The Awakening* remains an interesting contribution to the restricted economy of literary modernism.

There remains one other way a purely literary symbolism might suggest an ethical dimension relevant to ordinary life and practical human concerns. As I have argued, Chopin represents Edna's unsatisfied desire in art, philosophy, labor, and social relations in addition to the central thematics of sexuality and eroticism. In the simplest sense, some expansive notion of love would be required to satisfy Edna's desire as it calls to her through these different areas of her everyday activities of painting, thinking and reading, working at various tasks, and talking with others. At times, Chopin seems to equate the special cognition of the literary symbol with the kind of communication between subjects that respects differences and thus might be said to exemplify a new understanding of love. In Edna's most intimate and erotic moments with her lovers, we might expect just some hint of a more comprehensive notion of love that would coordinate her conflicting desires. These moments, however, are marked by her sudden exhaustion or her horror and loathing in the face of the violence that sexuality signifies in this patriarchal culture.

Alone with Edna, Arobin presses for intimacy by revealing a bit of his body, drawing up his cuff "to exhibit upon his wrist the scar from a saber cut which he had received in a duel outside of Paris when he was nineteen. . . . A quick impulse that was somewhat spasmodic impelled her fingers to close in a sort of clutch upon his hand. He felt the pressure of her pointed nails in the flesh of his palm" (*KCA,* 76). It is perhaps the most uncannily intimate moment Edna has in the text precisely because it exposes how profoundly masculine aggression and power have shaped relations of intimacy and sharing. That Edna repeats in miniature the Parisian duel by pressing "her pointed nails into the flesh of his palm" only confirms how illusory her "romantic escape" with Arobin is. " 'The sight of a wound or scar always agitates and sickens me,' " she said, " 'I shouldn't have looked at it' " (*KCA,* 76).

Edna experiences only the disgust occasioned by Chopin's recognition that *love* in this culture is simply another word for warfare. Touching Arobin's wound, Edna is accordingly repulsed and attempts to end her relation with Arobin by refusing to go to the races again because " 'I've got to work when the weather is bright, instead of—' " (*KCA,* 76). She is interrupted by him. He can hardly take the work of women with any seriousness. Arobin is cynical not only regarding the value of women but regarding himself. But it is also a sentence that Edna Pontellier cannot finish by herself; she is grateful for his interruption. Certainly Chopin's redefinition of love, suggested obliquely in Edna's brief moments of confidence with Mlle. Reisz and Adele, must be understood in terms of Edna's (or any subject's) ability to work and thus contribute to social value. In no sense could such an idea of love be equated with the romantic love offered by Arobin.

Unfortunately, Chopin is also unable to finish Edna's sentence, cryptically writing "love" as productive communication in the margins of *The Awakening*. Such a conclusion is perfectly modern in its affirmation of the power of literary modernism to negate social corruptions even as it denies its own power to create livable alternatives. Chopin's accomplishment is to have forced us to look at these sites of bodily violation, of wounding, to understand how completely social and human intercourse have failed. As they reenact the duel that Arobin fought in Paris when he was nineteen, Edna and Arobin merely reproduce the secret role of the individual in capitalism as soldier or pirate. Arobin's memory of Paris does not belong to him; it is something he has "recollected" from a cheap French romance.

The pathos of *The Awakening* is just this: The self has become a character in a melodrama. As such, the self is based on nothing, lacks substance, and only haunts the reader and Edna with the more substantial powers of natural transformation and social communication that in our fantastic postmodernity have become quaint memories. From our perspective, Chopin's undeveloped notion of social love seems merely sentimental. If we identify in that word Chopin's failure, we must also recognize our own failure to be capable of such love.

The Awakening: *The Economics of Tension*

DORIS DAVIS

Part of the impact of *The Awakening* lies in its skillful handling of economics. Chopin provides a text rich in monetary allusions that complement her heroine's quest for independence; in so doing, she establishes economics as a vital element of her characters' milieu. We are always aware of the economic pursuits in the novel—the business transactions of Mr. Pontellier, the Lebruns, and to some extent the Ratignolles. And we watch Edna in her pursuit of economic independence. But however much Chopin may have been intrigued by the financial world, she refrains from creating a Carrie Meeber in Edna Pontellier. Dreiser may enlist our concern for a character who struggles to acquire, but in *The Awakening* Chopin reverses the process, providing a protagonist who willingly strips herself of economic status.[1] Edna's voluntary relinquishment of economic security results in an underlying tension in the novel and ultimately ensures a more sympathetic reader.

Chopin's personal concerns with money may account for the economic tenor of much of *The Awakening*. A widow at thirty-two with six children to raise, she obviously had to devote attention to personal finances. Upon her husband's death in 1882, she carried on his work in Natchitoches for more than a year, corresponding with cotton factors in New Orleans, writing contracts and stocking the plantation store, which she on occasion ran. Her biographer Per Seyersted suggests that her success stemmed from her "vigor" and from "her knowledge of the value of money" (*CB*, 46). He suggests also that the family physician, Dr. Kolbenheyer, may have encouraged her to write, in part because "with six children and a rather limited income she could well use whatever she could earn" (*CB*, 49). That she attempted *The Awakening* when she did Seyersted attributes in

---

1. For two comparisons of Chopin and Dreiser, see *CB* and Emily Toth, "Timely and Timeless: The Treatment of Time in *The Awakening* and *Sister Carrie*," *Southern Studies*, XVI (1977), 271–76.

part to H. E. Scudder's observation of the greater possibility of her artistic and financial success with the novel than with short stories (*CB*, 73). We know that she kept records of what she was paid for a story, and she mentions on occasion her "commercial instinct" for writing (*KCM*, xiv–xv).

Even before her economic independence, Chopin evinced an interest in economic issues. In her youthful diary of 1869, she writes of the worldly success of a young woman whose attractions secured as a husband "one of the first merchants of New Orleans and a man worth $600,000" (*KCM*, 64). On her honeymoon, she writes of a "female broker" who instructs her to develop an interest in such issues as "commerce," to which she agrees (*KCM*, 69). And on that same trip in New York she describes her fascination with the finances of Wall Street: "I have heard the 'Bulls and Bears of Wall St.' bellowing and grunting in the Stock and Gold Boards—proceedings which interested me very much, though I was to some extent incapable of understanding their purport" (*KCM*, 69). In Europe she attributes the greatness of France to the "thrift and intelligence" of the lower classes (*KCM*, 84).

From these youthful comments about economics until her death in 1904, Chopin witnessed the tremendous financial growth of this nation and the stock market in particular. During her adult life, the transactions of the New York Stock Exchange increased from twenty billion dollars per year in the late 1860s to thirty billion shortly after 1900. Hers was the age of the railroad barons and the high-stakes entrepreneurs, of such men as William Henry Vanderbilt, Jay Gould, Jim Fisk, and John D. Rockefeller, an age in which great fortunes were made and lost. And she observed the financial panics of 1873, 1882, and 1893, crises that many Americans blamed on these "titans" of Wall Street. In each case, extravagant speculation, overinflated values, and lengthy cyclical depressions followed, the depression of the mid-1890s lasting almost until the end of the century.[2] The publication of *The Awakening* in 1899 saw the country emerging from a number of difficult years. Chopin, like other Americans, undoubtedly observed the rigors of economic speculation.

2. Donald L. Kemmerer and C. Clyde Jones, *American Economic History* (New York, 1959), 339; Harold U. Faulkner, *Politics, Reform and Expansion, 1890–1990* (New York, 1959), 143; John A. Garraty, *The American Nation: A History of the United States* (3rd ed.; New York, 1966), xiv.

Chopin brings her interest in finance to bear on the plots of both her novels. *At Fault* presents a protagonist who oversees the economy of a plantation, and *The Awakening* offers a background of speculative economics and a heroine who takes a positive if brief step toward financial independence. Although Seyersted comments that in *The Awakening* Chopin is "unconcerned with her protagonists's social and economic situation" (*CB*, 138), if we examine the novel closely we will find a heroine sensitive to the advantages of wealth.[3] She is enamored with beautiful things. She enjoys her "cool white muslin," the "dainty white gown," the "commodious wrapper," the "handsome reception gown," and the "satin gown [that] spread in rich folds" (*KCA*, 16, 44, 43, 50, 88). While Leonce may have chosen the furnishings for the "charming house on Esplanade Street," Edna is not immune to the aesthetic appeal of the "softest carpets and rugs," "rich and tasteful draperies," "paintings, selected with judgment and discrimination," "cut glass," "silver," and "heavy damask" (*KCA*, 50). These objects take on added appeal in the absence of her husband: "A feeling that was unfamiliar but very delicious came over her. She walked all through the house, from one room to another, as if inspecting it for the first time," trying the "various chairs and lounges" (*KCA*, 72).

Edna likes money, as Chopin points out, "as well as most women." On two occasions we see her enjoying the receipt of it. The first occurs on Grand Isle when Mr. Pontellier gives her cash before returning to the mainland, which she accepts "with no little satisfaction." She is happy "smoothing out the bills as she counted them one by one" (*KCA*, 9). On the second she counts her racetrack winnings, again gaining pleasure from possessing the money. Moreover, in thinking of those valuables she would relinquish for the sake of their children, she mentions money. " 'I would give my money,' " she asserts, along with her "life," for the children's contentment (*KCA*, 48). Money, for Edna, is valuable and desirable.

Edna's attraction to wealth makes the later scenes of her denial of Leonce's property more poignant. But though she likes money, her attitude toward it differs considerably from that of her husband. For Leonce, money signifies the world of enterprise with its accompanying transactions of buying and selling. His is an intense world of the mercurial stock market, of

3. Shirley Foster, "The Open Cage: Freedom, Marriage and the Heroine in Early Twentieth-Century American Women's Novels," in *Women's Writing: A Challenge to Theory*, ed. Moira Monteith (New York, 1986), 163.

commodities, speculation, and futures. It is an absorbing world that as Dr. Mandelet accurately observes, demands young men with the "fever of life still in your blood." It is a world that beckons Leonce to New York for a "big scheme," despite his knowledge of his wife's languor (*KCA*, 67). And it is a world that encourages evaluation of others in economic terms. Mr. Belthrop " 'could buy and sell us ten times over,' " Leonce tells Edna as he scolds her for neglecting her visitation days (*KCA*, 52). One critic correctly observes that Chopin "depicts the institution of business as an impediment to personal growth."[4] Leonce's absorption in his world of economics limits his development in other areas.

Edna has little appreciation of her husband's business endeavors, failing to understand Leonce's observation that the " 'way to become rich is to make money . . . not to save it' " (*KCA*, 53). For Edna, money represents conviviality, the enjoyment of herself as she converses with friends and pursues artistic interests.[5] It produces beautiful clothes and trips to carefree islands. But as she "awakens" in the novel, she begins to realize that money also represents freedom—her own. She must go beyond the rigidity of Leonce's financial world, however, to an evaluation of her own world, an investigation of her inner resources.

From the opening scene, Mr. Pontellier is obviously a man of the world, one who has already carefully read the "market report" of the papers. He delights in his financial success and in observing his wife, regarding her as one might "a valuable piece of personal property" (*KCA*, 4). He has been holding her rings as she swam with Robert, suggestive of his authoritative role. Edna by contrast is alternately gay and moody, whimsical and meditative. We glimpse the possible levity of her disposition as she frolics with Robert.[6] Pontellier's choice of words to Edna, to send Robert " 'about his *business* when he bores you' " (*KCA*, 5; emphasis mine), underscores his usual matter-of-factness. Chopin stresses the financial aspect of his personality once more in her description of his return

4. Thomas Bonner, Jr., "Kate Chopin: Tradition and the Moment," *Southern Literature in Transition: Heritage and Promise,* ed. Philip Castille and William Osborne (Memphis, 1983), 147.

5. Toth, "Timely and Timeless."

6. Jerome Klinkowitz, *The Practice of Fiction in America: Writers from Hawthorne to the Present* (Ames, Iowa, 1980), 40–41.

from Klein's Hotel that night. As he readies for bed, he piles his money on the dresser, "a fistful of crumpled bank notes and a good deal of silver coin" (*KCA*, 7). He reproaches his wife for her inattention to the children and himself. Against this scene of rigidity and monetary imagery Edna sheds her first tears in the novel.

Edna is attracted to Robert in part because he lacks the economic drive of her husband. A younger man, he has only a "modest position" in a mercantile establishment in New Orleans. He smokes cigarettes, he says, because he cannot afford cigars, and he gives most of his earnings to his mother for her support. He interests Edna with his plans to go to Mexico where "fortune awaited him" (*KCA*, 6). As Judy Little points out, she associates him "with fantastic images . . . of lovers in ships by moonlight who find treasure, or disappear forever among exotic islands."[7] As they set out for the Cheniere Caminada together, Robert speaks incessantly of adventures they will pursue and sparks her imagination about intrigue and fortune:

> "Then I'll take you some night in the pirogue when the moon shines. Maybe your Gulf spirit will whisper to you in which of these islands the treasures are hidden—direct you to the very spot, perhaps."
> "And in a day we should be rich!" she laughed.
> "I'd give it all to you, the pirate gold and every bit of treasure we could dig up. I think you would know how to spend it. Pirate gold isn't a thing to be hoarded or utilized. It is something to squander and throw to the four winds, for the fun of seeing the golden specks fly."
> "We'd share it, and scatter it together," he said.
> His face flushed. (*KCA*, 35–36)

For Edna and Robert, money represents spontaneity, adventure, mirth, and romance.

While the above passage suggests Robert and Edna's attitude toward money, it also underscores the economic overtones of the novel in the key words *hoarded, utilized,* and *squander.* A proper financial course, Chopin seems to suggest, is a delicate balance among these. In his emphasis on the accumulation of capital, Leonce becomes too absorbed in acquiring

7. Judy Little, "Imagining Marriage," in *Portraits of Marriage in Literature,* ed. Anne C. Hargrove and Maurine Magliocco (Macomb, Ill., 1984), 175.

and too rigid in his demand for the proper "utilization" of his wealth. His gambling and business transactions reflect a society bent on making money at the expense of other values. Yet Edna's actions strike us too often as irresponsible, a squandering of strength and resources.

If we turn from *The Awakening* for a moment to Chopin's short stories, we see her developing this notion of economic balance elsewhere in two pieces, "Polly" and "A Pair of Silk Stockings." Both contain pragmatic heroines who unexpectedly receive a sum of money and must decide on its best use. In the first story, Polly, a bookkeeper, receives one hundred dollars from an uncle with the stipulation that she use it all. He wants her to experience the exaltation of spending money. Instead of replacing her worn jacket, she buys attractive items for her parents and sisters—a lamp, rug, books, dishes, and so on. She does not squander the money or use it rigidly to get only what she needs; she creates joy for others and, indirectly, for herself.

The other story, "A Pair of Silk Stockings," depicts a mother, Mrs. Sommers, who when she unexpectedly receives fifteen dollars, considers first what she might buy for her children. But once in town she so enjoys the beauty of a pair of stockings that almost without thinking, she makes them her first purchase of the day, followed by other purchases such as gloves, boots, and theater tickets, all of which she thoroughly enjoys. Rather than focusing on the mundane on this occasion, Mrs. Sommers uses the money to nurture her sense of aesthetics, an action that Chopin seems to suggest is important for this character's development. Like Polly, Mrs. Sommers has developed a feeling of independence and fulfillment in her judicious use of money. Both characters might serve as models for Edna's emerging sense of autonomy. Experienced in directing their own finances, they realize the joy that accompanies the fruitful use of money.

Upon her return to New Orleans, Edna likewise pursues independence, but while her quest earns our admiration, it also creates a mounting tension as we consider the economic implications of her activities. We watch her grow more disenchanted with the insular nature of her life and more infatuated with Robert in his absence. She neglects her visiting days, loses interest in the management of the house, and argues with Leonce over financial matters. One of these altercations results in her breaking a crystal vase. Although occasioned by Leonce's words, the destruction symbolizes Edna's determination to set herself apart from her husband, emotionally and financially. In this same scene, Edna's attempt to destroy her gold wedding band also functions symbolically. When the maid recovers the ring and forces Edna to reclaim it, we feel the power Leonce has over her. Significantly, Edna fails to make the slightest "mark upon the little glittering circlet" (*KCA*, 53). Leonce's control, both legally and monetarily, is formidable.

In striving toward independence, Edna begins to cultivate a more serious interest in her art, eventually selling some of her work. To a certain extent she considers a positive assessment of her paintings as a reflection of her self-worth. On one occasion, she seeks the praise of Mme. Ratignolle even though she realizes that her friend lacks a knowledge of art. Edna simply needs encouragement. Significantly, Chopin chooses economic imagery in describing this scene of Adele's evaluation, using such terms as *value, venture, worth,* and *worthy* (*KCA*, 56). Chopin's economic terminology suggests that Edna needs to see herself as one capable of economic independence. She needs to be able to assess herself positively, to believe in her abilities.

As the possibility of financial independence becomes feasible, Edna grows more thoughtful about money. She acknowledges the importance of her racetrack winnings, becoming less willing to risk her money foolishly. During her father's visit, she had caught his fever for the racetrack, and with her knowledge of racehorses acquired from a youth spent in Kentucky, Edna instinctively places bets, playing for high stakes. The "fever of the game flowed in her cheeks and eyes, and it got into her blood and into her brain like an intoxicant" (*KCA*, 74). But with the need for economic balance, she wisely curtails these speculations.

In establishing her independence, Edna elects to leave the house on Esplanade. It is fitting that the unconventional Mlle. Reisz is the first to learn of Edna's plan to move from this large house to the little place nearby, the "pigeon house," practical but plain. " 'The house, the money that provides for it, are not mine,' " Edna argues (*KCA*, 79). She tells Mlle. Reisz of her plans to support herself with her mother's estate, her savings, and the livelihood derived through art—all of which strike us as admirable. Equally praiseworthy is her motive for moving, which becomes clearer to Edna as she confides in Reisz. "Instinct had prompted her to put away her husband's bounty in casting off her allegiance" (*KCA*, 80).

For her grand farewell dinner, Edna intends to use "all my best of everything—crystal, silver and gold, Sevres, flowers, music, and champagne to swim in" (*KCA,* 85). She offers a lavish display of Leonce's wealth, perhaps gloating over the control of his property in his absence. The imagery of the dinner clearly emphasizes wealth, suggesting a metallic quality. Chopin writes of the "pale yellow satin," the "brass candelabra," the "yellow silk shades," "yellow" roses, and silver and gold on the table (*KCA,* 86). Edna's gown has a "golden shimmer" (*KCA,* 88), and she wears her husband's latest present of diamonds. While some have seen the dinner as a parody of conventions, it seems also to function as Edna's farewell to the luxuries she has known and as an acknowledgement that she forgoes all for the right of privacy and independence—at the high cost of her possessions in marriage.[8] She will take with her only those things "acquired aside from her husband's bounty" (*KCA,* 84). In her comment " 'let Leonce pay the bills' " (*KCA,* 85) we see the cynicism that comes with her realization that she must leave behind all these beautiful objects.

At the dinner Edna breaks a glass when Victor sings a song reminiscent of Robert. As with the earlier act of destruction, Edna indicates her frustration with the confining nature of her life. She strikes out at all who would limit her independence, revealing her anguish at being another's emotional pawn. But Chopin uses the scene to indicate more than Edna's romantic interest in Robert. The breaking of the glass in this and the earlier scene marks Edna's sense of independence. In breaking the glass vase, Edna marks her frustration with living in her husband's home. In breaking the second glass Edna acknowledges that she is threatened by more than just her marriage. These acts of defiance—the willful destruction of her husband's property—strike at the crux of Edna's problem—her inevitable financial vulnerability.

Edna's bid for financial independence lasts only a few weeks, but during that time, she faces a number of difficult issues, her sexual relationship with the roué Arobin, her husband's imminent return to the city, Robert's reappearance and ultimate betrayal, and her responsibility toward her children. She continues to work on her art and even negotiates with a dealer to sell some studies the following winter. Yet we are tense about her ability

---

8. Robert White, "Inner and Outer Space in *The Awakening,*" *Mosaic,* XVII (1984), 97–109.

to succeed, wondering if one who has never before faced the challenge of independence will be able to attend successfully to all of these concerns.

Edna's failure at independence and ultimate suicide have occasioned varying interpretations. In terms of economics, one pertinent question we might ask is, Why is Edna unable to secure contentment and independence through her artistic work? Anne Goodwyn Jones believes that Edna fails to solve her dilemma because there are no female models of femininity and productivity in the novel.[9] Mlle. Reisz, though an artist and independent, is in some ways a repulsive woman, ungracious to most around her and physically unattractive. Her bleak living quarters, her "shabby, unpretentious little" rooms (*KCA*, 95), surely offend Edna's love of beautiful things. On Grand Isle, Edna had grown tired of her, and at the dinner party she finds her behavior "a little rude . . . but characteristic." As though deprived, the pianist is absorbed by the food on the table, all her attention "centered upon the delicacies placed before her" (*KCA*, 87).

The novel also lacks any female examples of economic success. Mlle. Reisz suggests the economic hardships of an independent woman. Chopin emphasizes the meager aspects of her livelihood: the "small rooms," "small table," "lumpy sofa," "old buffet" (*KCA*, 62). She lives away from the rest of humanity, where others cannot bother her. Drab too is her clothing, with its "shabby lace" and artificial violets. Mme. Lebrun, in her widowhood, also demonstrates the difficulties of female independence. Chopin tells us early in the novel that the house on Grand Isle had been a "summer luxury" of the Lebruns, but now Mme. Lebrun must manage cottages to help maintain her standard of living. On several occasions Chopin indicates the sons' financial support, mentioning that Robert sends her money even when he is in Mexico. And when Edna considers financial independence, her standard of living must be dramatically altered from a prestigious house to one derisively termed the "pigeon house" by the servants.

These allusions to financial difficulties sustain a point made by Charlotte Perkins Gilman in *Women and Economics*, published only one year before *The Awakening*. Gilman maintains that financial independence is

9. Ann Goodwyn Jones, *Tomorrow Is Another Day: The Woman Writer in the South, 1859–1936* (Baton Rouge, 1981).

crucial for women to develop their abilities, but she points out the difficulties: "And, when the woman, left alone with no man to 'support' her, tries to meet her own economic necessities, the difficulties which confront her prove conclusively what the general economic status of the woman is." [10] In leaving Leonce, Edna legally gives up all that was hers in marriage. According to the laws of Louisiana at the time, whatever Edna had accumulated in marriage, even her earnings and her clothes, belonged to her husband. [11]

To succeed in her bid for independence, Edna needed a strong sense of economic and personal drive, traits that she unfortunately fails to develop, as Emily Toth points out. Toth suggests that Edna reflects John Stuart Mill's criticism of women of the higher classes who lack "continuity of effort." [12] She detests this drive in Leonce but fails to realize its necessity in a modified way for her survival. Often she appears listless, without direction, abandoning herself to "Fate" to await the "consequences" (*KCA*, 103). She has lived in a society that has conditioned femininity and strength as separate entities for her class, and she thus lacks the fortitude and endurance to meet her problems head-on and come out the victor. She has acquired the love of beautiful things, experienced this force of her femininity and sexuality, responded to the call of her individuality and motherhood, but awakened only partially to the energy within that would have sustained her.

Winfried Fluck suggests that Chopin uses her fiction to explore varying feminine roles set against a background of American Victorianism. [13] Among those roles Chopin investigates with Edna is that of the upper-class woman who having been provided for all her life, determines to make her own way. The pressures would be immense, as Chopin knew firsthand, but the struggle an absorbing story, eliciting compassion for a character who gives up her possessions in marriage with dignity and strikes out on her

10. Charlotte Perkins Gilman, *Women and Economics,* ed. Carl N. Degler (1899; rpr. New York, 1966), 10.

11. Margaret Culley, "The Context of *The Awakening,*" in *KCA,* 118.

12. Emily Toth, "Kate Chopin's *The Awakening* as Feminist Criticism," *Louisiana Studies,* XV (1976), 250.

13. Winfried Fluck, "Tentative Transgressions: Kate Chopin's Fiction as a Mode of Symbolic Action," *Studies in American Fiction,* X (1982), 151–71.

own. In her experiment, Chopin allows her character only a brief fight for independence against complex obstacles. To succeed, she needs the "courageous soul that dares and defies" (*KCA,* 114). Granted, Edna fails to find a solution to her problems, but rather than being critical, we find integrity in her pursuit. We sympathize with one who pays for her failure with what is most dear—the currency of her life. The waste of her life and talents gives renewed poignancy to Mary Wollstonecraft's celebrated question, now almost two hundred years old: "And, who can tell, how many generations may be necessary to give vigour to the virtue and talents of the freed posterity of abject slaves?" [14]

14. Mary Wollstonecraft, *A Vindication of the Rights of Woman, 1792,* in *Feminism: The Essential Historical Writings,* ed. Miriam Schneir (New York, 1972), 15.

IV Reawakenings and Romantic Self-Deceptions 🍏

We must learn to reawaken and keep ourselves awake, not by mechanical aids, but by an infinite expectation of the dawn, which does not forsake us in our soundest sleep.

—Henry David Thoreau, *Walden*

Kate Chopin and the Dream of Female Selfhood

BARBARA C. EWELL

Alexis de Tocqueville, the French observer of American life, noted in his chapter "Of Individualism in Democratic Countries" that "*individualism* is a novel expression, to which a novel idea has given birth."[1] That "novel idea," individualism, shaped the nineteenth century and its version of the American Dream. To be a self, to be independent in a democracy of independent men (for only men were meant), to become self-conscious, even self-created, the "self-made man," or in R. W. B. Lewis's memorable formulation "the American Adam"—these were, and remain, important elements of the dream of America. This "novel idea" also fueled a number important social movements, including the abolition of slavery and the drive for women's suffrage, both efforts that sought citizenship and the affirmation of personhood for groups whose essential humanity had long been denied. Even the waves of European immigration and the push west to the frontier, that final bastion and symbol of rugged American individualism, were shaped by this ideal of autonomy.

The notion of individualism, of self-possession, also had important philosophic and imaginative expressions. We have only to think of Walt Whitman's *Song of Myself,* Thoreau's *Walden,* Mark Twain's *Adventures of Huckleberry Finn,* or any number of works by Ralph Waldo Emerson. Indeed, Emerson describes the times as dominated by the idea: "The key to the period appeared to be that the mind had become aware of itself. Men grew reflective and intellectual. There was a new consciousness. The former generations acted under the belief that a shining social prosperity was the beatitude of man, and sacrifice uniformly the citizen to the State. The modern mind believed that the nation existed for the individual, for the guardianship and education of every man. This idea, roughly written in revolutions and national movements, in the mind of the philosopher had

1. Quoted in F. O. Matthiessen, *American Renaissance: Art and Expression in the Age of Emerson and Whitman* (London, 1941), 5–6.

far more precision: the individual is the world."[2] Emerson represents an important dimension of the nineteenth-century version of the American Dream. His writings continually affirm the sovereignty of the self, the recognition that we are not wholly defined by such externalities as social conventions, institutions, property, roles, or even laws. To be a self, to define oneself as a subject with an independent inner life, was for Emerson the goal of human consciousness. As he writes in "Self-Reliance" (1841), "Nothing is at last sacred but the integrity of your own mind."[3]

This goal of selfhood had particular significance for nineteenth-century women, whose struggle for suffrage mirrored the larger aim of achieving the recognition of their personhood in society and in law. That greater struggle proved much more formidable than achieving the right to vote. In the United States as in most nations and cultures, patriarchal custom explicitly defined women as self-less. They were named and described only in terms of their relationships to men—*daughter, wife, mother, sister, widow*—or more specifically, in terms of their sexual relationships to men: *virgin, whore, mistress, spinster.* Women were, as Simone de Beauvoir so eloquently explained, simply men's "other," defined as whatever men were not: not rational, not strong, not self.[4] Women were not subjects but objects, of sexuality, of discourse, of art—of men.

For women writers, this definition of women as self-less was, and is, especially problematic, for to write is precisely to assert a self, to "master" language and discourse as a subject. It is to open the space in which meaning is created rather than to be the object or matter on which meaning is imposed. The dream of selfhood for women, then, offers a paradox, a paradox that suggests the crux of our current epistemological dilemma, the trap of our oppositional, binary, either-or consciousness. That consciousness insists that to be subject is not to be object, that meaning is or is not, that truth opposes the false, that good is not bad, that presence is not absence, that gender is male or female, that to write is to be a self is not to be female.

But as our greatest contemporary philosophers and critics are explain-

2. Ralph Waldo Emerson, "Life and Letters in New England," in *The Complete Writings of Ralph Waldo Emerson* (New York, 1929), 1043.
3. Emerson, "Self-Reliance," in *Complete Writings*, 139.
4. Simone de Beauvoir, *The Second Sex* (1952; rpr. New York, 1974).

ing, such a consciousness effaces the possibilities of differences without hierarchy or oppression, of diversity without opposition, and of meanings without finality. And in locating many of the most troubling consequences of such thinking in the relationships of gender, these philosophers have indicated the importance of redefining one of our most fundamental notions.[5]

Given the significance of this paradox, examine briefly how one important nineteenth-century writer, Kate Chopin, attempts to show in her fiction what it means to be a female self, how that self is defeated in its struggles by those very external forces that Emerson declared to be the least authentic, the least true to selfhood.

To understand Chopin's articulation of the dream of female selfhood, it is important to note her view of the goal of writing fiction. In 1896, Chopin made a revealing comment about the significance of the French writer Guy de Maupassant for her writing:

> About eight years ago there fell accidentally into my hands a volume of Maupassant's tales. These were new to me. I had been in the woods, in the fields, groping around; looking for something big, satisfying, convincing, and finding nothing but—myself; a something neither big nor satisfying but wholly convincing. It was at this period of my emerging from the vast solitude in which I had been making my own acquaintance, that I stumbled upon Maupassant. I read his stories and marvelled at them. Here was life, not fiction; for where were the plots, the old-fashioned mechanism and stage trapping that in a vague unthinking way I had fancied were essential to the art of story-making. Here was a man who had escaped from tradition and authority, who had entered into himself and looked out upon life through his own being and with his own eyes; and who, in a direct and simple way told us what he saw. When a man does this, he gives us the best that he can; something valuable for it is genuine and spontaneous. He gives us his impressions (*CW,* 700–701).

For Chopin, writing was a means of exploring and articulating what she saw—life—particularly the life of women and their struggle to achieve selfhood, the "sacred integrity" that Emerson and others saw as essential

5. See Alice A. Jardine, *Gynesis: Configuration of Woman and Modernity* (Ithaca, 1985), and Christopher Norris, *Deconstruction: Theory and Practice* (London, 1982), for a discussion of these issues.

to the American Dream. Chopin began to write in the years in which she was trying to come to terms with her individuality, making her acquaintance with the "wholly convincing" self that was no longer defined by her husband or indeed, since the death of her mother in 1884, by any adult relations. It was a painful time, a time she described in an 1894 diary entry as "the years of my growth—my real growth" (*KCM*, 92). What Chopin found in Maupassant was what she also admired in the New England writers Sarah Orne Jewett and Mary Wilkins Freeman: a model for expressing "what [she] saw."

But while Chopin found inspiration in Maupassant's fiction, her short stories at first remained a fairly superficial version of his injunction to write what she saw. Relying on the techniques of the popular mode of "local color" and exploiting the regional eccentricity and diversity of her thirteen years in Louisiana, Chopin's early stories tend to focus on the externals of experience. Those surfaces, despite their vividness and charm, did not yet adequately reveal the psychological realities that were to become her principal subject. The development of Chopin's use of those regional surfaces and her increasing skill in allowing them to disclose the deeper issues of identity and perspective can be briefly suggested in the differences between a relatively early (and justly famous) tale, "Desiree's Baby" (1893), and the equally striking later "Story of an Hour" (1894).

In the former story, a woman's inability to define a self outside the conventional identities of mother, wife, white, or black, results in her virtual erasure from the story—death. In the latter, a woman's belated recognition of a self cannot withstand the reimposition of her husband's definitions, his reappearance as husband and her forced return to the self-destructive limits of wifehood. Although in each story the woman dies, the latter reveals a creative struggle toward selfhood that the former suppresses, and the surfaces of "Story of an Hour" disclose more distinctly than the earlier tale the conflicting perspectives that frustrate Louise Mallard's survival.

Even in Chopin's most successful novel, the woman dies. But the story of her struggle is perhaps the nineteenth century's most vivid and sustained rendering of what it means for a woman to try to achieve the selfhood that Emerson described as the most sacred task of human being—the American Dream of becoming an individual, a self. But, I would argue, Edna's death reveals that the achievement of such integrity is finally a specifically *male* dream, one whose terms virtually exclude women, who cannot ignore or resist the role that "others" play in defining our lives.

The Awakening tells the story of Edna Pontellier, a young Kentuckian woman of twenty-eight in a conventional marriage with two sons. Her husband, Leonce Pontellier, is a successful New Orleans businessman, a rather typical American male who sees his wife as his possession, his assistant (not unlike his hired clerk) whose chief duty is to help him "keep up with the procession" toward financial success. The couple vacation with other French Quarter families on Grande Isle, a popular resort on the Gulf Coast, whose relaxed, sensuous atmosphere releases in Edna an unaccustomed sensuality. Vague at first, her desires become focused on Robert Lebrun, a young man who tends to be serially devoted to unavailable (married) women in his social set.

When Edna returns to New Orleans, her restlessness leads her eventually into an adulterous affair, not with Robert, who is too "honorable" and flees to business in Mexico, but with a well-known rake, Alcee Arobin. "Awakening" at last, Edna recognizes not only her sexual identity (the desires of her self) but also the emptiness of her marriage with Leonce and the untenability of her situation. For while her attraction to Alcee is purely physical and circumstantial, her beloved Robert is frankly shocked by her new self-possession. In despair, Edna returns to Grande Isle and walks down to the beach where she sheds her clothing, naked "like some new-born creature, opening its eyes in a familiar world that it had never known," and swims out into the safe, close embrace of the sea. (*KCA*, 113).

Like Desiree, Edna Pontellier lives in a society that defines women according to their relationships with men: daughter, sister, wife, mother. But unlike Desiree, Edna is "awakened" to the possibility, the dream, that she, like Emerson (whom she falls asleep reading!), can become a self: "In short, Mrs. Pontellier was beginning to realize her position in the universe as a human being, and to recognize her relations as an individual to the world within and about her" (*KCA*, 14–15). That Chopin, if not Edna, recognized the difficulty of this dream is evident in the wry continuation of the passage: "This may seem like a ponderous weight of wisdom to descend upon the soul of a young woman of twenty-eight—perhaps more wisdom than the Holy Ghost is usually pleased to vouchsafe to any woman" (*KCA*, 15).

Indeed, for most women, as both Desiree and Louise reveal, society's decree is selflessness, being for others. Edna's confidante, Adele Ratignolle, is a model of the type, in her romantic sexual beauty and her self-denying relationships with her husband and children. Adele is the classic "mother-woman" (*KCA*, 10). But for Edna, such self-effacement requires a sacrifice of "the essential," a loss of that core of identity for which each human being is responsible and without which no human being is possible. As she explains to Adele, " 'I would give up the unessential; I would give my money, I would give my life for my children, but I wouldn't give myself. I can't make it more clear; it's only something which I am beginning to comprehend, which is revealing itself to me' " (*KCA*, 48).

What leads Edna to a recognition of that essential core is her sensual awakening, her recognition that she does have desires (unlike Desiree, who is only "desired"), that her body is her own. This connection of the body, the physical, with selfhood is a frequent motif of literature by women. Women are often defined in terms of their bodies—as wombs, as sexual objects and parts—but as bodies that belong to others, the objects of male desire, the passive receptacle of male possession and passion. But even as they immerse themselves in this identity, becoming obsessed with their physical beauty, their sexual attractiveness to men, women become unaware of, even oblivious to, the reality of their bodies as their own.

Often enough, however, a woman is recalled to herself by that very physicality. In recognizing that her body is not merely another's (sexual object) but hers and the subject of her own desire, such a woman also encounters a self. The physical languor of the seaside nudges Edna toward just such a discovery: "She stretched her strong limbs that ached a little. She ran her fingers through her loosened hair for a while. She looked at her round arms as she held them straight up and rubbed them one after the other, observing closely, as if it were something she saw for the first time, the fine, firm quality and texture of her flesh" (*KCA*, 37). Eventually, that awareness of her body and its desires leads to the affair with Arobin. His is "the first kiss of her life to which her nature had really responded. It was a flaming torch that kindled desire" (*KCA*, 83). To discover her body and its passions is a revelation of an autonomy she had never experienced and an intimation of a selfhood she cannot resist.

Unlike Desiree, who fails to recognize any desire as her own, Edna rejects the false definitions that have been imposed upon her: Leonce's wife and possession, a self-less "mother-woman," or merely the mistress of Arobin (whom she does not love) or Robert (who is too conventional himself to understand how any respectable woman would expect—would *desire*—to have a self apart from the defined role as desired and owned by a man, in marriage). Talking with her friend Mlle. Reisz about her painting and moving to her "pigeon house," both emblems of her growing independence, Edna reflects her resolve "never again to belong to another than herself" (*KCA,* 80). Later, she simply laughs at Robert when he dreams of getting her freed from Leonce with a divorce: " 'You have been a very, very foolish boy, wasting your time dreaming of impossible things when you speak of Mr. Pontellier setting me free! I am no longer one of Mr. Pontellier's possessions to dispose of or not. I give myself where I choose. If he were to say, "Here, Robert, take her and be happy; she is yours," I should laugh at you both.' . . . His face grew a little white. 'What do you mean?' he asked" (*KCA,* 107).

But Edna is finally mistaken in thinking that a woman of her time can achieve such self-possession, that she can have the integrity that Emerson and other nineteenth-century male Americans described as the essence of the American Dream. Ironically, Edna is not so different from Huck Finn, the great model of American (masculine) identity. Like him, Edna is simply trying to follow her conscience, her inner light. Huck too struggles with false social constructions like racism and other bigotry that would destroy his personal relationship with Jim. But when he finally recognizes that these external definitions interfere with his integrity as an individual, he simply escapes to new adventures "in the territory." Edna's discovery that society, "civilization," is in conflict with selfhood and personal identity is similar. For her too, one's desires cannot be realized on shore or in a conventional marriage. But Edna cannot escape to the raft or to the territories because to be a woman is to be defined by the society, to live on the shore, without any separate raft of self.

For Edna, then, to be a self, to have desires, is to be no longer selfless, which is the essential condition for women. But to reject that role is to tread an unfamiliar and solitary ground. Adele, who epitomizes female selflessness, cannot even imagine having a self or anything other than her physical life to give up, so absorbed is she by the desires of others. And in the final analysis, neither can Edna escape those definitions by others. For unlike the orphaned, unrelated Huck, she cannot abandon or even deny her relations and responsibilities on the shore: her children. Though she has produced them without choosing, without understanding her desires, they are hers and make claims upon her. As she begins her final swim, "she thought of Leonce and the children. They were a part of her life. But they need not have thought that they could possess her, body and soul" (*KCA*, 114). Nevertheless, as Edna insists to the sympathetic Dr. Mandelet, she doesn't want "to trample upon the little lives" of her sons. She knows that she can neither return to the empty marriage with Leonce and abandon her newfound self nor accept the succession of lovers that she foresees, imposing on her children the pain of scandal, of others' definitions of her as unrespectable, as selfish. What Edna can give up is her life, (selflessly) sacrificing her body while preserving her essential self.

Edna's choice—and Chopin's tone in its description—gives *The Awakening* perhaps the most ambivalent conclusion in all American literature. Clearly, Edna is defeated in her quest for a self, but just as clearly, she is victorious. She does achieve and preserve a self—the essential, which women are categorically denied—and she *is* a woman who acts selflessly in giving up her life for her children.

But in the ambivalence of this ending Chopin affirms the difficulty of the dream of female selfhood in a society that defines women as selfless. More importantly, perhaps, Chopin also reveals the limits of the late nineteenth century's definitions of selfhood. At its base, such a self affirms an ego, an I, that is only and always in control. Such a self is ever subject, never subjected to its responsibilities and relations to others, as women inevitably are. In Edna's dilemma Chopin exposes the dream itself, the fantasy of male selfhood that is epitomized by Huck Finn: the dream that we can escape the definitions of our community, our language, the others about us.

In revealing the tragic impossibility of that dream for women, who are *other*, she underlines its illusoriness for men, who have created that otherness to deny their own—a convenient raft on which to avoid the responsibilities and contingencies that shore-born creatures must sometimes find disconcerting. At the same time, however, in Edna's triumph Chopin suggests the hope of a self that is also selfless, one not wholly defined by others or wholly careless of the responsibility of others, neither wholly object nor subject of desire. In that ambivalent triumph, then, lies a revolutionary image of the dream of female selfhood.

Finding the Self at Home: Chopin's The Awakening and Cather's The Professor's House

KATHERINE JOSLIN

> "I would give up the unessential; I would give my money, I would give up my life for my children; but I wouldn't give myself."
> —Kate Chopin, *The Awakening*

> He loved his family, he would make any sacrifice for them, but just now he couldn't live with them. He must be alone.
> —Willa Cather, *The Professor's House*

Willa Cather read Kate Chopin's *The Awakening* when it was published in 1899 and found the novel so disturbing that she reviewed it for the Pittsburgh *Leader* under the pen name "Silbert" (*KCA,* 153). Chopin's novel irritated Cather, as it did many of her contemporaries, but Cather's criticism went beyond mere prudery, the insistence on genteel literary etiquette. Although Cather credited Chopin with an "exquisite and sensitive, well-governed" style, she spoke against the "trite and sordid" retelling of a woman's familiar tale.[1]

Edna Pontellier, like Emma Bovary and Anna Karenina before her, wanted out of the house, that is, out of the monotony and restriction of domestic life. They represent a group of women "clamoring," in Cather's words, for more romance out of life than reasonable people can expect: "The unfortunate feature of their disease is that it attacks only women of brains, at least of rudimentary brains, but whose development is one-sided; women of strong and fine intuitions, but without the faculty of observation, comparison, reasoning about things" (*KCA,* 154).

According to Cather's reading of Chopin, Edna Pontellier works against herself, in the end annihilates herself, by nurturing a passion that exists only in her fancy, in her brain, in an ideal world, instead of living in the more

1. Willa Cather, "Books and Magazines," Pittsburgh *Leader,* July 8, 1899 p. 6, *KCA,* 153.

prosaic but ultimately healthier domestic world around her. In nineteenth-century fiction, women who go against the conventions of their social group, especially where sexual rules are in question, meet with disaster almost without exception. Why write another version of this already standard tale? Cather lectured Chopin.

When she wrote *The Professor's House* (1925), Cather, although she never acknowledged it as such, gave a literary response to Chopin's tale. The argument could also be made for Cather's novel *A Lost Lady,* her response to the Bovary theme. The story of Godfrey St. Peter's rebellion against domestic life revises the Edna Pontellier story by focusing on the male's resistance to marriage and parenthood. Reading the two novels together reveals how clearly Cather's novel reconsiders the domestic theme of Chopin's. Like Edna Pontellier, Godfrey St. Peter awakens to the burden of domestic obligation; his quest, like Edna's, is to find room for the self at home.

Kate Chopin's theme of female suffocation in the home arose from cultural changes taking place around her. The creation of separate spheres of life in nineteenth-century America, the doctrine that relegated men to the world of work outside the home and the woman to work within, broke down, late in the century. No longer content with the role of domestic angel, women grew more educated, more forceful, more visible outside the house. The tension born of this struggle provided Kate Chopin with her story about the Pontellier marriage. Clearly, Leonce considers Edna a chattel, garbs her in fashionable clothes, and houses her and his children in a home that announces his social standing. Edna, surprising her husband but not us, responds by moving out.

The theme of female rebellion against domesticity is so well known in American culture and literature that one has to wonder (at least I have for years) how Cather shifted the conflict by giving the traditional female lament to the male. Godfrey St. Peter (albeit a university professor and by definition eccentric, atypical of men in general) argues essentially the same line Edna does: Domesticity does not allow him a sense of self. In his makeshift office upstairs he could escape the responsibilities of domestic life, but "on that perilous journey down through the human house he might lose his mood, his enthusiasm, even his temper."[2]

2. Willa Cather, *The Professor's House* (New York, 1973), 27, hereinafter, cited parenthetically in the text as *PH*.

Since when did the man have to worry about such domestic peril? The answer may lie in the difference of twenty-five years between the two novels. As Margaret Marsh, in "Suburban Men and Masculine Domesticity, 1870–1915," has uncovered in her coining of the nearly oxymoronic term *masculine domesticity,* as many women moved into the man's sphere late in the nineteenth century, many men moved into the woman's—not as willingly, perhaps, or as thoroughly, but as surely. Her research into advice literature, architectural design, recreational patterns, and personal papers from the Progressive Era questions our current acceptance of the early twentieth-century cult of masculinity. By masculine domesticity, Marsh means "a model of behavior in which fathers would agree to take on increased responsibility for some of the day-to-day tasks of bringing up children and spending their time away from work in playing with their sons and daughters, teaching them, taking them on trips. A domestic man would also make his wife, rather than his male cronies, his regular companion on evenings out."[3] This new breed of men who coupled their work outside the home with their tasks as husbands and fathers in the home Willa Cather sought to capture in her novel. Godfrey St. Peter echoes Edna Pontellier in responding to the personal cost of socially engaged living.

An easy way of explaining the similarity between Edna and Godfrey is to argue that the professor is not really a male character but a masked female. In that reading, his lament echoes Edna's because both are, on a deeper level, women. Such a reading, however, is reductive. It posits that Willa Cather's lesbianism and her cross-dressing explain her imaginative art: Godfrey St. Peter as Willa Cather in disguise. Such a reading suggests that gender differences can never be bridged, that only women can artistically conceive women and men, men. Yet Godfrey St. Peter remains to many critics and readers a convincing man. I agree with Cather's biographer Sharon O'Brien that "a character like Godfrey St. Peter in *The Professor's House,* however 'feminine' his sensibility, should be considered male. Not to do so would be to overlook Cather's redefinition of male and female roles and identities."[4] Redefining gender roles included Cather's exploration of what Marsh has discovered in early-twentieth-

3. Margaret Marsh, "Suburban Men and Masculine Domesticity, 1870–1915," *American Quarterly,* XL (June, 1988), 166.

4. Sharon O'Brien, *Willa Cather: The Emerging Voice* (New York, 1987), 217.

century American culture, the movement of the man into the female sphere, literally and figuratively into the house.

The question for both Kate Chopin and Willa Cather was how to tell the tale of domestic life in America. Our society has always resisted the novel of manners, the story of the self at home and in society, preferring instead the romance, the tale of the self in nature, away from society and domesticity. The "damned mob of scribbling women," as Nathaniel Hawthorne dubbed female writers in the nineteenth century, often told the tale of domesticity. According to Elaine Showalter, writers like Susan Warner, E.D.E.N. Southworth, Louisa May Alcott and Elizabeth Stuart Phelps wrote popular novels that comfortably situated the heroine in a world of marriage and motherhood.[5] At the same time, male writers like Hawthorne, Edgar Allan Poe, Herman Melville, and even Mark Twain placed their heroes outside marriage and fatherhood. The female domestic story was regarded by male writers, critics, and readers as merely a popular genre. The romance, on other hand, became the genre of "serious" literature. In the traditional canon, therefore, the American quest has been depicted largely as a male journey away from the domestic, social world of women toward the open road.

Kate Chopin's *The Awakening* and Willa Cather's *The Professor's House* explore the conflict between the romantic desire for an autonomous self and the prosaic demands of feminine and masculine domesticity. Both writers sought a fusion of the domestic novel with the romance. They wanted to write "serious" literature about the possibilities for selfhood in the home. Unlike novelists who celebrated domesticity, Chopin and Cather presented the restrictions imposed on the individual, the demands on time and energy required by spouses and children. Edna Pontellier rebels against marriage and motherhood in many of the ways Godfrey St. Peter rebels against marriage and fatherhood. Over the course of the novels, they get, as Godfrey puts it, "isolation, insulation from the engaging drama of domestic life" (*PH,* 26). Outside the absorbing, enervating tasks of family life, away from spouses and children, Edna and Godfrey find the solitude they desire. Yet escape fails to cure their malady. In presenting their di-

---

5. Elaine Showalter, "Tradition and the Female Talent: *The Awakening* as a Solitary Book," in *NEA*.

lemma, Chopin and Cather question the possibility, even the desirability, of such romantic selfhood.

Domestic life differs in the novels, but both present marriages and family lives typical of their day. In the Pontellier domestic arrangement, the leisure of the wife, even her dress and her fair skin color, mark the status of the family. Leonce has acquired, rather than married Edna. She succeeds by spending his money well, being what Thorstein Veblen, in *The Theory of the Leisure Class* (also published in 1899), called a "conspicuous consumer."[6] Moreover, like the men of his time, Leonce expects the woman to shoulder all responsibility for the care and guidance of their children. He criticizes Edna for her inattention to their sick child Raoul: "If it was not a mother's place to look after children, whose on earth was it? He himself had his hands full with his brokerage business. He could not be in two places at once; making a living for his family on the street, and staying home to see that no harm befell them" (*KCA,* 7). The fact that they were on vacation, that he had plenty of time to care for his son, even that the children were boys and not girls, all mean nothing.

The domestic role for women of the day was managing the house and raising the children. As Charlotte Perkins Gilman observed in *Women and Economics* (again, 1899), such division of labor caused distortions. The woman became, along with the house and the children, the property of her husband. In order to catch a male provider, the woman had to become "oversexed," developing in lopsided fashion those sexual charms that might ensnare a man and neglecting other traits such as intellect and reason.[7] In that scheme, the man lost as much as the woman. He was forced by social custom to work doubly hard to support his wife and their children. If they did not have enough money for both to stay at home, their social status was marked by the woman's leisure, her relegation to the house, alone with her children. As a consequence of the long hours of work away from the home, the man lost his role as companion to his wife and guide to his children. He found himself, quite literally, outside the house.

In the novel, Leonce finds the world away from home to his liking: "He

6. Thorstein Veblen, *The Theory of the Leisure Class: An Economic Study in the Evolution of Institutions* (New York, 1899).

7. Charlotte Perkins Gilman, *Women and Economics: A Study of the Economic Relations Between Men and Women as a Factor in Social Evolution* (Boston, 1899).

was eager to be gone, as he looked forward to a lively week in Carondelet Street" (*KCA,* 9), the New Orleans equivalent of Wall Street. He leaves in the morning between nine and ten o'clock to go to work and returns between six-thirty and seven in the evening, allowing him time to dine with his wife, not his children, before retiring. When domestic discord develops in his marriage, Leonce dines in the homosocial world of his male club. His career allows him to escape domestic life altogether by traveling to New York on a lengthy business trip.

Cather's novel reverses this conflict in a way. Unlike Leonce Pontellier, Godfrey St. Peter has managed to merge the worlds of domesticity and work. He lives in the world of masculine domesticity. Cather describes the juggling Godfrey must do to devote himself to his family, his profession, and his writing:

> If someone in the family happened to be sick, he didn't go to his study at all. Two evenings of the week he spent with his wife and daughters, and one evening he and his wife went out to dinner, or to the theatre or a concert. That left him only four. He had Saturdays and Sundays, of course, and on those two days he worked like a miner under a landslide. . . . All the while that he was working so fiercely by night, he was earning a living during the day; carrying full university work and feeding himself out to hundreds of students in lectures and consultations. But that was another life. (*PH,* 28)

His life differs significantly from Leonce's in that he works in the house. That proximity to his family allows, even demands, engagement in the regular running of the household. Not unlike women who work at home, he finds that to leave his study is to encounter his family. Like the suburban men Marsh studied, he found time to devote to raising his children. Although he has male colleagues and his sons-in-law feud over membership in male clubs, Godfrey prefers to spend his one weekly evening out with his wife. Unlike the unawakened Edna, he must live two lives "very intensely" if he is to satisfy his family and himself. But like the awakened Edna, he finds creativity and productivity are in reverse proportion to the claims of everyday domestic life.

Their spouses, by contrast, have accepted traditional roles in their marriages. Lillian St. Peter abides in her own sphere, first in the old house, "as ugly as it is possible for a house to be," and later in the new house, a modern structure announcing their rise in status. As befits her role, she attempts to coax him into submission to the demands of the domestic world. There is evidence that she accepted the compromise she has had to make with domesticity. At the opera he hears in her voice "an old wound, healed and hardened and hopeless" (*PH*, 94). Finally she responds to Godfrey by virtually ignoring him; she builds, as Edna does, a house more to her liking. She even insists that her husband have a separate room there, a move that allows her a room of her own. When Godfrey resists the European vacation, she goes anyway, leaving him to work out his own dilemma. Her duties as mother and mother-in-law consume her time and energy.

As befits his role, Leonce Pontellier tries to manage his wife by demands and then by manipulation. Edna's father has warned him to use the power of the masculine presence: " 'Authority, coercion are what is needed. Put your foot down good and hard; the only way to manage a wife. Take my word for it' " (*KCA*, 71). Using such power, the colonel had "coerced his own wife into her grave." Leonce, a man of the newer order, is unwilling to exercise such brute power over his wife, yet the conflict over the role itself, ironically, sends his wife to the grave. Leonce's response to her oddities is finally to bury himself in his work, to allow his traditional social role, like Lillian's, to consume his time and energy.

The novels focus on Edna and Godfrey because they are at odds with their social roles, as is usually the case with American heroes. Both resist, in Bartleby fashion, the requirements of their society. In their resistance to socially imposed identities, Edna Pontellier and Godfrey St. Peter are not unlike Ahab or Huck. Both novels offer a version of the standard male quest in that both present a protagonist who desires to go beyond society, to escape the defining limits of domesticity, to discover how much of human nature is left outside the web of social ritual and attachment. Edna begins her awakening outside the Pontellier house. The family is vacationing on Grand Isle; natural forces begin at once to alter her physically and psychologically. After seeing her sunburn, her husband complains of the change he sees: " 'You are burnt beyond recognition' " (*KCA*, 4). Over the course of the novel, she becomes unrecognizable to someone who sees her only through the traditional lens. In seeming contrast, *The Professor's House* begins with St. Peter at home, yet his very house has become the world outside; his wife has moved, along with their belongings, to the new house. By refusing the new life, Godfrey has been in a sense left outside his marriage and family.

Both characters seek a place outside the home, a space that better suits them, a room and finally a house to themselves. Edna begins her flight from her family by designing an attic room, her atelier, modeled after Mlle. Reisz's garret with its open windows allowing light and air into the room. The desire for an upstairs retreat with a view of nature is featured in both novels. Godfrey St. Peter too has retreated to an atelier, the makeshift sewing room he shares with the seamstress Augusta. Cather even includes the details of the view of water and the ominous gasoline stove from Reisz's studio. The attic room stands both literally and figuratively for the artistic life, as Virginia Woolf made clear.[8] (Cather herself had an attic room when she was a child and again as an adult. By contrast, Chopin, a mother of six, had no such space to herself, indeed wrote with her children in sight.) Given his role as economic provider, such a study for a scholarly man would have to be tolerated by Godfrey's family. His younger daughter, Kathleen, so abides by the rule of his privacy that she sits outside the door with a severe wound until his time for study is over.

That same space for a woman is another matter. A single woman, like Reisz or Cather herself, might be allowed that freedom of thought and activity, but a married woman preferring such a retreat is such an anomaly that Edna's husband questions her sanity. " 'It seems to me,' " Leonce lectures Edna, " 'the utmost folly for a woman at the head of a household, and the mother of children, to spend in an atelier days which would be better employed contriving for the comfort of her family' " (*KCA*, 57). His point is that he has "employed" her by marrying her and that therefore her time belongs to him and his children. Edna has no right to a second career, especially one that takes time away from her family. Her attempts to escape his employment make Edna seem "a little unbalanced mentally" to her husband.

Once Godfrey has used his sewing-room–study to write his volumes of history and has thereby earned enough money to provide comfortably for his wife and himself, the family grows resentful of his right to such seclu-

8. Virginia Woolf, *A Room of One's Own* (New York, 1928).

sion. That is, once his employment as a scholar is no longer necessary to the financial well-being of his family, his role as provider loses its former status. Lillian, along with her newly wealthy daughter, Rosamond, and her upwardly mobile husband, Louis Marcellus, discourages Godfrey's continued seclusion. He, like Edna before him, is considered strange for not abandoning his retreat. The family uses the five hundred pounds he won from the Oxford prize in history to build the more expensive house to mark the family's rise in status. His dilemma is how to leave the attic room, the symbol and abode of his intellectual life.

As a consequence of gender, the woman's awakening comes far earlier than the man's. Edna is twenty-eight, Godfrey fifty-two. Over the years of his career, the professor has been allowed to devote much of his time to his own pursuits and has consequently not needed to "awaken" until his retreat is challenged. Edna has never been allowed any serious time to herself. When she takes her Tuesday "visiting day" for her own interests or leaves her children to go to her studio to paint, she immediately arouses the anger of her husband. Yet even the much younger Edna refers to the years lost to her: " 'The years that are gone seem like dreams—if one might go on sleeping and dreaming—but to wake up and find—oh! well! perhaps it is better to wake up after all, even to suffer, rather than to remain a dupe to illusions all one's life' " (*KCA,* 110).

Both Edna and Godfrey, in a sense, have slept through the routines, the expectations and obligations, of their domestic lives. For them to awaken, they must transcend that automatic role and find a new self, "to realize [their] position in the universe as a human being, and to recognize [their] relations as an individual to the world within and about [them]" (*KCA,* 14–15). Their awakening, ironically, sends them deep into themselves. Godfrey's state is, in Cather's words, only "semi-awake." He is a man who never before dreamed, preferring to live in a literal, material world. "But now," Cather explains, "he enjoyed this half-awake loafing with his brain as if it were a new sense, arriving late, like wisdom teeth" (*PH,* 263). His new state of "mental dissipation" is a clear echo of Edna's. Without the worry of social obligation, the usual round of perfunctory duties, where might the mind wander?

Edna's and Godfrey's quest for the self takes them outside the house, away from the quotidian world, to literal and symbolic realms of mystery and adventure. Both dream of a boat, lost or wrecked, beyond the constraints of society. Edna's dream takes the form of a story, a "pure invention" that she tells to her husband, father, and Dr. Mandelet of a woman who "paddled away with her lover one night in a pirogue and never came back." In telling the tale, she fires its fiction with the reality of her passionate longing so that "they could feel the hot breath of the Southern night; they could hear the long sweep of the pirogue through the glistening moonlit water, the beating of birds' wings, rising startled from among the reeds in the salt-water" (*KCA,* 70).

The doctor translates this fantasy into a fairly accurate reality by assuming that Edna is in the midst of an affair. Her desire, however, goes beyond mere sexual passion; she wishes to awake to an unknown world, one beyond the confining parameters of her domestic life. Later, her children and husband gone, she reads Emerson, not an unlikely choice for a romantic American hero to read, but (as critics have noted) the reading makes her sleepy. Yet she cannot sleep and remains restless because once outside the world of domestic obligations and definitions, she does not know who she is.

Cather's hero also dreams of a world away from the constraints of his real life. Like Edna, Godfrey first dreams of lost lovers. " 'My dear,' " he tells her, " 'it's been a mistake, our having a family and writing histories and getting middle-aged. We should have been picturesquely shipwrecked together when we were young' " (*PH,* 94). She admits to the same fantasy, although over the years she has given it up to " 'go on living.' " As Godfrey goes to sleep that night, feeling little of Edna's restlessness, he finds the perfect day in his history for the desired wreck: "Indeed, nobody was in it but himself, and a weather-dried little sea captain from the Hautes-Pyrenees, half a dozen spry seamen, and a line of gleaming snow peaks, agonizingly high and sharp, along the southern coast of Spain" (*PH,* 95). His final dream, then, excludes his wife, landing him safely beyond domesticity into a fantasy version of the scholarly work that has made up his professional life. The source of his fantasy had been a trip to visit the Thieraults, a family of sons who seemed closer to him than brothers. Alone with Charles Thierault, he sailed on a little brig, *L'Espoir,* with a captain from the Hautes-Pyrenees and a spare crew of seamen, and on their voyage the plan of his history of the Spanish explorers unfolded before him (*PH,* 106).

As their fantasies reveal, Edna and Godfrey associate self-exploration and discovery with the movement, the sensation, the depth of water, a dominant symbol in both novels. Edna, as a young woman relatively unschooled in life, cannot swim at the beginning of the novel. Her goal is to learn "to swim out far, where no woman had swum before" (*KCA,* 28). The beckoning yet fearful sea operates, as it does in so many American romances, as the symbol of self-knowledge outside society, away from the shore. Chopin's novel is held together by its seductive image: "The voice of the sea is seductive; never ceasing, whispering, clamoring, murmuring, inviting the soul to wander for a spell in abysses of solitude; to lose itself in mazes of inward contemplation. . . . The voice of the sea speaks to the soul. The touch of the sea is sensuous, enfolding the body in its soft, close embrace" (*KCA,* 15). The sea symbolizes consciousness, the stream of images that includes sensation and memory. Learning to swim awakens Edna to her sensuality and passion, repressed at puberty. The movement of the water across her body calls up memories of grass across her body when she was young and, by association, her sexual desire for the cavalry officer, a surrogate of her father, and later the actor whose picture likewise aroused her.

Lake Michigan has somewhat the same effect on Godfrey St. Peter. Unlike Edna, he knows how to swim, in fact learned as a boy and as an adult is a strong swimmer. Yet, like her, he delights in the sensation of being in the water: "But the great fact in life, the always possible escape from dullness, was the lake. The sun rose out of it, the day began there; it was like an open door that nobody could shut. The land and all its dreariness could never close in on you. You had only to look at the lake, and you knew you would soon be free" (*PH,* 30).

The lake reminds him of his youth, sends him backward in memory as it does Edna. At the age of eight, the young Godfrey had been abruptly and forcibly taken from his lakeside farm by parents eager to settle in Kansas. As an adult, he buys the old house because it will allow him a view of Lake Michigan, and whenever he is depressed, he goes to the lake to swim. The sensation of his body in water frees Godfrey, as it does Edna, from the claims of the domestic world.

Being in the water evokes in Edna the memory of a time when her body essentially belonged to her and not to her husband and children. It is that theme, it seems to me, that Willa Cather failed to understand fully. To

Cather's mind, Edna Pontellier's desire for freedom stops at sexual passion, yet Edna espouses the feminism of her day. Leonce complains to Dr. Mandelet, "She's making it devilishly uncomfortable for me. . . . She's got some sort of notion in her head concerning the eternal rights of women" (*KCA*, 65). That argument separates her from Emma Bovary and Anna Karenina. Her quest, at least in part, is to find a new self beyond the heterosexual bond.

Edna seeks, as Godfrey does with men, to develop a bond with other women, a bond she apparently did not have with her mother. As Sandra Gilbert has noted, on Grand Isle, itself a colony of women and children, Edna responds to her "sensuous susceptibility to beauty" by beginning an intimacy with Adele Ratignolle, a relationship she had never before experienced.[9] Later, with Mlle. Reisz, Edna seeks a different kind of intimacy with a woman, one based on aesthetics, even intellect. In fashioning a new self, Edna is caught between these two models. She cannot go back to Ratignolle's submissive role and hasn't the strength to go forward to Reisz's independent one. Reisz appropriately warns her of the price of her quest: " 'To be an artist includes much; one must possess many gifts—absolute gifts—which have not been acquired by one's own effort. And, moreover, to succeed, the artist must possess the courageous soul' " (*KCA*, 63). Edna's quest, then, is for courage, the soul that "dares and defies." Instead of reading the story as a feminist awakening, Willa Cather read the story in her review as a Bovary-like tale of a woman who pursues the sensual, the passionate life at the expense of her intellect, her ability to reason.

To revise the story of Edna Pontellier, therefore, Willa Cather excluded the theme of heterosexual passion, insisting that Godfrey St. Peter's quest avoid such a "sordid" theme. Once a marriage has gone stale, as the St. Peter marriage has, a middle-aged man might seek a renewal of youthful passion by taking a mistress. Such a tale is trite. That was Cather's criticism of Chopin, and we would therefore expect her to reject it in her revised story. Consequently, unlike Edna, who returns to puberty, Godfrey returns to latency, to his presexual self, the young boy he had to repress, abandon, to take up his social roles as husband, father, teacher.

The Tom Outland section, the centerpiece of Godfrey's journey back to

9. Sandra Gilbert, Introduction to *The Awakening* (New York, 1985).

youth, functions as a romance within the domestic tale. As Cather explained, "In my book I tried to make Professor St. Peter's house rather overcrowded and stuffy with new things; American proprieties, clothes, furs, petty ambitions, quivering jealousies—until one got rather stifled. Then I wanted to open the square window and let in the fresh air that blew off the Blue Mesa." [10] The passion he finds is homosocial; his young student Tom Outland leads him back to a world without women. Outland's life on the Mesa with Roddy, the men's world of Western adventure, is a version of the scholarly history Godfrey St. Peter has devoted his life to. That is, both are versions of the male quest, the journey out of the house, away from the world of women.

As Leslie Fiedler pointed out, the American romance is full of such partnerships. [11] Godfrey sees this passion for Tom Outland as a romance "of the mind—of the imagination" (*PH,* 258). Instead of a sexual affair, Godfrey has an intellectual one: "Just when the morning brightness of the world was wearing off for him, along came Outland and brought him a kind of second youth" (*PH,* 258). Cather extends the story beyond the homosocial relationship between the professor and Outland to his relationship with himself. Godfrey St. Peter finds his way through the retelling of the Outland story back to another boy, "the boy the Professor had long ago left behind him in Kansas, in the Solomon Valley—the original, unmodified Godfrey St. Peter" (*PH,* 263). In reuniting with his own youth, the professor seeks to get in back of the social overlay. To him that early life was "the realest of his lives," and the intervening years "had been accidental and ordered from the outside" (*PH,* 264).

The true self, the imaginative, creative self, is for both Godfrey and Edna the child, the self before socially imposed gender roles. But the desire to return to a life without their families is as much a fantasy as their dreams of shipwrecks. Likewise, they both find it difficult to move forward alone into a new life. Chopin's first title, *A Solitary Soul,* would have served both novels well. Both protagonists seek a new abode, a house to themselves. Edna's cottage, her "pigeon house," simplifies her life by requiring less space, fewer servants, less furniture—providing, in the end,

---

10. O'Brien, *Willa Cather,* 192.
11. Leslie Fiedler, *Love and Death in the American Novel* (New York, 1960).

no room for her husband and children. Godfrey solves his problem by simply refusing to give up the old house. There in his study, the sewing forms around him (the only form of female company he apparently desires), he no longer has to risk encounters with his family. Both get what they say they want. They escape domesticity, both the feminine and masculine versions.

What is truly unsettling about these journeys is the ultimate failure of such quests. To remove the self from the social, domestic life is to succumb to depression, alienation, despair. With differing degrees of commitment, both attempt suicide, although, presumably, only Edna succeeds. She cannot envision a role beyond wife, mother, or lover. Once out of her family house, she cannot return and has no other comfortable place to live. In her revision of Chopin's story, Cather adds the deus ex machina in the form of Augusta and forces her hero to rerelinquish his boyhood self to return to the adult world, joyless though it may be. Both novels suggest that in a sense there is no place beyond the house, no transcending the domestic world.

Kate Chopin and Willa Cather, both cool-eyed realist writers, regard the romantic quest with skepticism. Individuals are caught in the fabric of social living, a weave that often constricts but ultimately forms the self. In writing their versions of the domestic novel, Chopin and Cather explore the restrictions on the socially engaged individual and the failure of the romance to find a satisfactory way to define the self outside the social arrangement. We must find the self at home, their novels suggest, if we are to find the self at all.

Taming the Sirens: Self-Possession and the Strategies of Art in Kate Chopin's The Awakening

LYNDA S. BOREN

> For she was the maker of the song she sang.
> The ever-hooded, tragic-gestured sea
> Was merely a place by which she walked to sing.
> —Wallace Stevens
> "The Idea of Order at Key West"

In 1888, Rollman and Sons of St. Louis published a sprightly polka for piano by Kate Chopin. It was entitled the "Lilia Polka," perhaps (although with a variant spelling) after Chopin's only daughter, Lelia, or after George Sand's novel of the same name. Listening to Chopin's polka, one can sense the vitality and playfulness of her spirit, the passion that infused her life and her art.

Chopin's musicality dictates moods, themes, and structures in *The Awakening,* which is, when one considers it against the backdrop of traditional novelistic discourse, a highly experimental foray into modern techniques of *self*-expresion, a "reaching out" on the writer's part "for the unlimited in which to lose herself" (*KCA,* 29). A lyrical composition of sounds and voices, human or otherwise, drifts in and out of Chopin's retelling of an old story (adultery and its consequences), sweeping her listeners up, like Edna, into the colorful ambience of Louisiana's sumptuous bonhomie. One is not only a reader but also a listener; she composes not in silence but at the keyboard, and her appeal is the universal one of music—to our desires, our emotions.

We awaken at the end of the book to discover that poor Edna is, after all, dead, that she suffered unbearably, and that her life was unfulfilled, coming full circle as it does to the ironic medley of sensations that overcome her: the stern voice of her father and that of her sister, chains that confine a barking dog, clanging spurs, humming bees, and the "musky odor of pinks" (*KCA*, 114). If Edna succumbs at the end of Chopin's story, to *what* does she surrender? To take Chopin at her word is to reach only one conclusion: Edna drowns in a sea of sensations. The predominant one, the sensation of sound, overwhelms her. "The voice of the sea is seductive; never ceasing, whispering, clamoring. . . . The voice of the sea speaks to the soul" (*KCA*, 15).

While the apparently incongruous mixture of sounds at the end of the novel lends itself to a superficial commentary on Chopin's thematic mingling of eros and thanatos in the portrayal of Edna's tragedy, it is also, in terms of musical composition, a resolution of discord with harmony, an unholy alliance between seemingly warring factions—in this case between the patriarchal world of Edna's birth and the overwhelming forces of nature. Neither world could sustain Edna's passionate soul or answer the demands of her defiant will. When she turns at last to the embracing arms of the fatal mother, to the overwhelming finality of the sea, it is because she has been duped.

Edna's search for self-fulfillment is bound to her desire for creative achievement, her evolution as an artist. Unfortunately, she is never given the chance to sprout wings, much less to "soar above the level plain of tradition and prejudice" (*KCA*, 82). It is Chopin who achieves that victory. The "ideal" woman never emerges in Chopin's novel, and Edna, whom Chopin uses as the ostensible heroine of her romance, is meant to illustrate how easily the woman artist might fall victim to her own unlimited and unlimiting desire. Edna is the creative will without form, a voice cut off and ultimately smothered in its infancy.

We should not be surprised at Edna's defeat. While Chopin was no doubt given to moods of darkness and despair, she achieved that self-realization that Edna never could—as a mother, a wage earner, and an artist. Chopin sacrifices her heroine to make a point: Art is an expression of self, a struggle for dominance. The woman artist achieves liberation only when she assumes the authority of her own voice. As Edna discovers in her intimate conversations with Adele Ratignolle, "she was flushed and felt intoxicated with the sound of her own voice and the unaccustomed taste of candor. It muddled her like wine, or like a first breath of freedom" (*KCA*, 20).

Throughout *The Awakening*, we are given examples of women who "dare and defy": Mme. Lebrun, with the clatter of her sewing machine, is the self-reliant commercial woman (but most unpleasant and obviously bitter); Mlle. Reisz is a "slave" to the great musicians of the past whose work she interprets, thereby "scavenging" from a male-dominated tradition (a "bust of Beethoven [scowls] at [Edna]" from Reisz's "mantelpiece," [*KCA,* 79]); and even Adele Ratignolle, who is given to murmuring in soft undertones (*KCA,* 18) and basking in the bliss of motherhood, cries out in her childbearing torment, "'This is too much! . . . Mandelet ought to be killed! . . . Is it possible I am to be abandoned like this—neglected by everyone?'" (*KCA,* 108). Work, art, motherhood—each, taken separately as a consuming, exclusionary, *self*-defining role, is lacking. There is only one solution: to be master of all and slave to none; to have, in the end, a voice and a self of one's own.

As Plotinus so aptly put it, "We ourselves possess beauty when we are true to own own being; our ugliness is in going over to another order; our self-knowledge, that is to say, is our beauty; in self-ignorance we are ugly."[1]

The portrait of Edna is that of a woman who attempts this mastery. Unlike Reisz, she seeks not to interpret or mimic the great art of others (primarily men) but to sing her own songs. Sadly, she is defeated. All the more reason, Chopin warns in her portrayal of Edna's demise, to seek in art not the delusion of escape but the power of self-realization.

Edna's awakening is conveyed to us in lyric form, as is her death. Readers, however, do not like to acknowledge that they have been mesmerized by Chopin's art, that their rational, moralizing, judgmental faculties have been suspended and that they have sleepwalked through the sordid spectacle of Edna's melodramatic demise.

In spite of the high praise given to the craft of *The Awakening,* resentment lingers over the elusive nature of Chopin's narrative strategy. Even Willa Cather, who was anything but naïve when it came to music, claimed irritation with the novel, but, again, it is clear that Cather was most offended by the ambiguous nature of Edna's value as a heroine: "Edna Pontellier and Emma Bovary are studies in the same feminine type. . . . Both

---

1. Plotinus, "On the Intellectual Beauty," trans. Stephen MacKenna, in *Critical Theory Since Plato,* ed. Hazard Adams (New York, 1971), 113.

women belong to a class, not large, but forever clamoring in our ears, that demands more romance out of life than God put into it.''[2] Chopin's laughing rejoinder to her critics, however, takes us back to the essential irreverence of her approach to the written word. When she had "found out" what Edna Pontellier was "up to, the play was half over and it was then too late."[3]

If she failed to be as upset as her contemporaries over the amoral tone of *The Awakening,* it was because Chopin was able to make a clear distinction between art and real life, between passion wed to form (as we encounter in music) and the formless, futile passion of Edna Pontellier's pathos. The wit of Oscar Wilde's Vivian in *The Decay of Lying* affords a lens through which to view Chopin's attitude about the essential incompatibility of art with the turmoil and chaos of real life. As Vivian quips, " 'Art is our spirited protest, our gallant attempt to teach nature her proper place.' "[4] *The Awakening* was in the final analysis a work of fiction in spite of its bold investigation of one woman's attempt at defiance. What bothered the readers of Chopin's day (and what still bothers some) was their own seduction, the beguiling force of Chopin's compositional witchery. "It is sad and mad and bad, but it is all consummate art," wrote one critic.[5] "The spell of the book—it is something to be 'dreamed upon,' " wrote another.[6] If anything, Chopin's novel portrayed the dangers of misdirected passion. Her reader is forced to participate in Edna's seduction, however, and thereby hangs the tale.

We might well imagine Chopin's humorously ironic response to what is recognizably a distrustful, puritanical attitude toward art itself, particularly the notion that art might exist simply for "art's sake" alone, unfettered by

2. Willa Cather, "Books and Magazines," Pittsburgh *Leader,* July 8, 1899, p. 6, cited in *KCA,* 153.

3. "Aims and Autographs of Authors," *Book News,* XVII (July, 1899), 612, cited in *KCA,* 159.

4. Adams, ed., *Critical Theory Since Plato,* 673.

5. C. L. Deyo, "The Newest Books," St. Louis *Post-Dispatch,* May 20, 1899, p. 4, cited in *KCA,* 149.

6. Frances Porcher, "*The Awakening*: Kate Chopin's Novel," St. Louis *Mirror,* May 4, 1899, p. 6, cited in *KCA,* 145.

moral platitudes or idealistic convictions. Perhaps for this reason, many critics have gone astray in trying to make more of Edna's character than is actually there. She is not a "Creole Bovary," as Cather claimed, nor does she encompass the complexity and awareness of memorable heroines like Isabel Archer or George Sand. She is, on the other hand, a woman undone by delusion. And if at the end of the book we are led to rhapsodize on the transcendent beauty of Edna's watery death, we too have been undone, by our own penchant for confusing sonatas with the silent rapture of mystical ecstasy.

Why is it so difficult to discuss *The Awakening* simply as art? For Kenneth Eble, the novel added a new dimension to American fiction, "an example of what Gide called the *roman pur.*"[7] And as Daniel Rankin pointed out over fifty years ago, "The philosophy of Schopenhauer, the music of Wagner, the Russian novel, Maeterlinck's plays—all this she absorbed" (*CS*, 173–75). Perhaps we can begin by listening to some major compositional elements in the structure of Chopin's novel.

First there is *repetition*, the mindless screech of the parrot. "*'Allez vous-en! Allez vous-en! Sapristi!* That's all right!'" (*KCA*, 3). The voice of the parrot is a transforming device; it translates the human voices of Grand Isle into a meaningless composition of haphazard sound. Lacking this human element, the parrot's screech, musically considered, is atonal, mechanical, and discordant; intrusive, noisome, and irritating. To open one's novel in such a way is to perform a feat of modern symbolism. The words of Mme. Lebrun—an unhappy, frustrated widow—are transmogrified through the inhuman grotesque image of an encaged bird. Sound and symbol merge, setting the tone for Chopin's depiction of feminine pathos. "I have no leaning towards a parrot," Chopin wrote in her diary. "I think them detestable birds with their blinking stupid eyes and heavy clumsy motions. I never could become attached to one" (*KCM*, 171).

A mockingbird hangs on the other side of the door, "whistling his fluty notes out upon the breeze with maddening persistence" (*KCA*, 3). How are we to read the mockingbird? Per Seyersted interprets the birds as beings that imitate, engaged and enslaved. One repeats "its master's words, the

7. Kenneth Eble, "A Forgotten Novel: Kate Chopin's *The Awakening*," *Western Humanities Review*, X (Summer, 1956), 261–69, cited in *KCA*, 165.

other [echos] the voice of other species" (*CB,* 159). Speculatively, the mockingbird might also represent the South, its native habitat, but it is a *he*-bird, and in contrast to the parrot, the mockingbird is rarely if ever caged. We equate with it freedom and wildness. In addition, the mockingbird, unlike the parrot, lacks the ability to mimic the human voice. He is a singer of pure music; words are unknown to him.

Because these annoying birds belong to Mme. Lebrun, they "had the right to make all the noise they wished," and Mr. Pontellier relinquishes his newspaper in disgust. Chopin, with the ear of a musician and the reputed ability to mimic, opens her novel with discordant noises: a screeching parrot (encaged dehumanized voice); a whistling mockingbird (defiant, persistent sounds of nature); and an exclaiming husband: " 'What folly! to bathe at such an hour in such heat!' " (*KCA,* 4). Parrot, mockingbird, Mme. Lebrun, Leonce Pontellier, and the Farival twins (demonically pounding out their "Zampa" duet on the piano) offer Chopin's reader a startling, distasteful introduction to life on Grand Isle. Playing with our moods, Chopin offers a soothing contrast with the silent distant images of the lady in black, the quadroon nurse with a "far-away, meditative air," and the slowly approaching white sunshade that advanced at a "snail's pace" as it covered Mrs. Pontellier and the "young Robert Lebrun" (*KCA,* 4).

Thus far, we are held in limbo between two realities: the noise of frustrated, confined existence and its alternatives—religious solitude, dreams, or death—just as the caged birds exemplify equally untenable zones of expression: to parrot or to mock. As though bound irrevocably to the "noise" of existence (the stock market, machines), Mr. Pontellier shouts, argues, and demands his way through the novel. This is his role and his sound. He is disruptive and discordant in reaction to the disruption and discord that impinge on his quest for a dignified, orderly life. He reproaches, questions, and at one point commands Edna, as though she were a child, " 'You must come in the house instantly!' " (*KCA,* 32). The sound of her husband's voice is monotonous, insistent to Edna, just as the sounds of the birds and Mme. Lebrun had been to him, and herein lies the essence of Chopin's humor. "Noise," or atonal discord, is picked up and repeated in different contexts, forming a leitmotif or running commentary on the psychological distress of Chopin's characters.

To the mother of the Farival twins, their playing would hardly have sounded like noise. Under normal circumstances, the calls of the mockingbird are entertaining. And the voice of one's husband is, under loving conditions, welcome. Chopin's use of sound, then, constitutes an experimental language that supplies an interesting access to multiple ironies in the novel. To hear the subtle counterpoints, aided by associative memory, is to leave *The Awakening* with more complex insights and a more sophisticated interpretation than not to hear them. In music, a change in speed and emphasis can change the mood and effect of a melody. Chopin's "Lilia" polka, delivered in impromptu, improvisational fashion, can have many moods. Jazzed up, with a flourish here and there, it seems to capture the capricious, romping nature of a child at play. Rendered slowly, it suggests the poignant longing of lost love. Context, reader sensitivity, and rendition work in concert to produce meaning or impressions. If these impressions remain unconscious, the listener is moved but fails to recognize why.

During her four and a half years in the Cane River region of Louisiana, Kate Chopin's home became the center of society; she was known for her gaiety, tact, and sense of humor, her musical and conversational talents. Considering the pessimistic message of *The Awakening,* a novel that ends with the watery suicide of its lonely heroine, it is highly probable that Chopin considered her work an experiment in form, depicting the inevitable consequences of a young impressionable woman from "good old Kentucky Presbyterian stock" being suddenly dropped into the sensuous milieu of Louisiana's Creole life.

Applying musical science to her narrative lyricism, Chopin, like Mlle. Reisz, manipulates her reader's response. Surrounded on all sides by temptations and dangerous influences and lacking, it would seem, from earliest childhood, the loving, guiding hand of a caring mother, Edna is the ideal subject for scientific analysis. Edna is not only surrounded by temptations; Chopin also subjects her to looming threats. As Edna's Kentucky-colonel father announces to her husband, Leonce: "'Authority, coercion are what is needed. Put your foot down good and hard; the only way to manage a wife. Take my word for it.'" "The Colonel was perhaps unaware," continues Chopin, "that he had coerced his own wife into her grave" (*KCA,* 71). Rounding out her list of ingredients, Chopin tosses in Mlle. Reisz, a thinly disguised witch, who seduces Edna with heavy doses of Frederic Chopin's most evocative music. All of these elements recall similar events in the melodramatic episodes of Henry James's fiction, specifically those sinister images of Mme. Merle in *The Portrait of a Lady* (1881), her back to Isabel as she enchants her listener with a rendition of Schubert, or little Miles in *The Turn of the Screw* (1889), distracting the governess with the same instrument so that his little sister, Flora, can slip away undetected. Chopin's depiction of Edna reflects a similar ambivalence toward the hypnotic power of a rarified Emersonian idealism. Under the spell of such unyielding "otherworldliness," the enchanted victims move, as in a trance, to their unhappy conclusions. Conveyed through the primitive impulses of pure lyric, transcendental persuasion extends beyond the limits of rational discourse to the more chaotic, wilder regions of the human psyche.[8]

Edna Pontellier's psyche is extremely vulnerable. She seems to suffer from unaccountable fluctuations in mood; at least she seems to be only half aware of why she feels the way she does, even though Chopin's readers comprehend Edna's justifiable reactions to the suppression of her natural vivacity. Edna is either unable or unwilling to parcel out her emotional life, as does Adele Ratignolle, who confines her emotions to the socially safe *soirée musicale*, with its light music and proper settings. Instead, she succumbs to the overpowering spell cast by Mlle. Reisz's artistry and the strains of Chopin.

Subscribing to Nietzsche's argument in *The Birth of Tragedy from the Spirit of Music* (1872), it follows that Edna's latent Dionysian desires for irrational ecstasy are brought to the surface by certain types of music, while the Apollonian demand for order, required by art, is only feebly realized or negatively imaged as "encaging," "paternalistic," "silencing."[9]

The nineteenth century reveled in the music of abandon and passion. As Casimir Wierzynski's rhapsodic praise of Chopin illustrates, Chopin, most of all, spoke to the soul with his music. "He made the piano sing," wrote Wierzynski. "From his childhood he had a passion for opera, espe-

8. Lynda Boren, *Eurydice Reclaimed: Language, Gender and Voice in Henry James* (Ann Arbor, 1989), 45. See also Lynda Boren, "The Performing Self: Psychodrama in Austen, James and Woolf," *The Centennial Review*, XXX (Winter, 1986), 1–24.

9. Friedrich Nietzsche, *The Birth of Tragedy and the Spirit of Music,* 1872; rpr. as *The Birth of Tragedy and the Genealogy of Morals,* trans. Francis Golffing (New York, 1956).

cially Italian opera. He understood instinctively that a melody, if it is not to sound mechanical, must breathe like a human voice, and he commanded the piano to breathe. Thus was born his famous *tempo rubato.*" Hailed as the poet of musicians, whose music moves Edna to tears, Chopin was by nineteenth-century standards no ordinary composer. As Wierzynski insists, "Chopin mixed sounds as paints are mixed on a palette, and produced colors that had not even been imagined before. He . . . opened up new horizons of musical poetry." [10] Side by side with such rapturous, almost religious adoration of Chopin and the power of music were the meticulous, scientific experiments conducted by Hermann Helmholtz based on the auditory properties of the ear, physiological factors, and so on.

Helmholtz's classic study, *The Sensations of Tone,* sought to offer an alternative to the mysticism that had dominated both music and math from the age of Pythagoras. Helmholtz journeyed to America in 1893 at the age of seventy-two when he was sent by the German government to the Electrical Congress in Chicago. His ideas ran counter to the romanticism and idolatry of music, which he studied, as any scientist would, in terms of its sensational effects on the body, and it is highly likely that Chopin in the course of her salon discussions was exposed to his discoveries. Halbert Britan's study *The Philosophy of Music* (1911), however, continues to insist, years after Helmholtz's experiments, that "the natural, instinctive effect of rhythm is emotional, that it never loses its fundamental psychological character." [11] Whatever comes first, the physical or the psychic, it is apparent that Chopin, at least in her composition of *The Awakening,* took more than a casual interest in the science of music.

Kate Chopin's knowledge of music, particularly that of Chopin and Wagner, is apparent in *The Awakening.* It is also highly likely that she took a scientific interest in it. Through the influence of Dr. Kolbenheyer, who encouraged Chopin to begin her literary career, the writer's home became a center for intellectual and creative discussions. William Schuyler— writer, critic, composer, and champion of Wagner—often attended Cho-

10. Casimir Wierzynski, *The Life and Death of Chopin,* trans. Norbert Guterman (New York, 1949), x.
11. Hermann Helmholtz, *The Sensations of Tone* (1877; rpr. New York, 1954); Halbert Britan, *The Philosophy of Music* (New York, 1911), 81.

pin's gatherings. Chopin's "closer friends were, in Felix Chopin's words, 'pink-red liberals' who believed in intellectual freedom" (*CB*, 63–64). The profile of Chopin at this time in her life leads one to believe that she was very much caught up in the reform movements and language-theory movements closely allied to symbolism and the fin de siècle experimentation illustrated by *The Yellow Book*. Music as a medium for psychological and social change was thoroughly championed. It was hailed as the universal language, a language of the masses, who were often locked out of the cultural sharing that comes with literate comprehension. George Bernard Shaw's linking of musical structure, particularly that of the human voice, to his social dramas about equality and sexual liberation encouraged further experimentation with music and politics.

That Chopin took an active interest in these aspects of music is clear. According to Seyersted, "She was familiar with the topics and movements of the day and loved to be mentally stimulated by spirited discussions, particularly with her male friends." Joining the Wednesday Club of St. Louis (founded by T. S. Eliot's mother and forty other women), "Chopin read a paper to them on 'Typical Forms of German Music.'" In a characteristic display of independence, however, "the next year, when it became compulsory to belong to a specific study group, she gave up her membership" (*CB*, 65).

By inserting the music of Chopin and Wagner into *The Awakening*, demonstrating their effect on Edna at the hands of Mlle. Reisz, Chopin allowed herself the freedom to explore the difficulties faced by a heroine caught between the Dionysian and Apollonian forces of her existence and also to explore the prevalent scientific and psychological theories espoused by her coterie.

Edna Pontellier may be seen as a woman caught between centuries. Pulled by the strong romantic stereotypes of forbidden passion, with the tempestuous musician figure at the center of her fantasies, Edna is yet scrutinized scientifically by Chopin, who lets us examine her behavior while allowing us only partial glimpses into her motivations. She is a woman struggling to be modern, held back by outmoded notions of romantic love and fulfillment. Caught between the physicianly but useless "wisdom" of Dr. Mandelet, who considers "most women to be moody and

whimsical," and the sorceress Mlle. Reisz, who violates Edna's very soul
with her musical machinations, Edna is imprisoned by the inflexible polar
antagonisms of her confusing options.

If Edna were a different person genetically, Chopin hints, her life might
have been spared. But Edna is especially sensitive—to light, to sound.
Thus Chopin introduces a naturalistic, physiological, predetermined aspect
to Edna's fate. Edna suffers from an unnamed malady that throws her into
fits of despondency. She needs the sun; she becomes depressed on cloudy,
dark days; she is highly susceptible to changes in the weather and the
effects of passionate music.

Edna's search for spiritual fulfillment finds its greatest solace in the
haunting sounds of a southern dreamscape: "the hooting of an old owl in
the top of a water-oak, and the everlasting voice of the sea, which broke
like a mournful lullaby upon the night" (*KCA*, 8). This longing is artifi-
cially satisfied by the music of Reisz, who beguiles Edna into believing
that she can dwell forever in its ethereal, passionate realm. Edna becomes
the sensitive instrument upon which Reisz works her magic. With her
small wizened face and eyes that glow, Reisz is decidedly demonic. She
seems to read Edna's thoughts or feelings, and as Edna listens to Reisz
play, she is overcome with passions of solitude, hope, longing, and despair, passions that lash and sway her soul just "as the waves daily beat
upon her splendid body" (*KCA*, 27).

Although Edna is obviously overcome by the music, we are forced to
question the viability of Reisz's genius. Is it Reisz's music or Edna's sensitivity that creates the emotion? Or does the music itself take over? And
if so, are Edna's feelings spiritual or physical? If Chopin wished to dramatize the struggle between Dionysian and Apollonian forces, she could not
have chosen a more intellectually provocative battleground. Listening to a
certain piece of music, Edna creates pictures in her mind as a visual ac-
companiment. Her body is not involved, only her intellect, her imagination. When Reisz begins to play Chopin, however, Edna's body is possessed; she trembles and weeps uncontrollably.

Edna's lack of control over her emotions is an inherent weakness. As
Chopin illustrates, she has never learned to withhold her feelings and thus
subjects herself to a dangerous vulnerability. Edna presses the hand of the
pianist convulsively; Reisz merely pats her on the shoulder with a few gruff

words. There is a grim lesson to be learned in Reisz. She avoids the water, some say because of that natural aversion for water sometimes believed to accompany the artistic temperament. She lives meagerly in a small dingy apartment. She has never been touched by passion, and she feels no remorse in evoking the passions of others, in binding Edna to her, enslaving her, we might almost say, through her music.

The images of the parrot and the mockingbird in the opening of Chopin's novel become more ominous as Reisz's hold on Edna tightens. Through witchery, she would prompt Edna to the move that brings her to the "pigeon house" where, like a bird in a domestic cage, Edna suffers from unbearable depression. The evening of her grand dinner party had been filled with wine, song, poetry, mandolins. "But as she sat there amid her guests, she felt the old ennui overtaking her, the hopelessness which so often assailed her, which came upon her like an obsession, like something extraneous, independent of volition. It was something which announced itself; a chill breath that seemed to issue from some vast cavern wherein discords wailed" (*KCA*, 88). If one listens carefully enough to this passage, its evocations are multiple: Negro blues or soul-wrenching jazz instrumentals, the imagined singing of desolate Sirens. It is hauntingly reminiscent of an underworld of agony and despair. Reisz becomes uncharacteristically intoxicated at Edna's dinner party, making a fool of herself and diminishing her image as the supposed artist who "dares and defies."

At Grand Isle, Reisz constantly greets Edna by creeping up behind her, touching her on the shoulder, and interrogating her with probing personal questions. As though in a spell, Edna passively responds to Reisz's probing until she recognizes something evil in Reisz's speech or manner, at which point, seeming to awaken from a dream, Edna looks down at her companion wondering how she could have listened to her venom for so long. She escapes Reisz by plunging into the sea. "She had not intended to go into the water; but she donned her bathing suit, and left Mademoiselle alone, seated under the shade of the children's tent. . . . She remained a long time in the water, half hoping that Mademoiselle Reisz would not wait for her" (*KCA*, 49). "But Mademoiselle waited," we are told. During the walk back, she raves about Edna's appearance in her bathing suit and encourages her to come visit her when they return to New Orleans.

Even though she is not sure that she likes Mlle. Reisz, Edna seeks her out in the city. As Edna had confessed to Robert after hearing Reisz play that fatal evening, " 'I wonder if I shall ever be stirred again as Mademoiselle Reisz's playing moved me tonight. I wonder if any night on earth will ever again be like this one. It is like a night in a dream' " (*KCA,* 30).

With each visit to Reisz's apartment, we notice a change in Edna. At her first, "the little musician laughed all over when she saw Edna." She takes Edna's hand "between her strong wiry fingers, holding it loosely without warmth, executing a sort of double theme upon the back and palm" (*KCA,* 62). In this first visit, Reisz aggressively manipulates Edna, withholding a letter from Robert Lebrun until she has Edna under her influence. Quoting from the letter, Reisz recalls Robert's words: " 'If Mrs. Pontellier should call upon you, play for her that impromptu of Chopin's, my favorite. I heard it here a day or two ago, but not as you play it. I should like to know how it affects her' " (*KCA,* 63). Reisz produces the letter only after Edna begs to hear the impromptu. As Edna reads the letter, Reisz begins to play a soft interlude, an improvisation, her body settling into ungraceful curves and angles that give it an appearance of deformity. Reisz's body is possessed by a grotesque will (ugly, demonic) that overrides any concern for Edna's well-being. Gradually and imperceptibly, the interlude melts into the soft opening minor chords of the Chopin impromptu. At the end of this session, Reisz picks up the letter, crumpled and damp with Edna's tears. She smoothes the letter out, restores it to the envelope, and replaces it in her table drawer.

Shortly thereafter, Mr. Pontellier consults Dr. Mandelet about Edna's behavior. " 'Has she,' asked the Doctor, with a smile, 'has she been associating of late with a circle of pseudo-intellectual women—super-spiritual superior beings? My wife has been telling me about them.' . . . 'That's the trouble,' broke in Mr. Pontellier, 'she hasn't been associating with any one. She has abandoned her Tuesdays at home, has thrown over all her acquaintances, and goes tramping about by herself, moping in the street cars, getting in after dark. I tell you she's peculiar. I don't like it; I feel a little worried over it' " (*KCA,* 65–66).

However, Edna's determination to perfect her artistry during this period of delicious solitude is weakened by some deep absence or loss in her life that overcomes her. Only Reisz's music has the power to free her soul.

After a disappointing evening with friends, Edna returns home to prepare a solitary feast. In the preparation of this repast, Edna begins to take on the witchlike characteristics of Reisz, as though she were indeed possessed. "She rummaged in the larder and brought forth a slice of 'Gruyere' and some crackers. She opened a bottle of beer which she found in the icebox. Edna felt extremely restless and excited. She vacantly hummed a fantastic tune as she poked at the wood embers on the hearth and munched a cracker" (*KCA,* 75). That evening, Edna dreams of Mr. Highcamp "playing the piano at the entrance of a music store on Canal Street" while his wife says to Alcee Arobin as they board an Esplanade streetcar: " 'What a pity so much talent has been neglected!' " (*KCA,* 75).

During Edna's second visit, Reisz gives her a letter from Robert that she has secreted under a scowling bust of Beethoven. This time, Edna does not begin at once to read Robert's letter; she listens first to Reisz's music. "She sat holding the letter in her hand, while the music penetrated her whole being like an effulgence, warming and brightening the dark places of her soul. It prepared her for joy and exultation" (*KCA,* 80). In this intense encounter, Edna seems to get the better of Reisz, however. Her love for Robert is too strong a spell even for the witchery of Reisz. " 'If I were young and in love with a man,' " says Reisz, turning on the stool and pressing her wiry hands between her knees as she looks down at Edna on the floor holding the letter, " 'it seems to me he would have to be some *grand esprit,* a man with lofty aims and ability to reach them; one who stood high enough to attract the notice of this fellow-men. It seems to me if I were young and in love I should never deem a man of ordinary caliber worthy of my devotion' " (*KCA,* 81). " 'Now it is you who are telling lies and seeking to deceive me,' " Edna rejoins. " 'Or else you have never been in love and know nothing about it. Why,' she continues, clasping her knees and looking up into Reisz's twisted face, 'do you suppose a woman knows why she loves? Does she select?' " (*KCA,* 81).

Edna's reunion with Robert, as might be expected, takes place in Reisz's apartment. By this point, Edna has begun to pluck at the piano keys as if to summon up on her own the magic that had first inspired her. "Edna seated herself at the piano, and softly picked out with one hand the bars of a piece of music which lay open before her. A half hour went by. There was the occasional sound of people going and coming in the lower hall. She was growing interested in her occupation of picking out the aria, when there was a second rap at the door" (*KCA,* 96). One glance from Robert, however, dispels the enchantment of music. "She found in his eyes, when he looked at her for one silent moment, the same tender caress, with an added warmth and entreaty which had not been there before—the same glance which had penetrated to the sleeping places of her soul and awakened them" (*KCA,* 97).

So much has transpired in Edna's life since Robert's departure, so fatal has Reisz's touch been to her spirit, however, that a life with Robert is now impossible. As Edna witnesses the torture of Ratignolle's childbirth, the awakening alluded to might not only inform the title of Chopin's work (which she agreed to change from *A Solitary Soul*) but also signify Edna's final realization that nothing, not even Robert, can fulfill the longing of *her* soul. "There was no one thing in the world that she desired. There was no human being whom she wanted near her except Robert, and she even realized that the day would come when he, too, and the thought of him would melt out of her existence, leaving her alone" (*KCA,* 113). Edna swims away to solace, away from the painful passions that had enslaved her, even those inspired by Reisz's music. "She thought of Leonce and the children. They were a part of her life. But they need not have thought that they could possess her, body and soul" (*KCA,* 114). The final images attending Edna's drowning, especially that of the chained dog, offer an ironic contrast to her will to freedom.

Behind the enslavement of Edna in a world she did not make and from which she was powerless to escape, lies the darker world of slavery in the South, a fact often overlooked in interpretations of Chopin's novel. The enslavement by desire is reinforced by the lingering traces of Louisiana's slave culture and rigid caste system from which there was no escape. Walter Benn Michaels, however, calls to our attention the fact that at least in the case of one of Chopin's predecessors, Harriet Beecher Stowe, the depiction of slavery was closely tied to the overarching troublesome mercantile ethos that controlled American life. "What slavery proved to Stowe was that even the possession of one's own body could not be guaranteed against capitalistic appropriation." [12] Simon Legree symbolizes a grim

12. Walter Benn Michaels, "Romance and Real Estate," in *The American Renaissance Reconsidered,* ed. Walter Benn Michaels and Donald E. Pease (Baltimore, 1985), 176.

truth only thinly disguised by the charm of the Cane River region, with its sprawling magnificent plantations. No doubt Chopin's many images of encagement and bondage derive an intensified ominous quality from their association with the apparently genteel, gracious life of Louisiana's Creoles.

In contrast to the caged birds, Edna at the conclusion of the novel feels totally free, totally self-possessed. Ironically, however, she is totally circumscribed, totally self-deluded. Edna, like an obedient somnambulent child, swims to her death, another statistic in a long list of American protagonists done in by the promise of paradise. To quote Leo Marx, "In the end the American hero is either dead or totally alienated from society, alone and powerless, like the evicted shepherd of Virgil's ecloque. And if, at the same time, he pays a tribute to the image of a green landscape, it is likely to be ironic and bitter. The resolutions of our pastoral fables are unsatisfactory because the old symbol of reconciliation is obsolete." [13] Chopin continues the tradition set by her male counterparts. Without parroting or mocking, she sings in her own voice in a style that gives the victory ultimately to art itself.

Edna—like that equally ephemeral American figure Billy Budd, who in death "ascended; and, ascending took the full rose of the dawn"—has been appropriated in the service of art. As R. W. B. Lewis asserts, "Billy's death transforms the sailors' mutinous anger into acceptance. . . . For them, Billy is the subject of song and fable thereafter." No doubt Melville's observation at the conclusion of Billy's story has applications for Chopin's portrait of Edna: "The symmetry of form attainable in pure fiction cannot so readily be achieved in a narration essentially having less to do with fable than with fact. Truth uncompromisingly told will always have its ragged edges; hence the conclusion of such a narration is apt to be less finished than an architectural finial." Like the Siren of old, Kate Chopin's music tricks us into believing—as long as we are under its spell—that Edna triumphs precisely at the moment she forfeits her own life. However, in the words of Melville's Captain Vere, who muses on Billy's catastrophe, " 'With mankind . . . forms, are everything; and that is the import couched

13. Leo Marx, *The Machine in the Garden: Technology and the Pastoral Ideal in America* (Oxford, Eng., 1964), 364.

in the story of Orpheus with his lyre spellbinding the wild denizens of the wood.' " [14] Edna dies because she fails to comprehend this wisdom. In life, the successful artist, with "measured forms," insists on the full possession of a voice, a self, and a life of her own. She lives to swim another day.

14. Herman Melville, *Billy Budd, Sailor,* in *The Norton Anthology of American Literature* (2nd ed.; New York, 1986), 1045, 1047–48; R. W. B. Lewis, *The American Adam: Innocence, Tragedy and Tradition in the Nineteenth Century* (Chicago, 1955), 151.

V   *The Lesser-Known Fiction*

Chopin's Movement Toward Universal Myth

SARA DESAUSSURE DAVIS

The recent appearance of *A Vocation and a Voice* provides the collection of stories, which was never published in Chopin's lifetime, the same physical wholeness, the same published reality, as *Bayou Folk* and *A Night in Acadie*.[1] Reading *Vocation* as a whole provides a new sense of the direction of Chopin's writing style as she began to shift from Bayou myth toward a more universal one. The *Vocation* collection was deliberately experimental and seems at first miscellaneous in selection, unresolved in its complexities, that is, in its pointed differences from Chopin's earlier two volumes of short fiction. From 1893 to 1900, *Vocation* became Chopin's repository of troublesome pieces, the majority difficult to place, five not accepted anywhere during her lifetime, others published in newspapers (a last resort), in a short-lived magazine, or in *Vogue,* which gave her latitude but lacked a clear sense of its own fledgling critical tastes. The major national magazines that rejected individual stories that would later compose the *Vocation* manuscript, as well as the publishers who successively rejected the *Vocation* collection, no doubt anticipated something of the censure that erupted after *The Awakening.*

They would have been right too because these stories contain the novel's controversial subjects, its themes, symbols, psychological realities, particularly the new areas of women's experience (new, that is, to a fictional portrayal of them). It seems unlikely that Chopin could have written *The Awakening* without first having written the majority of the *Vocation* stories. Even the language of the title, a *vocation* and a *voice,* declares the coming artistic triumph of *The Awakening.* Chopin did not consider the fictional pieces a volume until 1896 when she had written the title story, "A Vocation and a Voice," though subsequently she would add eight more stories. By having a young male protagonist in the title piece, she deliber-

1. Emily Toth, ed., *A Vocation and a Voice,* (New York, 1991). Since I did not have this edition as I wrote the essay, my references are to Seyersted's *CW*.

ately disguises her investment in the female point of view that dominates both the collection and the novel.

As the outrage that followed publication of *The Awakening* and the canonization of it that occurred in our generation equally attest, Chopin captured a culturally, socially, and politically important moment for American men and women. Although the social context is Victorian, New Orleansian, and upper middle class, the viewpoint definitely female, the realistic qualities of the novel become subsumed in the lyrical writing, so that Chopin's inherent feminism appears not as tract or treatise but as myth. Sandra Gilbert's tour de force introduction to the Penguin edition of *The Awakening* analyzes the myth of Aphrodite underlying the story of Edna and the feminist desires of Chopin.[2] Gilbert shows that myth provides freedom from nineteenth-century restrictions, artificialities, pretenses; in short, provides a fantasy world where characters can be in touch with the vital forces of nature and a different vision of society. In the two short-story collections that made her literary reputation prior to *The Awakening,* Chopin created an Acadian and Bayou myth that served the same function as the Greek. In Acadia she could explore freely the French, black, and Spanish people living out of the mainstream of much American life. She could reveal, almost with impunity, aspects of human nature that would not be acceptable if the setting and people were more recognizably mainstream, urban, middle class, and Anglo-Saxon. What distinguishes *Vocation* is that the central Louisiana "mythical" grounding largely disappears, and dreams, in a myriad forms, take its place, providing access to the larger mythic world.

More precisely, dreams in the world of *Vocation* mean altered states of consciousness in which a character transcends mundane reality and enters a fantasy, an illusion, a dream, a vision, to return with different options, a changed perspective. In *Vocation* the enabling mechanism or inducement to an altered state might be one or more of several change agents: shocking news, the death of the husband in "Story of an Hour"; a wife's affair, "Her Letters"; the recovery of sight, "The Recovery"; sexual passion, "A Vocation and a Voice," "The Falling in Love of Fedora," and others; music, "A Vocation and a Voice," and "A Morning Walk"; hypnotism, "A

2. Sandra M. Gilbert, ed., *"The Awakening" and Selected Stories* (New York, 1984).

Mental Suggestion"; idleness accompanied by fatigue or world-weariness, "An Idle Fellow" and "The Night Came Slowly"; or drugs, "An Egyptian Cigarette."

This list does not exhaust the twenty-one stories of *A Vocation and a Voice,* but it does indicate a pervasiveness in the collection. Two patterns emerge, both relevant to *The Awakening:* something so forceful and compelling that it wrenches one from daily habit and quotidian life or something so soothing, it relaxes, then beguiles one out of the clutches of the mundane. The major example of the first pattern from *The Awakening* occurs at the pivotal childbirth scene followed by Robert's abandonment, culminating in Edna's vision in the Gulf. The major example of the second pattern is when Edna "that summer at Grand Isle . . . began to loosen a little the mantle of reserve that had always enveloped her" (*KCA,* 15). She says to Mme. Ratignolle, " 'Sometimes I feel this summer as if I were walking through the green meadow again; idly, aimlessly unthinking and unguided' " (*KCA,* 18).

In these altered states, generated by a force over which the character exercises little or no control, the character moves out of the ordinary world, out of the historical moment, and into a mythic world within reach of wisdom. Often the resultant vision or dream state frightens and appalls, as it does the narrator of "An Egyptian Cigarette." She writhes in burning sands, tortured in her hallucinogen-induced dream-vision by the contemptuous cruelty of her lover's desertion: "The weight of centuries seemed to suffocate my soul that struggled to escape, to free itself and breathe. I had tasted the depths of human despair." Similarly, for Edna "there were days . . . when it did not seem worth while to be glad or sorry, to be alive or dead; when life appeared to her like a grotesque pandemonium and humanity like worms struggling blindly toward inevitable annihilation. She could not work on such a day, nor weave fancies to stir her pulses and warm her blood" (*KCA,* 58).

In *The Awakening* the aura of Louisiana settings and characters no longer offers the reader the protection granted by Bayou myth in *Bayou Folk* and *A Night in Acadie* because Chopin portrays an urbane social class recognizable to her readers as belonging to a social reality uncomfortably closer to their own than that of Bayou folk. She worked her way toward this stance in the *Vocation* stories composed prior to the novel.

"An Egyptian Cigarette" was the last fictional piece Chopin wrote before beginning *The Awakening*. The story resembles the longer work in both tone and technique (not to mention its similar use of the bird, serpent, and water symbolism) and, most importantly, embodies a perceptible shift in Chopin's writing. In fact, Chopin accomplishes the shift in most of the *Vocation* stories, merely extending it in *The Awakening*. Chopin changes her readers' relation to her fictional material by removing the distancing Bayou myth. Instead, her writing in *Vocation* and *The Awakening* becomes an intense fusion of realistic historical time with a mythopoetic style, so that reality becomes both knowable and bearable, at least for those characters (and readers) prepared to accept it. Chopin transfigures disturbing actualities of nineteenth-century life into more broadly universal characteristics. The transcendence of time allowed by myth generates a space or vision that alters reality, or one's perception of it.

The structure of "An Egyptian Cigarette" suggests how this works. A recognizably middle-class reality frames the central story of smoking a hashish cigarette. Pointedly, an architect provides the female narrator with the cigarettes from his travels to the Orient. An architect is a maker of physical reality, an artist, in some sense also a designer of the future. In these ways his occupation approximates Chopin's as both realistic writer and purveyor of mythic visions.

The Egyptian cigarette induces a transcendent state that lasts according to the clock merely fifteen minutes but takes the narrator to a mythic underworld where she experiences excruciating psychic despair and where time is eternal. The narrator's horrific journey ends as the drug loosens its hold, whereupon she destroys the remainder of the cigarettes, aware of the loss of "other visions . . . what might I not find in their mystic fumes? Perhaps a vision of celestial peace; a dream of hopes fulfilled; a taste of rapture, such as had not entered into my mind to conceive" (*CW*, 573). She then receives a ritualistic coffee from the architect, signaling her return to reality and real time.

The compelling social facts underlying this brief tale point to the ways they also underlie the lyricism of *The Awakening*. The "Egyptian" of the title euphemistically and exotically denies a not uncommon *American* phenomenon of Chopin's day. Nineteenth-century American distilleries often added opium derivatives to their products to induce addiction and additional sales. The products included soda-fountain drinks, tonics of all sorts, whiskies, and cigarettes.[3] In *The Awakening* M. Ratignolle "advised a tonic" for Edna when he notices her changed appearance since her return from Grand Isle (*KCA*, 56). This detail passes modern readers almost unnoticed, except for the cumulative effect of drug references and metaphor in the novel. In fact, opophagia, or opium eating, was a major if untalked-about medical and social problem in Chopin's day. Chopin, in her own way, talks about it. The fact that it was a widespread middle-class phenomenon would have made Chopin aware of it, even if her friend, the physician and obstetrician Dr. Frederick Kolbenheyer, did not. (John Haller and Robin Haller note that opium products were often prescribed for "female ailments.") Among drug addicts in nineteenth-century America, women outnumbered men three to one. Not counting prostitutes, the ratio was two to one. The most typical users were affluent middle-class women.[4] Among contemporary literary examples, one need only remember Edith Wharton's heroine Lily Bart in her descent from upper- to lower-class existence and her death by chloral.

One medical history states, "The Victorian age . . . not only witnessed the culmination of the opium trade with China, but also marked the development of morphia and a long list of opium alkaloids." Opium and its derivatives were astonishingly available to purchasers, who became easily addicted. Commenting on the high percentage of women addicts, Haller and Haller quote one contemporary physician who said the cause of their addiction was "their lives—doomed, often to a life of disappointment, and, it may be, of physical and mental inaction."[5] Other doctors speculated that female drug dependency "stemmed from women's refusal to maintain their natural position within the proper limits of the home circle." Leonce Pontellier says much the same thing.

Before looking at Chopin's poetic transformation of this prevalent social reality into artistic form in *The Awakening,* I would argue that the recurrence of sleep, night, and death as a mythic triad among the *Vocation* stories suggests Chopin's knowledge that these ancient Greek deities—

3. John S. Haller, Jr., and Robin M. Haller, *The Physician and Sexuality in Victorian America* (Urbana, 1974), 276.

4. *Ibid.,* 174, 281, 175.

5. *Ibid.,* 279.

Hypnos, Nyx, and Thanatos—all wore wreaths of poppy, the source of opium and its derivatives.[6] "A Mental Suggestion," written the year before "An Egyptian Cigarette," explores the frontiers of Hypnos, of hypnotism, its induced trances, its altered realities, especially as those affect sex and marriage.

Although in *The Awakening* Chopin uses drug terms and the psychology of addiction with clinical precision, she presents nothing resembling the pathology of Fanny's alcoholism in *At Fault*. Rather, she transforms the terminology of addiction into poetic metaphor, evoking a universal condition even as it draws on specific historical realities of women's lives in the late nineteenth century.

Readers have long recognized the ways Grand Isle's lush tropical setting and the incantatory power of the Gulf lull Edna's Protestant sensibilities so that she can "'awaken . . . out of a life-long stupid dream,'" as she says to Robert. But the more crucial drug passage concerns Alcee Arobin, whose presence during Robert's absence gradually becomes a *habit* in her life. Chopin tellingly calls Alcee's effect upon Edna "*narcotic*," something that induces sleep and with prolonged use becomes addictive: "She lit a candle and went up to her room. Alcee Arobin was absolutely nothing to her. Yet his presence, his manners, the warmth of his glances, and above all the touch of his lips upon her hand had acted like a narcotic upon her. She slept a languorous sleep, interwoven with vanishing dreams" (*KCA*, 77). Narcotics characteristically induce a dreamlike state or stupor. Alcee, like a drug, is not so important in himself as in the state he produces: He is "absolutely nothing to her," for "'Today it is Arobin; tomorrow it will be some one else'" (*KCA*, 113). The addiction matters, the drug not at all. Alcee's effect upon Edna, we are repeatedly told, is entirely physical— "it was not the kiss of love"—and thus Alcee becomes the artificial substitute for the love and passion she cannot have with Robert. Alcee eases, one might say numbs, Edna's pain and disquietude.

The drug references unite Edna's experience with Alcee to the pivotal scene of Adele's delivery. There, chloroform disguises the sensations of birth pangs much as sexual pleasure with Alcee addictively numbs life's pains. With Adele, Edna recalls one of her own accouchements, thus, "an

6. *Ibid.*, 175.

ecstasy of pain, the heavy odor of chloroform, a stupor which had deadened sensation" (*KCA*, 108–109). Note the order of the phrases here, chloroform mediating between "ecstasy of pain" and "a stupor." At both poles of women's sexual experience, as lover or mother, Edna finds intense physical experience paradoxically accompanied by the means of deadening it to insensitivity. Like her relationship with Alcee, however, Adele's delivery produces both new life out of darkness and insight out of pain.

Earlier Edna wanted life's *delirium* in contrast to the Ratignolles' domestic harmony. The medical meaning of *delirium* is "mental confusion, clouded consciousness resulting from high fever, shock, or intoxication characterized by tremors, hallucinations, delusions, and incoherence." This definition suits as well the condition of the narrator in "The Egyptian Cigarette" when she experiences the hallucinatory trance. To Edna, the fevered pitch, the ecstasy of such a condition, seems clearly preferable to the insensate complacency of the Ratignolles (he is, significantly, a pharmacist), yet a delirium is after all confused, uncontrolled, trancelike, a kind of drugged state.

In her confusion, Edna often fluctuates radically, randomly, between the "old ennui" and heightened states of pleasure or excitement. Edna's condition resembles what one nineteenth-century physician had to say of women opium addicts: "Before long, her mind would begin to rise above the paltry things of every-day life, and wander forth in the land of glorious dreams where everything seems to be possible and where [she was] always on the eve of accomplishing some great object." [7]

Pleasurable and dangerous as altered states of being may be, Chopin explores them not only for what they suggest about the desire to escape reality but also because they enable another kind of reality—frontier states of consciousness that provide refuge even as they require exploration before and until social reality can change. In this conjunction between altered states of reality and social reality, Chopin finds nineteenth-century drug addiction a way of expressing the historical reality of women's lives and a means of probing new possibilities for other lives. The sea, both Eros and Thanatos for Edna, beckons with just that seductive, paradoxical promise.

7. J. S. Weatherly, "Increase of the Habit of Opium-Eating," *Transactions*, Medical Society of the State of Alabama (1869), 67, as quoted in Haller and Haller, *Physician and Sexuality*, 281.

All through her work Chopin proclaims her disinterest in the past and her fascination with the present and future. She values myth, accessible through the dream world, not because it returns us to the past but because it removes us from the fixity of the current historical moment and enables a radically different vision of reality.

Reverie, stupor, languor, delirium, dreams, drunkenness, a drugged state—all these images from the novel and from the *Vocation* stories are ways of protecting oneself from the intense pains of nature, society's demands, a lover's failure to provide the real thing. These Edna awakes from, as she puts it to Dr. Mandelet, " 'rather than to remain a dupe to illusions all one's life.' " But they are also the enabling agents of awakening with new insight and vision. If Chopin as artist and woman had responded only to the pain and loss accompanying vision or awakening, she never would have produced the art she did. Unlike Edna, she does not walk into the Gulf. Nor does she blunt the pain. Fortunately, as an artist she dared keep and smoke those dangerous Egyptian cigarettes.

Kate Chopin's "Charlie"

ANNE M. BLYTHE

Kate Chopin's story "Charlie"—written in 1900, the year following the publication of *The Awakening,* but not published until 1969—has been almost completely neglected by critics, and what attention it has received has done it little justice. The longest and one of the strongest and most moving of her stories, "Charlie" has with few exceptions been misread and misunderstood by literary critics since it was first made generally available in Per Seyersted's 1969 edition of Chopin's writings (*CU,* 638–70).

Seyersted began the critical misreading of the story when he dealt with it briefly in his 1969 biography of Chopin. Discussing it in light of Chopin's theme of "female self-assertion," Seyersted says that the author "allows herself to disable a man . . . thus subtly hitting back at the males who labeled her a disgrace and silenced her literary gun because she had represented a woman taking liberties of a man" (*CB,* 183). He is referring to the critical reception of *The Awakening* and the episode in the story where Charlie, the tomboy heroine, practicing her target shooting in the woods with a pistol, accidentally wounds a male stranger in the arm. But the analogy is farfetched. The wound is not only unintentional; it is in his arm, and it is slight—and Charlie is deeply embarrassed. Seyersted unfortunately goes a step further in misreading the story when he suggests a tendency toward incestuous feelings between Charlie and her father. Although he somewhat downplays this accusation by enclosing it within parentheses, he nevertheless puts forth the unhappy idea that a "Freudian would call it [the relationship between Charlie and her father] a fixation and point to the secret outing of the two where they feel 'like a couple of bees in clover' " (*CB,* 183).

This is nonsense. Her father loves Charlie and misses her when she is away. She loves him. There is no hint of anything abnormal or unhealthy in the feelings of either, no suggestion that this healthy father-daughter relationship is in any way delaying or hampering her maturing as a young woman or growing in need and ability to respond to other men.

The great injustice done by this reading lies in the fact that because Seyersted as editor and biographer was the most important Chopin scholar who had yet written about her and his critical judgments were usually carefully weighed and sensible, it was perhaps inevitable that later critics would use this original prurient reading of the text as a springboard for further, if brief, misconstructions and distortions of the story.

One critic, though she asserts that "Charlie" is "probably the only good piece [Chopin] wrote after *The Awakening* debacle," joins Seyersted in his Freudian reading of the story and goes even further, saying that the story "shows a troubled imagination." She believes that Charlie must "become 'masculine' and lose her sensual life, or become 'feminine' and lose her independence; [that] in fact, to have independence a woman *must* become 'male.'" She sees the story as one with a "saddening conclusion." Another critic dismisses it as sentimental and misreads the ending: "Not even Chopin's earliest stories surpass in sentimentality 'Charlie.' In it a girl grows up, falls in love, loses a man to her sister, and dedicates the rest of her life to helping her father." Barbara H. Solomon, in her edition of Chopin, follows and slightly elaborates Seyersted's interpretation.[1]

Such distorted and inaccurate interpretations have succeeded in denying a proper place in American fiction to what may be Kate Chopin's finest characterization of a young woman and one of her finest short stories. I propose that "Charlie" be read as an exceptionally strong and forthright story of the growth into womanhood of a young girl of unusually fine qualities and potential. To read the story in any other light is to ignore too many aspects of it that the author stresses—for example, the happy ending. For at the conclusion, Charlie is preparing to marry a good man, a man who loves her, who is her match in both temperament and physicality. She will marry a man she knows and understands and has grown to love, a man her father knows and respects.

"Charlie" is the story of a seventeen-year-old tomboy, Charlotte Laborde, the second of seven daughters, who runs free and wild on the family's Louisiana plantation. Charlie (as nearly everyone calls her) is intelligent

---

1. Anne Goodwyn Jones, *Tomorrow Is Another Day* (Baton Rouge, 1981), 139, 144; Peggy Skaggs, *Kate Chopin* (Boston, 1985), 63–64; Barbara H. Solomon, *The Awakening and Selected Stories of Kate Chopin* (New York, 1976).

and imaginative, physical and courageous, loved but not always approved of by the people who live in that self-contained world. She is especially close to her father, a widower, and is worshiped by her younger sisters (her older sister, Julia, is too ladylike to approve of her entirely). She is constantly getting into and out of scrapes, and her father, her sisters, her aunts, and her teacher are all worried that this daring, imaginative, impetuous young girl is going to have a difficult time in the adult world unless her boundless energy can be channeled into activities more conventional than racing along the levee and around the plantation on horseback and on a bicycle—a nice combination that Chopin uses to show that Charlie can be equally at home in a changing modern world and an older traditional and rural one.

When we meet her first, she is hot, mad, and in trouble. Our first impression is the one shared by her sisters in the schoolroom. Distracted from their studies by a figure "galloping along the green levee summit on a big black horse, as if pursued by demons," they then identify by "a clatter of hoofs upon the ground below" and a voice "pitched rather high" berating a boy for not currying Tim, her horse, their tardy and wayward sister's approach (*CW*, 639). When she finally enters the classroom, she is the picture of vigor and health, "robust and pretty well grown for her age" (*CW*, 639), but at this moment red-faced and perspiring. Chopin's precise phrase, "pretty well grown for her age," is aptly descriptive of her not-quite womanhood. Charlie is dressed in a costume of her own devising, a sort of "divided skirt," a practical but not unfeminine garment she has shaped to suit the life of an active and energetic tomboy whose physical development is just beginning to belie her boyish ways.

Although Charlie hates the cramped artificiality of the plantation schoolroom and the rigid controls imposed upon her freedom by Miss Melvern, the governess, she is instinctively drawn to certain of the arts as well as the natural world outdoors. Chopin tells us that "Charlie had a way, when strongly moved, of expressing herself in verse" (*CW*, 641). Banished from the schoolroom, she sits on the porch at the back of the house writing a poem about Miss Melvern but letting herself be distracted by all the activity of the plantation yard. The fat Negro cook affectionately abuses her son who is sharpening the ax, and one of the little "Cadian" girls from down the lane comes up with chickens to sell. Charlie at first watches the life around her, still writing the poem, then, because it is impossible not to, lays it aside and joins them. Her poetic impulse is genuine but untrained, undisciplined. Along with her natural exuberance, there are traces of irresponsibility. Charlie is honest, headstrong, and brave, but still capable of being thoughtless.

Her poems are not the only sign of her creative imagination. She next pays a visit to the Bichou family's cabin where she spins a fantastic impromptu tale about tigers and bears and her magic ring. The Bichou children are spellbound. "They had a way of believing everything she said—which was a powerful temptation that many a sterner spirit would have found difficult to resist" (*CW,* 645–46). When she starts back home through the woods, Ma'am Bichou, worried about "that Charlie," sends her young son Xenophore with her to see that she makes it home safely. The two sit down to rest beside a fallen tree, and Charlie confides in her young friend: " 'I tell you what it is, Xenophore, usually, when I come in the woods, after slaying a panther or so, I sit down and write a poem or two. . . . There are lots of things troubling me, and nothing comforts me like that' " (*CW,* 646–47). Charlie is acknowledging the changes that are beginning to stir within her, mysteriously to her mind, even before her encounter with Firman Walton.

This meeting takes place after she has revealed her deepest secret to the little boy, her possession of a pistol. " 'I think I'll practice my shooting; I'm getting a little rusty; only hit nine alligators out of ten last week' " (*CW,* 647). A stray shot hits Walton, who is taking a short cut through the woods on the way to pay a business call upon Charlie's father. Mistaking her for a boy at first, he speaks angrily to her: " 'You young scamp! I'll thrash the life out of you.' " But on discovering that she is a girl, he is apologetic.

Walton is encouraged to remain a few days with the family to recover from his wound, and he does so quite cheerfully. Indeed he feels that he has suddenly found himself in heaven among seven beautiful maidens. One evening when all her sisters have gone off for their dancing lessons, Charlie (who has stayed at home because she doesn't *like* dancing lessons) is brooding on the porch steps when Walton joins her. Sitting down beside her, he earnestly begins to say again how sorry he is about the accident. Knowing perfectly well that the shooting was her fault, not his, genuinely puzzled and piqued by his insistence, she speaks somewhat condescendingly to him and brushes him off. At that moment, young Xenophore slips quietly up the steps and within Walton's hearing delivers a message to Charlie from Gus Bradley, her longtime companion around the plantation.

Although she does not articulate her feelings, a pleasurable confusion about them is obviously stirring within her. The two men paying their respects could not be more different: Firman Walton is a slick city sophisticate Charlie knows she does not understand; Gus Bradley is a man she understands perfectly. Walton is described as "good looking, intelligent looking" (*CW,* 650). In contrast, Bradley is described as a shy man with a smooth face that "looked as if it belonged to a far earlier period of society and had no connection with the fevered and modern present day" (*CW,* 654). He is described in terms of Charlie's familiar world, for he is a big man and "in the saddle or out in the road or the fields he had a fine, free carriage" (*CW,* 654). With new awarenesses beginning to form in her mind, Charlie lingers on the porch with Walton until dusk when "the moon was already shining in the river and breaking with a pale glow through the magnolia leaves" (*CW,* 654). When her sisters return from their dancing lessons, Charlie slips upstairs with them, "bent upon making a bit of toilet for the evening" (*CW,* 652).

The accidental shooting of Walton has convinced everyone, including Charlie, that it is time to send her to boarding school in New Orleans. This idea, which has always been abhorrent to her, she is "exceedingly astonished" to discover is now "not at all distasteful"; she finds herself marveling at the mystery (*CW,* 654). This significant change in her character, we come to see, is probably due to her feeling attracted to Walton, apparently the first time she had felt such an emotion. She is also "secretly in hopes" (*CW,* 652) that her sister Amanda will lend her a dress to wear that first evening when her father orders her out of her "trouserlets." When Gus is surprised and flustered at seeing her in a dress with "frills and furbelows," Charlie replies impatiently: " 'Oh, well, I have to begin some time' " (*CW,* 655). Secretly she would like this big change, from divided skirt to feminine dress, to pass by unnoticed. However, once committed to a course of action, her instinct is to plunge forward headlong and unhesitating. And she handles this stepping into the feminine world of lace, ruffles, sailor hats, and baubles characteristically—with unbridled enthusiasm.

Now, thrust brand-new and untried into rich city life, Charlie stuns everyone in charge of her with a "violent" acceptance of her change in lifestyle. She also surprises with her extravagance. The only examples of womanhood she has had in her family are sorely lacking in both passion and creativity; in other words, she has no idea what it means to be a grown-up woman except what she has seen in her older sister, whatever she recalls of her mother (who died when she was eleven) and her aunts. She is doggedly determined to become "a fascinating young lady" (*CW*, 657), but she knows instinctively that she is out of place in this artificial world. She senses more and more intensely her awkwardnesses and tries with the aid of creams and curling irons and hat pins to conform to that world's standard of beauty. It is worth noting at this point too that during those two weeks of preschool "preparation" and initiation, Charlie finds herself frequently in the company of Firman Walton, who, although he distinctly prefers the company of the more beautiful and polished Julia, does not mind toying with the wild heart of her younger sister.

An episode that takes place soon after she enters the school and that warrants close and careful examination is the greatly misunderstood scene of Mr. Laborde's visit. The decision to send her to the boarding school was not an easy one for her father. All his daughters are described as individuals—each has been encouraged to grow according to her natural bent—but Charlie has a more restless spirit than the others. We must remember too that of all the daughters, Charlie is the one who knows best the working world of her father's plantation. That Mr. Laborde loves this wayward daughter is obvious. That he enjoys her company especially because she can ride, shoot, and fish better than the other girls is also apparent. And that he misses her sorely when she must be sent off to school cannot be doubted. But he believes that Charlie must be tamed, that she must learn for the sake of her own happiness to conform to the polite ways of the civilized world.

When he comes to visit her, he rejoices in seeing her, and she in him; he delights in discovering how well she has made the adjustment. He encourages what he assumes is her natural (but hitherto dormant) feminine frivolity, and they have a fine afternoon together. To play the role of a stern disciplinarian is not something that comes easily to Mr. Laborde, and now that he can enjoy his daughter's company without constant worry, he does so "like a school boy on a holiday" (*CW*, 661).

But to read this scene as incestuous is absurd. It is quite likely that if Mr. Laborde was separated for several months from his six-year-old twins, with whom he is equally affectionate—they count the gray hairs on his temples "perched on either arm of his chair" (*CW,* 644)—he would be "hungry" for them too. But the key to their relationship in this scene is the conversation between Charlie and her father at the lake café where they enjoy their second breakfast of the day, blissfully unaware of the rest of the world. Charlie proudly holds out her hand (newly creamed) for him to inspect. " 'What do you think of that, dad?' " she asks him. He looks carefully, examining the ring she always wears, then says, " 'No stones missing, are there?' " How well he knows his daughter! When she tells him with some exasperation to inspect the whiteness of her hand, and to compare it with her sister Julia's, he immediately understands the importance of her question. She is asking him for a confirmation of her femininity. Having long been aware (and disdainful of the fact) that Julia's hands were soft and white whereas hers were tanned and strong, she now feels pride that she has accomplished so successfully one of the more considered requisites of feminine appearance. Mr. Laborde takes her question seriously and gives a good father's careful answer. " 'I don't want to be hasty,' " he tells her. " 'I'm not too sure that I remember, and I shouldn't like to do Julia's hand an injustice, but my opinion is that yours is whiter' " (*CW,* 662).

This episode carries all the tenderness, gentle humor, and trust that can be asked of a father and a seventeen-year-old daughter, and Chopin accomplishes this with a fleeting moment's conversation. To read this scene as corrupt is an ultimate in critical misreading and falsification, and to use such a misreading to show Chopin as warped and embittered (by her critics!) at this period in her career is to be as false to the writer as to her work.

As Charlie continues to strive to adjust to the new environment of school, friends, dress, habits, and conventions, there is one carryover from the old familiar world. That is her poetry, which continues to be her confidante. It becomes more and more the vehicle for trying to understand her new and confusing emotions.

All of her schoolmates like Charlie enormously, although they don't understand her and are privately shocked at her lack of refinement in certain ways. But they recognize and respond to her generous heart and offer to help her learn the conventional graces. When it comes to light that Charlie is a poet, and a good poet at that, she is universally acclaimed and made to share with her friends the lines she has been writing. She shares her artistry shyly, trying hard "to look indifferent" (*CW,* 659). She shares all of her poems but one. This she had written immediately following the two-week preparation for school, and it is different from the rest of her poetry. It is written "in the smallest possible cramped hand . . . folded over and over and over" (*CW,* 658) until it is tiny enough to fit underneath a picture in her cherished locket. She keeps her love poem to herself.

Charlie is smitten by Firman Walton. And she suffers her first heartache because of his casual, meaningless flirtations. But this experience becomes a vital part of Charlie's realization that she does not belong in Walton's (and her sister Julia's) world of fashioned manners and sophisticated affectations. Indeed her heart recovers much as Walton's arm recovers from the flesh wound. Both wounds are inflicted primarily by accident (although Walton should have been more aware of his effect upon her), and both wounds seem at first to be far more serious than they are.

Then comes the terrible news of her father's near-fatal accident at the plantation. Charlie returns home and remains to help nurse him. While there, she receives the news of Julia's engagement to Walton.

In a period of a few months, Charlie has suffered the disgrace of being banished from the plantation to boarding school, the shock of her father's near-fatal accident, and the humiliation of rejection by a man she believed genuine in his attentions. When she learns of her sister's engagement, she responds with violent passion. In "a voice hideous with anger" she denounces her sister in front of the younger sisters, resumes her trouserlets, mounts her horse, and takes off blindly and furiously on a "mad ride" (*CW,* 666–67). We know, as Charlie knows, that she is purging her mind, her body, and her heart of what is not good and natural for her. And in that ride she throws off "the savage impulse" that caused her outburst against Julia. "Shame and regret had followed and now she was steeped in humiliation such as she had never felt before." She apologizes to her sisters for her words and behavior. The result of this sequence of emotions— rejection, bitterness, and rage, ending in humiliation and purgation—is that the "girlish infatuation which had blinded her was swept away in the torrents of a deeper emotion," leaving her now "a woman" (*CW,* 667).

Charlie, then, does not return to and remain on her father's plantation as a defeated girl (or woman). She does not have to shed her femininity and "become 'masculine' and lose her sensual life" to maintain her independence. On the contrary, she achieves a clearly defined sense of purpose and makes a deep and lasting commitment to a life of usefulness and hard work, a life rich in potential for creativity and emotional growth. As her father slowly recovers, she and Gus naturally begin working together, restoring the plantation gradually to its condition before the accident. They are both physical people, unafraid and unashamed of the dirt, sweat, elements, and creatures of their world, and their work together brings them steadily closer. Gradually they also learn to communicate their feelings and emotions. The conversation between them at the end of the story is full of shyly revealed emotions as they both come to realize how their relationship has changed and grown deeper. She tells him, " 'It seems to me I've always liked you better than any one, and that I'll keep on liking you more and more.' " She then tells him good night and runs "lightly" into the house, leaving him "in an ecstasy in the moonlight" (*CW,* 669).

Why did Chopin not publish so fine a story? The most reasonable answer is that it is a very long story and she may have sent it out to one or more magazines only to have it rejected because of its length. Another possibility is that Chopin had indeed "withdrawn," not from her continuing creative strength as an artist but from the public eye after the critical rejection of *The Awakening.* Perhaps she wrote "Charlie" much as she did "The Storm," which because of its direct sexuality could not have been published in her lifetime, wrote it to complete something for herself alone, for her own satisfaction as a writer.

I believe that Kate Chopin put a great deal of herself into her tomboy creation. But what she did *not* put into the story is fear of failure. No fear or resentment of outside opinion informs this work.

"Charlie" is a rich and rewarding story with an unforgettable heroine. It deserves a high place in American short fiction before World War I.

Insistent Refrains and Self-Discovery: Accompanied Awakenings in Three Stories by Kate Chopin

NANCY S. ELLIS

In *The Awakening*, Mlle. Reisz's piano music triggers Edna Pontellier's first emotional arousing: "The very first chords . . . sent a keen tremor down Mrs. Pontellier's spinal column. It was not the first time she had heard an artist at the piano. Perhaps it was the first time she was ready, perhaps the first time her being was tempered to take an empress of the abiding truth. . . . The very passions themselves were aroused within her soul, swaying it, lashing it, as the waves daily beat upon her splendid body. She trembled, she was choking, and the tears blinded her" (*KCA*, 27). Throughout the novel, Edna continues to be awakened in various ways, one of which is Mlle. Reisz's music. Another is the consciousness of physical touch, which Chopin expresses frequently with hand imagery.

But Edna is not the first of Chopin's characters to be stirred to an emotional awakening by music. In an early story, "With the Violin," she uses the "pleading, chiding, singing" tones of the instrument to rescue a despondent man from suicide. His experience is dramatic, but so are others in the early fiction. The character development on which the author focuses in "After the Winter" and "At Cheniere Caminada" grows from an awakening born of a single distinct musical experience. In both stories the notes of a church organ stimulate in the lives of two men profound emotional changes that most likely would not have occurred otherwise.

The 1896 novel by Harold Frederic, *The Damnation of Theron Ware*, also describes the passionate power of music. Frederic's descriptions are as moving and intense as Chopin's:

> There fell upon this silence—softness so delicate that it came almost like a progression in the hush—the sound of sweet music. . . . Then it rose as by a sweeping curve of beauty, into a firm, calm, severe melody, delicious to the ear, but as cold in the mind's vision as moonlit sculpture. It went on upward with stately collectedness of power, till the atmosphere seemed all

alive with the trembling consciousness of the presence of lofty souls, sternly pure and pitilessly great.

Theron found himself moved as he had never been before. He almost resented the discovery, when it was presented to him by the prosaic, mechanical side of his brain, that he was listening to organ-music, and that it came through the open window from the church close by: He would fain have reclined in his chair and closed his eyes, and saturated himself with the uttermost fulness of the sensation.[1]

Reminiscent of Edna's sessions with Mlle. Reisz, Chapter XIX of *The Damnation* (197–209) is filled with passages descriptive of music, specifically by Frederic Chopin, including the "Berceuse" that Kate Chopin used in "Wiser than a God."

Yet another awakening associated with music dominates Chopin's "A Vocation and a Voice." But this awakening seems to prefigure Edna Pontellier's. Rather than the experience of one moment, music becomes a refrain that continues to stir the boy to an awareness of himself and his world.

"After the Winter," written on December 31, 1891, and published in the New Orleans *Times-Democrat* on April 5, 1896, is such a simple story that the reader can hardly miss Chopin's thematic symbols (*CW,* 1011). Chopin's M. Michel experiences an awakening, a rebirth, on an Easter Sunday and thus right "after the winter." M. Michel has lived a misanthrope's life for the past twenty-five years after returning home from the Civil War and finding his child dead and his wife gone wanton. His bitter withdrawal from society has naturally inspired intriguing, murderous stories about him that fascinate the local children.

Trezinie, the blacksmith's daughter, longs to have wonderful flowers to add to the altar decorations of Easter morning, and her sense of pride compels her to try to outdo the others who have already taken flowers to the church. Chopin creates a vivid awareness of the young girl's spirit and environment by pointing out that the child has tried unsuccessfully to make her charred yard beautiful with colorful flowers. But the resourceful youth is inspired by the idea of gathering wildflowers fresh on Easter morn. Her resourcefulness and determination to work with what she has is reminiscent of Fifine in Chopin's "A Very Fine Fiddle." She, Cami (the cobbler's son),

1. Harold Frederick, *The Damnation of Theron Ware* (1896; rpr. Cambridge, Mass., 1960), 79–80.

and La Fringante (a little Negress) go into the forest early Easter morning to gather fresh wildflowers. When they come upon Michel's crude empty cabin, they examine it with childlike curiosity before they strip the hillside of its flowers.

M. Michel, returning to his cabin, finds that "his woods had been despoiled." He grows angry not because he cares about the flowers but because someone has invaded his privacy: "Why had these people, with whom he had nothing in common, intruded upon his privacy and violated it? What would they not rob him of next?" Because he has recently been to town, he knows that it is Easter and that the flowers are being used "to add to the mummery of the day." In his anger he determines to "go down among those people all gathered together, blacks and whites, and face them for once and for all. He did not know what he would say to them, but it would be defiance—something to voice the hate that oppressed him" (*CW*, 185).

After entering the church and removing his hat as a mulatto tells him to do, he finds that being surrounded by people after so many years of being alone "affected him strangely." Still he resolves to speak out, "just as soon as that clamor overhead" stops. But this clamor, the music of the organ "filling the small edifice with volumes of sound" and the "voices of men and women mingling in the 'Gloria in excelsis Deo,' " confuses and stirs him. Chopin describes the intensity of his experience:

> The words bore no meaning for him apart from the old familiar strain which he had known as a child and chanted himself in that same organ-loft years ago. How it went on and on! Would it never cease! It was like a menace; like a voice reaching out from the dead past to taunt him. "Gloria in excelsis Deo!" over and over! How the deep basso rolled it out! How the tenor and alto caught it up and passed it on to be lifted by the high, flute-like ring of the soprano, till all mingled again in the wild paean, "Gloria in excelsis!"
>
> How insistent was the refrain! and where, what, was that mysterious hidden quality in it; the power which was overcoming M'sieur Michel, stirring within him a turmoil that bewildered him? (*CW*, 185–86)

Compelled to flee the church filled with music and people, Michel is followed by the sounds of "Bonae voluntatis" and the refrain " 'Pax! pax! pax!'—fretting him like a lash."

The description of Michel's experience recalls an 1867 diary entry, a composition on Christian art that Chopin wrote as a seventeen-year-old.

> There remains yet to be considered the influence of Christianity upon music, that art so powerful as an agent in awakening the slumbering passions in the heart of man. From the time that David tuned his harp in Salem, and Jeremiah with prophetic voice sang forth his "Lamentations," music has continued to gain in perfection of expression and harmony without entirely abandoning the mutation of the voices of nature. It arose to the dignity of an art, only when Christianity ennobled the muses, by accepting their services to add to the splendor of her ceremonial; then was heard for the first time beneath the Gothic arches of the Cathedral of Milan the exultant strains of the "Te Deum" which have lost none of their original power after sixteen centuries—then was heard amid the pillard isles of the Cistine Chapel the harmony of that wondrous "Miscrera," now, now stealing forth from the darkness like the first wail of a broken heart, growing fainter and fainter while it dies away in silence as if the grief were too great for the strain; then leaping forth, not like the voice of song, but on agony—floating and swelling with irresistible power till it sinks again into the low broken tunes of intense anguish (*KCM*, 54).

Chopin continues to emphasize the emotional power of the music. Even when Michel is back in his hut, the music of the organ and choir echoes within him and causes "restlessness" and "a driving want for human sympathy and companionship . . . [to reawaken] in his soul." His reawakened desire for human companionship will be echoed in Mme. Martel's experience that is "born" on a Christmas Eve ("Madame Martel's Christmas Eve"). Both of these characters, wedded to the past with worship or hatred, enter scenes filled with music and create a small stir. Michel responds to this need by retracing a path he has not taken in years. He returns to his former homesite, expecting it to be grown over totally. Instead, under the beautiful moonlight, he finds his house and fields waiting for him. His old friend and neighbor Joe Duplan, magically appearing and explaining that he has been taking care of the place, offers this advice: " 'Let the past all go, Michel. Begin your new life as if the twenty-five years that are gone had been a long night, from which you have only awakened.' "

Chopin uses the music of the organ and the choir as the experience that awakens Michel and the refrain "Pax!" that accompanies his flight from the church as the song of his rebirth that returns him to his place among men.

Antoine (Tonie) Bocase, an innocent fisherman, is another Chopin character awakened by the power of music. Unexpected music from the usually silent church organ stirs Tonie, initiating him into his first experience with love in "At Cheniere Caminada."[2] Shy and clumsy, the simple fisherman, who still lives with his mother, has "no desire to inflame the hearts of any of the island maidens." However, the unexpected music at mass one morning changes Tonie.

Emphasizing the importance of music's role in Tonie's awakening, Chopin describes what happens while the priest chants the mass in "measured tones" that rise and fall "like a song":

> Some one was playing upon the organ whose notes no one on the whole island was able to awaken; whose tones had not been heard during the many months. . . . A long, sweet strain of music floated down from the loft and filled the church. . . .
>
> It seemed to Tonie . . . that some heavenly being must have descended upon the Church of Our Lady of Lourdes and chosen this celestial way of communication with its people. But it was no creature from a different sphere; it was only a young lady from Grand Isle. A rather pretty young person with blue eyes and nut-brown hair. (*CW*, 309–10)

From this moment on, Tonie is in love. Catching a glimpse of his celestial organist after church, Tonie wanders aimlessly around the island. He is not alert to anything and cannot answer his mother's customary questions when he returns home. But she has some information for him; she gives him the name of the organist, Claire Duvigne. Simply knowing Claire's name captures Tonie even further.

From then on, nothing is normal for Tonie. He cannot even work. In his innocence and inexperience, he does not recognize "the powerful impulse that had, without warning, possessed itself of his entire being," but instinctively he obeys the impulse "as he could have obeyed the dictates of hunger and thirst." He is awakened to a part of his own nature he cannot identify. Claire's image, "connected with that celestial music which had

---

2. Written in October, 1893, and published in December, 1894, in the New Orleans *Times-Democrat*. See *CW*, II, 1016.

thrilled him and was vibrating yet in his soul," is stamped in his mind. He abandons the repair work on his lugger and sails to Grand Isle where he hires out his boat and runs errands. Rather than turning to society as Michel does, Tonie isolates himself by spending his summer days, one by one, watching Claire with the other young people. Only once does Claire hire his boat alone. While they are out on the water, she is able to sense his love for her and flippantly finds it amusing "to pose" for "even a rough fisherman—to whom she felt herself to be an object of silent and consuming devotion. She could think of nothing more interesting to do on shore." The force and extent of Tonie's infatuation, which Chopin describes as a "savage instinct of his blood," is beyond Claire's ability to understand. Finally the ringing of the angelus bell and Claire's "musical voice" telling him to return to shore startle Tonie out of his passionate reverie. As memories of the Sunday that he heard the organ return to him, Tonie once again sees Claire as "that celestial being whom our Lady of Lourdes had once offered to his immortal vision."

Tonie's internal struggle between his passionate instinct and his spiritual vision continues when the insensitive young woman, maintaining her pose and playing romantic heroine, pays him with a silver chain from her wrist. The simple "touch of her hand fire[s] his blood." Tonie presses the chain to his lips, watching her walk away. His thoughts, prompted by the passion that has been awakened, are surprising in their intensity:

> "He was stirred by a terrible, an overmastering regret, that he had not clasped her in his arms when they were out there alone, and sprung with her into the sea. It was what he had vaguely meant to do when the sound of the Angelus bell weakened and palsied his resolution. . . . He resolved within himself that if ever again she were out there on the sea at his mercy, she would have to perish in his arms. He would go far, far out where the sound of no bell could reach him. There was some comfort for him in the thought." (*CW*, 315)

Following Tonie's dramatic confession, Chopin advances from the summer to the next January when Tonie is in New Orleans on business. By this time, he is a "wretched-hearted being" because he has not seen Claire. He has finally told his mother of his consuming love for the organist, and his mother fears that Tonie will not return, "for he had spoken wildly of the rest and peace that could come only to him with death." In New Orleans, Tonie meets Mme. Lebrun and her mother from Grand Isle, who are in the city "to hear the opera as often as possible," and from them Tonie learns that Claire Duvigne has died "simply from a cold caught by standing in thin slippers, waiting for her carriage after the opera." Stunned by the news, Tonie gets drunk; however, "from that day he felt that he began to live again." Her death releases him.

Later, talking to his mother, he explains that he had known he had no chance of winning Claire's love because he was only a rough fisherman and had no way to compete with the men who were always around her. He knew that one day she would marry, have children, and return with them to Grand Isle. Since Claire is now in heaven "where she belongs," he feels he has a chance to win her love because at last "she will know who has loved her best." Although Chopin does not express the idea directly, Tonie is obviously a man frightened by his intense feelings of love. He is more comfortable with his images of Claire as a "celestial organist" and an inhabitant of heaven than with the real woman.

Part of the importance of this story lies in its connections with *The Awakening* through shared characters and locations, and similar incidents. Tonie, his mother, and Mme. LeBrun reappear in the novel, which begins and ends on Grand Isle. Edna Pontellier and Robert Lebrun spend a day on Cheniere Caminada, Tonie's home. When Edna flees from mass at the church where Tonie hears Claire play the organ, she and Robert spend the afternoon at Mme. Antoine's. Tonie later takes the two back to Grand Isle in the same boat with the red lateen sail that he had once sailed for Claire. Chopin even mentions Claire by name as the "sunlight" in which Robert spent two previous summers. Claire died between the seasons spent at Grand Isle (*KCA,* 12). Chopin also uses hand imagery, the potential sensuousness of the simple touch, in both stories. Perhaps the most interesting connection between the novel and the story lies in Tonie's desire to perish in the sea with Claire because of his unattainable love, foreshadowing Edna's suicide in the same waters.

Regardless of the connections with *The Awakening*, "At Cheniere Caminada" needs to be considered on its own merit. While the organ music in "After the Winter" awakens Michel to a rebirth, the unexpected music from the organ awakens the unprepared Tonie to new emotions that nearly destroy him. The surging, assailing, instinctive passions that Tonie feels are also experienced by the boy in "A Vocation and a Voice." These emotional awakenings illustrate that Chopin was not simply a feminist. She understood human nature in all its complexity, not just the woman's plight that many critics like to demonstrate through Edna Pontellier. As Arthur Hobson Quinn writes, "There is an unusual understanding of man's passion in 'At Cheniere Caminada,' in the depiction of Antoine Bocaze's relief when the summer visitor whom he has been hopelessly worshipping at a distance dies, and the torturing thought that some other man may possess her is over."[3]

Joyce Coyne Dyer describes Tonie's first emotions as "marked by sentimentality and juvenile idealization" and later ones as "an issue of sexual need rather than childish infatuation." She goes on to claim that "Chopin assures us symbolically . . . that there are natural forces within each man that he cannot resist":

> Not only Chopin's women slumber and awake. The recent popularity of *The Awakening* has given many the idea that Chopin is a woman who writes best about women and their nature. But a review of several of her best, though little-known, short stories indicates that she recognized and understood the passions and needs of men as well as women. Tonie and the boy of "A Vocation and a Voice" are sexually awakened and aroused by the soft skin, magical voices, or disturbing and mysterious personalities of women. . . . As these stories and others suggest, her true subject was both men and women. Her true subject was human nature."

Chopin does write that Tonie follows his new instincts as he would those of "hunger and thirst" and that there is a "savage instinct in his blood." Even though the angelus bell temporarily brings Tonie's imagination back to his first pictures of Claire, Dyer points out that "violent fantasies" quickly return and Tonie dreams of going beyond the reach of the bell.[4]

Tonie's desire to escape the reaches of his conscience suggests the strength of his physical feelings and indicates the struggle between his spiritual and physical natures. Chopin explores this conflict further in "A

3. Arthur Hobson Quinn, *American Fiction: A Historical Survey* (New York, 1936), 356.
4. Joyce Coyne Dyer, "Kate Chopin's Sleeping Bruties," *Markham Review,* X (1980–81), 11, 12.

Vocation and a Voice." And once again Chopin chooses to accompany an awakening with music. But this time, rather than a single musical experience, Chopin uses the musical sounds as an unworded vocal refrain heard at intervals throughout the story, even as the voice of the sea speaks to Edna in *The Awakening*. Peggy Skaggs also sees this relationship.[5]

The awakening in "A Vocation and a Voice" is a positive one, a joyous affirmation of life.[6] The story tells of an unnamed fifteen-year-old boy who leaves his makeshift home to join a pair of vagabonds who travel the countryside telling fortunes and selling patent medicines. Chopin emphasizes the boy's innocence of spirit and experience in many ways. She includes bits of information about his background as an altar boy; he "belonged under God's sky in the free and open air." Hungry for the outdoors, he thrives in the first weeks of roaming with the strange pair, Suzima and Gutro.

As the source for the recurring music, Chopin uses the beautiful singing voice of the "robust" and "comely" Suzima, a young woman of about twenty. At one time Suzima sang in the chorus of an opera company, and her youthful experience contrasts greatly with the boy's innocence. What is special about Suzima at first is her voice, although he does not yet know why the music moves him. When she "lifted her voice and sang," he thinks he has "never heard anything more beautiful than the full, free notes that come from her throat, filling the vast, woody temple with melody." Always she sings the same thing, a "stately refrain from some remembered opera." There are times when the boy sings with Suzima as she plays her guitar, but the days of their pleasing duets are cut short because as he matures, his voice changes. The young woman's companion, the rough Gutro, is always associated with his prized pair of mules. Gutro takes better care of the mules than of people. Frequently drunk, he often abuses Suzima and becomes "the beast" in the boy's thinking. Chopin uses both of these characters to awaken the boy to a knowledge of different aspects of his own nature.

After a while, the odd threesome settle into an abandoned cabin for the

5. Peggy Skaggs, "The Boy's Quest in Kate Chopin's 'A Vocation and a Voice,'" *American Literature*, LI (1979), 270–76.

6. Written in November, 1896, not published until March, 1902, when it appeared in the St. Louis *Mirror*. See *CW*, 1027.

winter. The lad has a chance to serve as an altar boy again and even works in the village to pay for new clothes required by his growth. Chopin gently lets the boy roam between the contrasting worlds of the little village and the independent vagabonds. Whenever his allegiance seems to lean toward the standards of the village and church, Chopin woos the lad through Suzima. An example of this occurs after the boy and Suzima have dinner with the village priest. The boy has been a little nervous about how Suzima will behave and is relieved when they head home. Feeling she has been "respectable" long enough, Suzima begins to sing the familiar "stately refrain." In fact, Chopin notes, it is so familiar that he has begun to hear it "sometimes in his dreams." Although Chopin describes the boy's next remark as delivered "impetuously," it is still a significant statement: " 'I'd rather hear you sing that than anything in the world, Suzima.' " Another example of Suzima's wooing the lad away from the village occurs when she informs him that they are going to start traveling again. She sits and waits, "a shadowy form . . . lurking nearby," while he takes leave of the villagers.

At this point the lad is more aware of being wooed by the woods and the seasons than by the young woman. The boy's thoughts and heart respond to the "breath of Spring abroad beating softly in his face, and the odors of Spring assailing his senses."

Spring, the season of love, brings new awakenings to the youth. Physically growing and thriving, the lad starts to grow in other ways. Gutro's tales told by the campfire stir him, sometimes leaving him "not so tranquil." Then Gutro, forced by pains in his leg, allows the boy to tend the prized mules, the most manly job Gutro knows. Taking the mules to the stream to water them, the boy sees Suzima sitting naked as she bathes. The change in him is instant. Her image burns into his brain and flesh "with the fixedness and intensity of white-hot iron" just as Claire's image was stamped on Tonie's mind. Quickly turning away and going on with watering the mules, the boy reacts later in rage: "For the first time in his life he uttered oaths and curses that would have made Suzima quail." The awakening within him causes him to flee into the woods where he cries.

For a while, Suzima and the lad are irritable with each other. Then the moon comes out one night, and the vagabonds travel on, Gutro driving the wagon, the other two walking behind. Suzima sings her song that echoes "from a distant hillside" until she tires and climbs into the wagon to sleep. Her bare feet "peeped out, gleaming in the moonlight." Finally, "in submission to a sudden determination moving him, seemingly, without his volition," he springs into the wagon. Once again, Chopin's awareness of the powerful sensation of touch is important, but this time the touch is of bare feet, not hands. Soon Suzima is holding the lad "with her arms and with her lips." (A similar scene, though totally coincidental, can be found in Faulkner's *Light in August* when Byron Bunch struggles with thoughts of climbing into the truck beside Lena Grove. Byron is not welcomed, as the boy is, and runs off into the woods, like the boy.)

The changes in the boy in the next few days are great. His sexual initiation makes him totally responsive to nature all about him and to Suzima, who becomes the "embodiment of desire and the fulfillment of life." Her song is now clearly and symbolically powerful: "When she sang her voice penetrated his whole being and seemed to complete the new and bewildering existence that had overtaken him." But Chopin prepares another profound awakening. The lad discovers evil in himself. Trying to protect Suzima from one of Gutro's beatings, the boy comes close to killing the crude man with a knife. His sudden self-knowledge is the crux of one of the main conflicts in the story. "He had always supposed that he could live in the world a blameless life. He took no merit for he could not recognize within himself a propensity toward evil. He had never dreamed of a devil luring unknown to him, in his blood. . . . He shrank from trusting himself with this being alone. His soul turned toward the refuge of spiritual help, and he prayed to God and the saints and the Virgin Mary to save him and to direct him" (*CW*, 542).

The lad retreats to a monastery the trio has passed recently and eventually becomes Brother Ludovic, "hero of the wood" to the other brothers and students. His interest in nature and his strength are outstanding; he exhausts himself daily as protection from "that hideous, evil spectre . . . lurking outside, ready at any moment to claim him, should he venture within its reach." But Chopin understands the strength of human nature. There are still nights when he has "disturbing vision[s]" of "following, [but] never overtaking a woman—the one woman he had known—who lured him." With the determination of "a fixed purpose in life," Brother Ludovic undertakes to build a stone fence around the sacred grounds. It will be a solid stone wall, a "prison," some of the brothers joke.

Then comes the final awakening for the boy-man, which Chopin chooses to describe in terms of instinct. With the "mute quivering attention of some animal in the forest, startled at the scent of approaching danger," Brother Ludovic is flooded by vivid memories of Suzima—the day he saw her naked, the night he climbed into the wagon. His response becomes attentive rather than fearful when from a distance he recognizes the "voice of a woman singing the catchy refrain from an opera." Brother Ludovic watches the paradelike movement of the lone woman in the road below. Physically and symbolically, he crosses the wall, "conscious of nothing in the world but the voice that was calling him and the cry of his own being that responded." At last he follows the "voice of the woman."

The words in the title of this story are clever choices. *Vocation* seems to refer to the priestly calling of the boy-man, but it also can refer to any "calling," secular or religious. *Voice* seems to signify Suzima's song that casts its spell over the boy. But Chopin suggests another meaning for *voice* when she notes that Brother Ludovic is "hardly past the age when men are permitted to have a voice and a will in the direction of government." Thus *voice* also becomes a reference to one's being old enough to make his own decisions. Perhaps what Chopin is saying is not the obvious "priest and song" that come so quickly to mind but that each man must find and respond to his own calling. That is the ultimate awakening and the ultimate fulfillment.

The other awakening in "A Vocation and a Voice" stems from two levels of conflict that Chopin explores. Bert Bender sees the "opposed forces in this story" as "work, conventionality, orthodox religion, and the will" versus "idleness, unconventionality, a kind of pantheistic religion, and impulsiveness." He credits Suzima's voice that weaves in and out as the story's "lyric quality." Peggy Skaggs sees the story in terms of basic human drives: "the drives for a sense of belonging, for love relationships with others, and for selfhood."[7] But examining these conflicts, the first is the simple physical development and sexual initiation (awakening) of the lad. The other is a spiritual one that rages on several levels.

Not only is the boy torn between worship as he knows it in a liturgical sense and experiences it instinctively in nature, but he also finally awakens

7. Bert Bender, "Kate Chopin's Lyrical Short Stories," *Studies in Short Fiction*, XI (1974), 257–66; Skaggs, "Boy's Quest," 271.

to the struggle of good and evil, to a knowledge of sin within himself. (This struggle between the secular and the sacred is also evident in Chopin's "Lilacs" through the pull that Adrienne Farival experiences.) This knowledge does not come through physical awakening or sexuality but through Gutro, who is constantly associated with beasts.

At one point, Chopin seems to mock the boy's religious devotion through Suzima's fascination with seeing him serve mass. Elmo Howell comments that Chopin treats the church with respect and that "in describing the sensual, she never denies the validity of the spiritual."[8] The beautiful robes and mysterious language seem to be props not unlike those she and Gutro use to fool the people in the villages. Although the church is a refuge for the boy, his instinctive love of nature is also expressed romantically in terms of worship and religion. As the story opens, he is sitting in the park, speculating that heaven is "like this" rather than a "celestial city paved with gold." The first time he hears Suzima's voice, it fills "the vast, woody temple." When the boy wanders in the woods at night, he walks fearlessly, "holding communion with something mysterious, greater than himself, . . . something he called God." It is as if he were in Eden before the Fall. Just as Adam and Eve became aware of their nakedness and hid themselves, after seeing Suzima naked, the lad runs into the woods, hiding himself for a time. But early on, Chopin tells her readers: "He belonged under God's sky in the free and open air." The vocation this boy-man has is the one he must follow. His manhood cannot be found behind some solid stone fence. He must follow Suzima's song, long in his dreams.

Dyer takes the view that the boy is innocent about the nature of nature. He mistakenly thinks "nature is gentle" and thus remains "oblivious to its driving insistence." Seeing nature as "semi-divine," the boy's response is like a child's. Dyer interprets Suzima as representing "sexual desire"; Gutro, "violent tendencies." And by association the boy uncovers both within himself. Dyer notes that the boy tries to control his own nature and to recover his innocent belief in nature at the monastery, but Suzima's voice reawakens needs of his flesh that "are more imperative than those of this spirit." Dyer concludes that "Chopin was fascinated by the basic, primi-

8. Elmo Howell, "Kate Chopin and the Pull of Faith: A Note on 'Lilacs,' " *Southern Studies,* XVIII (1979), 104, 108.

tive desires of both men and women . . . who are complex creatures who have no choice but to discover their passion, in spite of risks, confusion, and guilt."[9]

Each of the major characters in these three stories experiences a significant self-discovery that the author deliberately initiates through musical experience. The awakenings of these men are as deeply passionate as the initial awakening of Edna Pontellier that Chopin also signals through music.

Music, as ordinary and extraordinary experience in secular and sacred situations, becomes a thematic and symbolic expression in the lives of her characters. Whether male or female, conventional or defiant, the people of Kate Chopin's stories are influenced and changed by the power of music.

9. Dyer, "Sleeping Bruties," 13–15.

Bibliography

Adams, Hazard, ed. *Critical Theory Since Plato*. New York, 1971.

Allen, Priscilla. "Old Critics and New: The Treatment of Chopin's *The Awakening*." In *The Authority of Experience: Essays in Feminist Criticism*, edited by Arlyn Diamond and Lee R. Edwards. Amherst, Mass., 1977.

Arthur, Stanley Clisby. *Jean Laffite, Gentleman Rover*. London, 1952.

Baudelaire, Charles. *Baudelaire: Selected Writings on Art and Artists*. Translated by P. E. Charvet. Middlesex, 1972.

Bauer, Dale Marie, and Andrew M. Lakritz. "The Awakening and the Woman Question." In *Approaches to Teaching Chopin's "The Awakening,"* edited by Bernard Koloski. New York, 1988.

Baym, Nina. Introduction to *"The Awakening" and Selected Stories*. Modern Library Editions. New York, 1981.

Bender, Bert. "Kate Chopin's Lyrical Short Stories." *Studies in Short Fiction*, XI (1974), 257–66.

Bonner, Thomas, Jr. *The Kate Chopin Companion, with Chopin's Translations from French Fiction*. New York, 1988.

———. "Kate Chopin: Tradition and the Moment." In *Southern Literature in Transition: Heritage and Promise*, edited by Philip Castille and William Osborne. Memphis, 1983.

Boren, Lynda S. *Eurydice Reclaimed: Language, Gender, and Voice in Henry James*. Ann Arbor, 1989.

———. "The Music of Passion: Kate Chopin's Experimental Keyboard." Paper presented at MLA convention, New Orleans, December 28, 1988.

———. "The Performing Self: Psychodrama in Austen, James and Woolf." *Centennial Review*, XXX (Winter, 1986) 1–24.

Britan, Halbert. *The Philosophy of Music*. New York, 1911.

Buell, Lawrence. "The Thoreauvean Pilgrimage: The Structure of an American Culture." *American Literature*, LXI (1989), 175–99.

Carroll, Michael. *The Cult of the Virgin Mary: Psychological Origins*. Princeton, 1986.

Cather, Willa. "Books and Magazines." Pittsburgh Leader, July 8, 1899, p. 6.

———. *The Professor's House*. New York, 1973.

Chopin, Kate. "Aims and Autographs of Authors." *Book News,* XVII (July, 1899), 612.

———. *"The Awakening": An Authoritative Text, Contexts, Criticism.* Edited by Margaret Culley. New York, 1976.

———. *"The Awakening" and Other Stories by Kate Chopin.* Edited by Lewis Leary. New York, 1970.

———. *"The Awakening" and Selected Stories.* Modern Library Editions. New York, 1981.

———. *"The Awakening" and Selected Stories.* Edited by Sandra M. Gilbert. New York, 1984.

———. *"The Awakening" and Selected Stories of Kate Chopin.* Edited by Barbara Solomon. New York, 1976.

———. *A Vocation and a Voice.* Edited by Emily Toth. New York, 1991.

Collins, Robert. "The Dismantling of Edna Pontellier: Garment Imagery in Kate Chopin's *The Awakening.*" *Southern Studies,* XXIII (Summer, 1984), 176–90.

Davis, Sara deSaussure. "Chopin's *A Vocation and a Voice:* Its Relevance to *The Awakening.*" Paper presented at MLA convention, New Orleans, December 28, 1988.

de Beauvoir, Simone. *The Second Sex.* 1952; rpr. New York, 1974.

Delbanco, Andrew. "The Half-Life of Edna Pontellier." In *New Essays on "The Awakening,"* edited by Wendy Martin. New York, 1988.

Deyo, C. L. "The Newest Books." St. Louis *Post-Dispatch,* May 20, 1899, p. 4.

Douglas, Ann. "The Literature of Impoverishment: The Women Local Colorists in America 1865–1914." *Women's Studies,* I (1972), 3–54.

D.S.M. "Women Artists." *The Living Age,* CCXX (1899), 730–32.

Eble, Kenneth. "A Forgotten Novel: Kate Chopin's *The Awakening.*" *Western Humanities Review,* X (Summer, 1956), 261–69.

Elliott, Emory, ed. *Columbia Literary History of the United States.* New York, 1988.

Emerson, Ralph Waldo. *The Collected Works of Ralph Waldo Emerson.* Edited by Alfred R. Ferguson *et al.* 12 vols. Cambridge, Mass., 1971.

———. *The Complete Writings of Ralph Waldo Emerson.* New York, 1929.

Engels, Frederick. *The Origin of the Family, Private Property and the State.* 1884; rpr. New York, 1985.

Ewell, Barbara C. *Kate Chopin.* New York, 1986.

Faulkner, Harold U. *Politics, Reform and Expansion 1890–1900.* New York, 1959.

Fern, Fanny. *Ruth Hall.* New Brunswick, 1986.

Fiedler, Leslie. *Love and Death in the American Novel.* New York, 1960.

Fluck, Winfried. "Tentative Transgressions: Kate Chopin's Fiction as a Mode of Symbolic Action." *Studies in American Fiction,* X (1982), 151–71.

Foster, Shirley. "The Open Cage: Freedom, Marriage and the Heroine in Early Twentieth-Century American Women's Novels." In *Women's Writing: A Challenge to Theory,* edited by Moira Monteith. New York, 1986.

Fox-Genovese, Elizabeth. *"The Awakening* in the Context of the Experience, Culture, and Values of Southern Women." In *Approaches to Teaching Chopin's "The Awakening,"* edited by Bernard Koloski. New York, 1988.

———. "Edna's Suicide." Paper presented at MLA convention, New Orleans, December 27, 1988.

Frederick, Harold. *The Damnation of Theron Ware.* 1896; rpr. Cambridge, Mass., 1960.

Friedan, Betty. *The Feminine Mystique.* New York, 1963.

Fuller, Margaret (Ossoli). *Woman in the Nineteenth Century.* Boston, 1855.

———. *Woman in the Nineteenth Century.* 1855; rpr. New York, 1971.

Garraty, John A. *The American Nation: A History of the United States.* 3rd ed. New York, 1966.

Gilbert, Sandra. Introduction to *"The Awakening" and Selected Stories.* New York, 1984.

———. "The Second Coming of Aphrodite: Kate Chopin's Fantasy of Desire." *Kenyon Review,* V (Summer, 1983), 3–54.

Gilbert, Sandra M., and Susan Gubar, eds. *Norton Anthology of Literature by Women.* New York, 1985.

Gilman, Charlotte Perkins. *Women and Economics,* edited by Carl Degler. 1899; rpr. New York, 1966.

———. *Women and Economics: A Study of the Economic Relations Between Men and Women as a Factor in Social Evolution.* Boston, 1899.

Gilmore, Michael T. *American Romanticism and the Marketplace.* Chicago, 1985.

———. "Revolt Against Nature: The Problematic Modernism of *The Awakening."* In *New Essays on "The Awakening,"* edited by Wendy Martin. Cambridge, Eng., 1988.

Greer, Germaine. *The Obstacle Race: The Fortunes of Women Painters and Their Work.* London, 1979.

Haller, John S., Jr., and Robin M. Haller. *The Physician and Sexuality in Victorian America.* Urbana, 1974.

Heilbrun, Carolyn. *Writing a Woman's Life.* New York, 1988.

Helmholtz, Hermann. *The Sensations of Tone.* 1877; rpr. New York, 1954.

Histoire des grandes familles françaises du Canada: Aperçu sur le Chevalier Benoist et quelques familles contemporaires. Montreal, 1867.

Howell, Elmo. "Kate Chopin and the Pull of Faith: A Note on 'Lilacs.' " *Southern Studies,* XVIII (1979), 103–109.

Howells, William Dean. *Criticism and Fiction.* New York, 1891.

Ibsen, Henrik. *A Doll's House.* In *Eight Plays.* New York, 1951.

Irigary, Luce. *This Sex Which Is Not One.* Translated by Catherine Porter and Carolyn Burke. Ithaca, N.Y., 1985.

Jacobs, Jo Ellen. "*The Awakening* in a Course on Philosophical Ideas in Literature." In *Approaches to Teaching Chopin's "The Awakening,"* edited by Bernard Koloski. New York, 1988.

James, Henry. *The Portrait of a Lady.* Edited by Leon Edel. Boston, 1963.

———. *The Turn of the Screw.* Edited by Robert Kimbrough. New York, 1966.

Janeway, Elizabeth. *Man's World, Woman's Place.* New York, 1971.

Jardine, Alice A. *Gynesis: Configurations of Woman and Modernity.* Ithaca, N.Y., 1985.

Jones, Anne Goodwyn. *Tomorrow Is Another Day: The Woman Writer in the South, 1859–1936.* Baton Rouge, 1981.

Kelley, Mary. "Desiring Images/Imaging Desire." *Wedge,* VI (1984), 4–9.

———. *Private Woman, Public Stage: Literary Domesticity in Nineteenth-Century America.* New York, 1984.

Kemmerer, Donald L., and C. Clyde Jones. *American Economic History.* New York, 1959.

Klinkowitz, Jerome. *The Practice of Fiction in America: Writers from Hawthorne to the Present.* Ames, Iowa, 1980.

Koloski, Bernard, ed. *Approaches to Teaching Chopin's "The Awakening."* New York, 1988.

Kristeva, Julia. *Desire in Language.* Edited by Leon Roudiez, translated by Thomas Gora, Alice Jardine, and Leon Roudiez. New York, 1980.

Lant, Kathleen. "The Siren of Grand Isle: Adele's Role in *The Awakening.*" *Southern Studies,* XXIII (Summer, 1984), 167–76.

Leary, Lewis. Introduction to *"The Awakening" and Other Stories by Kate Chopin.* New York, 1970.

Lewis, R. W. B. *The American Adam: Innocence, Tragedy and Tradition in the Nineteenth Century.* Chicago, 1955.

Little, Judy. "Imagining Marriage." In *Portraits of Marriage in Literature,* edited by Anne C. Hargrove and Maurine Magliocco. Macomb, Ill., 1984.

Lukacs, Georg. *History and Class Consciousness.* Translated by Rodney Livingstone. Cambridge, Mass., 1985.

Marsh, Margaret. "Suburban Men and Masculine Domesticity, 1870–1915," *American Quarterly,* XL (June, 1988).

Martin, Wendy. Introduction to *New Essays on "The Awakening."* Edited by Wendy Martin. Cambridge, Eng., 1988.

Martin, Wendy, ed. *New Essays on the "The Awakening."* Cambridge, Eng., 1988.

Marx, Karl, and Frederick Engels. *Capital.* Translated by Ben Fowkes. New York, 1977.

Marx, Leo. *The Machine in the Garden: Technology and the Pastoral Ideal in America.* Oxford, Eng., 1964.

Matthiessen, F. O. *American Renaissance: Art and Expression in the Age of Emerson and Whitman.* London, 1941.

Melville, Herman. *Billy Budd, Sailor.* 1924; rpr. in *The Norton Anthology of American Literature.* New York, 1986.

Michaels, Walter Benn. *The Gold Standard and the Logic of Naturalism.* Berkeley, 1987.

———. "Romance and Real Estate." In *The American Renaissance Reconsidered,* edited by Walter Benn Michaels and Donald E. Pease. Baltimore, 1985.

Michaels, Walter Benn, and Donald E. Pease, eds. *The American Renaissance Reconsidered.* Baltimore, 1985.

Mills, Elizabeth Shown. *Chauvin dit Charleville.* Cane River Series. Oxford, Miss., 1976.

Mills, Gary B. *The Forgotten People: Cane River's Creoles of Color.* Baton Rouge, 1977.

Nietzsche, Friedrich. *Beyond Good and Evil.* Translated by Walter Kaufman. New York, 1966.

———. *The Birth of Tragedy and the Spirit of Music.* 1872; rpr. New York, 1956, as *The Birth of Tragedy and the Genealogy of Morals,* translated by Francis Golffing.

Nochlin, Linda. "Why Are There No Great Women Artists?" In *Woman in Sexist Society,* edited by Vivian Gornick and Barbara Moran. New York, 1971.

Norris, Christopher. *Deconstruction: Theory and Practice.* London, 1982.

The Norton Anthology of American Literature. 2nd ed. 1979; rpr. New York, 1986.

Novak, Barbara. *American Painting of the Nineteenth Century: Realism, Idealism, and the American Experience.* New York, 1979.

O'Brien, Sharon. *Willa Cather: The Emerging Voice.* New York, 1987.

Ohmann, Richard M. *G. B. Shaw, the Style and the Man.* Middletown, Conn., 1965.

Perspectives on Kate Chopin: Proceedings of the Kate Chopin International Conference. Natchitoches, La., 1990.

Plotinus. "On the Intellectual Beauty." Translated by Stephen MacKenna. In *Critical Theory Since Plato,* edited by Hazard Adams. New York, 1971.

Pollock, Griselda. *Vision and Difference: Femininity, Feminism and the Histories of Art.* New York, 1988.

Porcher, Frances. "*The Awakening:* Kate Chopin's Novel." St. Louis *Mirror,* May 4, 1899, p.6.

Porter, Carolyn. "Reification and American Literature." In *Ideology and Classic American Literature,* edited by Sacvan Bercovitch and Myra Jehlen. Cambridge, Eng., 1986.

Quinn, Arthur Hobson. *American Fiction: A Historical and Critical Survey.* New York, 1936.

Rankin, Daniel. *Kate Chopin and Her Creole Stories.* Philadelphia, 1932.

Scarry, Elaine. *The Body in Pain: The Making and Unmaking of the World.* New York, 1985.

Schneir, Miriam. Preface to *A Doll's House.* In *Feminism: The Essential Historical Writings,* edited by Miriam Schneir. New York, 1972.

Seyersted, Per, ed. *The Complete Works of Kate Chopin.* Baton Rouge, 1969.

Seyersted, Per. *Kate Chopin: A Critical Biography.* 1969; rpr. Baton Rouge, 1980.

———. "Kate Chopin's Wound: Two New Letters." *American Literary Realism,* XX (1987), 71–75.

Seyersted, Per, and Emily Toth, eds. *A Kate Chopin Miscellany.* Baton Rouge, 1979.

———. *Kate Chopin's Private Papers.* Bloomington, Ind., forthcoming.

Shaw, George Bernard. *The Perfect Wagnerite.* London, 1923.

———. *The Quintessence of Ibsenism.* New York, 1958.

———. *The Sanity of Art.* New York, 1908.

Showalter, Elaine. "Feminist Criticism in the Wilderness." In *The New Feminist Criticism: Essays on Women, Literature, and Theory,* edited by Elaine Showalter. New York, 1985.

———. "Tradition and the Female Talent: *The Awakening* as a Solitary Book." In *New Essays on "The Awakening,"* edited by Wendy Martin. Cambridge, Eng., 1988.

Skaggs, Peggy. "The Boy's Quest in Kate Chopin's 'A Vocation and a Voice.'" *American Literature,* LXI (1979), 270–76.

———. *Kate Chopin.* Boston, 1985.

Smith, Gayle. "Emerson and the Luminist Painters: A Study of Their Styles." *American Quarterly,* XXXVII (Summer, 1985) 191–215.

Smith-Rosenberg, Carroll. *Disorderly Conduct: Visions of Gender in Victorian America.* New York, 1985.

Solomon, Barbara H. Introduction to *"The Awakening" and Selected Stories of Kate Chopin,* edited by Barbara H. Solomon. New York, 1976.

Stanton, Elizabeth C. "'Womanliness,' an Address to the New York State Legislature, 1880"; "'Solitude of Self,' an Address Before the U.S. Senate Comm. on Woman's Suffrage, 1892." In *History of Woman's Suffrage,* edited by Mari Jo and Paul Buhle. Urbana, 1978.

Taylor, Helen. *Gender, Race, and Region in the Writings of Grace King, Ruth McEnery Stuart, and Kate Chopin.* Baton Rouge, 1989.

Thomas, Heather Kirk. "'Development of the Literary West': An Undiscovered Kate Chopin Essay." *American Literary Realism,* XXII (Winter, 1990), 69–75.

Toth, Emily. "Comment on Barbara Bellow Watson's 'On Power and the Literary Text.'" *Signs,* I (Summer, 1976), 1005.

———. *Kate Chopin: The Life of the Author of "The Awakening."* New York, 1990.

———. "Kate Chopin's *The Awakening* as Feminist Criticism." *Louisiana Studies,* XV (1976), 241–51.

———. "A New Biographical Approach." In *Approaches to Teaching Kate Chopin's "The Awakening,"* edited by Bernard J. Koloski. New York, 1988.

———. "The Shadow of the First Biographer: The Case of Kate Chopin." *Southern Review,* XXVI (April, 1990), 285–92.

———. "Timely and Timeless: The Treatment of Time in *The Awakening* and *Sister Carrie.*" *Southern Studies,* XVI (1977), 271–76.

Veblen, Thorstein. *The Theory of the Leisure Class: An Economic Study in the Evolution of Institutions.* New York, 1899.

Walker, Nancy. "The Historical and Cultural Setting." In *Approaches to Teaching Chopin's "The Awakening,"* edited by Bernard Koloski. New York, 1988.

Warner, Marina. *Alone of All Her Sex: The Myth and the Cult of the Virgin Mary.* New York, 1976.

Warnken, William P. "Kate Chopin and Henrik Ibsen: A Study of *The Awakening* and *A Doll's House.*" *Massachusetts Studies in English,* IV (1974–75), 43–49.

Warren, Robert Penn. *All the King's Men.* 1946; rpr. New York, 1974.

White, Robert. "Inner and Outer Space in *The Awakening.*" *Mosaic,* XVII (1984), 97–109.

Wierzynski, Casimir. *The Life and Death of Chopin.* Translated by Norbert Guterman. New York, 1949.

Wilde, Oscar. *The Decay of Lying.* 1889; rpr. New York, 1971, in *Theory Since Plato,* edited by Hazard Adams.

Wilson, Edmund. *Patriotic Gore.* New York, 1962.

Wilson, Maryhelen. "Kate Chopin's Family: Fallacies and Facts Including Kate's True Birthdate." *Kate Chopin Newsletter,* II (1976–77), 25–31.

———. "Women's Lib in Old St. Louis: La Verdon." *St. Louis Genealogical Society,* XIV (n.d.), 139–40.

Wolff, Cynthia Griffin. "Thanatos and Eros: Kate Chopin's *The Awakening.*" *American Quarterly,* XXV (October, 1973) 449–71.

Wollstonecraft, Mary. *A Vindication of the Rights of Woman, 1792.* In *Feminism: The Essential Historical Writings,* edited by Miriam Schneir. New York, 1972.

Woolf, Virginia. *A Room of One's Own.* New York, 1929.

Ziff, Larzer. *The American 1890's: Life and Times of a Lost Generation.* New York, 1966.

Zlotnick, Joan. "A Woman's Will: Kate Chopin on Selfhood, Wifehood, and Motherhood." *Markham Review,* III (1968), 2–6.

Contributors

JEAN BARDOT is chairman of the Department of French Studies and Foreign Languages at the American University of Paris. Bardot's Université de Paris dissertation, "L'influence française dans la vie et l'oeuvre de Kate Chopin" (1985–1986), established new connections between the Louisiana and French branches of the Chopin family. His historical and biographical researches have also led him to discover the definitive evidence, a baptismal certificate, establishing Kate Chopin's birthdate as February 8, 1850 (not 1851).

DEBORAH E. BARKER is assistant professor at the University of Mississippi. She received her Ph.D. from Princeton University and is currently working on a study of the representation of women painters in the nineteenth-century American *Kunstlerroman*.

MARTHA FODASKI BLACK is professor of English at Brooklyn College, City University of New York. The author of *George Barker: Twentieth Century Romantic* and many articles on modern poetry, fiction, and drama, she teaches a course on modern "Anglo-Irish" literature for Brooklyn College in Ireland every summer. A book-length manuscript on Emma Goldman and Margaret Sanger awaits revision until she has published her most recent study, "The Last Word in Stolen Telling: George Bernard Shaw and James Joyce."

ANNE M. BLYTHE is projects director for the Seajay Society (Research in Southern Literary and Cultural History), Columbia, South Carolina. Blythe has edited two books by Elizabeth Allston Pringle, *Rab and Dab* and *A Woman Rice Planter*, and has published an essay on William Gilmore Simms's *The Cassique of Kiawah*. She is currently writing and producing *South Carolina Women Writers*, a series for South Carolina Educational Television. She also plans an edition of Marjorie Kinnan Rawlings' unpublished first novel, "Blood of My Blood."

LYNDA S. BOREN served for two years on the planning committee for the Kate Chopin International Conference at Northwestern State University of Louisiana in Natchitoches. She also chaired a special session on Kate Chopin at the New Orleans meeting of the Modern Language Association in 1988. Boren's theoretical book *Eurydice Reclaimed: Language, Gender and Voice in Henry James* was published in 1989, and she has published essays on Constance Fenimore Woolson, Mary Wilkins Freeman, Jane Austen, Virginia Woolf, and Margaret Atwood. A former Andrew Mellon fellow and the recipient of a grant from the National Endowment for the Humanities, Boren has had two Fulbright lectureships abroad, one to the University of Erlangen-Nuremberg, Germany, and the most recent to Srinakharinwirot University, Bangkok, Thailand.

DORIS DAVIS, assistant professor of English at East Texas State University at Texarkana, has received several grants, including two from the National Endowment for the Humanities. Davis spent the summers of 1989 and 1990 securing grants for and directing citywide writing projects for one hundred schoolchildren. She also serves as director of the East Texas Writing Project. Her research interests include the relationship between economics and literature.

SARA DESAUSSURE DAVIS is associate professor of English and assistant dean for humanities and fine arts at the University of Alabama. Interested in late-nineteenth-century American fiction, Davis has published articles on Kate Chopin, Henry James, and Mark Twain and has coedited *The Mythologizing of Mark Twain*. She held a Senior Fulbright Lectureship at the University of Heidelberg and the University of Mannheim from 1980 to 1981.

NANCY S. ELLIS is an instructor of English at Mississippi State University. A church organist and former high school teacher of English and piano, Ellis has worked primarily on southern writers, from Faulkner and Welty to Chopin and Ellen Douglas. During summers she teaches a course in southern literature at the Mississippi Governor's School.

BARBARA C. EWELL is associate professor of English at City College, Loyola University in New Orleans. In addition to her articles and book on Chopin (*Kate Chopin*), Ewell has coedited (with Dorothy Brown) two collections of essays on Louisiana women writers. One appeared as a special issue of *New Orleans Review* (1988), the other is forthcoming from Louisiana State University Press (1992). She has also published on Margaret Atwood, John Barth, and feminist criticism. Having recently taught three National Endowment for the Humanities summer seminars for schoolteachers (and a fourth for the Louisiana Endowment for the Humanities) on the connections between region, gender, and genre in southern women writers, she is now writing a book on that topic.

DOROTHY H. JACOBS, associate professor of English, University of Rhode Island, has recently pursued her interest in drama with publications on American playwright David Mamet, an essay on modern British playwrights, and a work on daytime television drama. She is currently engaged in research on Trinity Repertory Theatre.

KATHERINE JOSLIN is assistant professor of English at Western Michigan University. Joslin is the author of *Edith Wharton* in Macmillan's Women Writers Series and has published several articles on the writer. She helped to found the Edith Wharton Society, serves on its executive board, and is the director of the 1991 international conference "Edith Wharton in Paris."

JOHN CARLOS ROWE, professor of English, Department of English and Comparative Literature, University of California, Irvine, was formerly chair of the department at Irvine. Rowe has published extensively on nineteenth- and twentieth-century American literature, particularly fiction. His publications include *Henry Adams and Henry James: The Emergence of a Modern Consciousness, Through the Custom House: Nineteenth-Century American Fiction and Modern Theory,* and *The Theoretical Dimensions of Henry James.* With Richard Berg he has recently edited *The Vietnam War and American Culture.*

HEATHER KIRK THOMAS is assistant professor of American literature at Loyola College of Baltimore. Thomas is currently preparing a documentary life of Kate Chopin. An essay by Thomas on Emily Dickinson has been reprinted in *On Dickinson: The Best from "American Literature,"* and one on Chopin appears in *American Literary Realism.*

EMILY TOTH, professor of English and director of women's studies, Louisiana State University, is the author of *Kate Chopin: A Life of the*

Author of "The Awakening," now the definitive biography. She is also founder-editor of the *Kate Chopin Newsletter* (1975–1979), coeditor, with Per Seyersted, of *A Kate Chopin Miscellany,* and editor of *A Vocation and a Voice.* She is at work on editing *Kate Chopin's Private Papers* (forthcoming). Emily Toth is also the author of the novel *Daughters of New Orleans* and a biography of Grace Metalious (*Inside Peyton Place*), and coauthor of *The Curse: A Cultural History of Menstruation.*

Index

DEMCO